The Algorithmic Trading Machine

Architecture, Engineering, and Automation

Victor Trex

Published by NobleTrex Press

For permissions and other inquiries, write to:
P.O. Box 3132, Framingham, MA 01701, USA

Contents

Introduction

Algorithmic trading is often described as a contest of models, but in practice it is a contest of machines. Profitable ideas are necessary, yet insufficient; they must be expressed as software that ingests imperfect data, reasons under uncertainty, acts through fragmented markets, and remains dependable under failure, scrutiny, and speed. This book, The Algorithmic Trading Machine: Architecture, Engineering, and Automation, treats the trading system itself as the central artifact-an evolvable, observable, and governed machine that binds research to production and transforms hypotheses into executed risk with feedback.

The volume is organized to reflect the life cycle of that machine. We begin with Market Foundations and Data Backbone, because every later decision is downstream of market structure and data quality. Readers will encounter the instruments traded, the venues that list them, the mechanics of orders and settlements, and the canonical schemas that make tick, book, and bar data consistent across time. Corporate actions, adjustments, lineage, and data quality controls are positioned not as housekeeping but as reliability engineering for truth. When the book speaks about "backbone," it means both the plumbing and the integrity guarantees without which research is theater and operations are fragile.

With a dependable substrate, the narrative turns to Quantitative Methods and Statistical Foundations. Here we develop the language of probability, inference, time-series modeling, and optimization that powers alpha discovery and risk estimation. Equal emphasis is placed on what not to do: multiple testing, leakage, and invalid cross-validation can inflate backtests while impoverishing live results. The goal is to equip readers with tools and habits that survive contact with markets, not merely the elegance of textbook proofs.

Architecture and Software Engineering for Trading Systems then bridges theory to deployable services. You will see how to choose languages and libraries for the right performance envelope, design interfaces that isolate change, encode data efficiently, and enforce correctness through tests and secure coding. The end-to-end blueprint outlines core services-strategy engines, risk and portfolio layers, market data and order management-so that teams can reason about boundaries, latency budgets, and failure domains before they manifest in production incidents.

Strategy Research, Backtesting, and Machine Learning addresses the creative heart of the enterprise. We structure hypothesis formation, feature engineering, model selection, and interpretability with an eye to the operational realities introduced earlier. Backtesters are treated as simulators of market microstructure and execution, not mere portfolio calculators. Walk-forward validation and robustness testing are configured to emulate the passage of time and the costs of adaptation.

Portfolio Construction, Risk, and Execution integrates signals into positions that can be held, hedged, and transacted. You will learn to translate objectives and constraints into optimization problems, to account for transaction costs and market impact, and to route orders intelligently across venues. Execution quality is framed as an engineering problem: queue position, latency, and venue behavior shape realized P&L as surely as forecast accuracy.

Because modern electronic markets reward determinism and penalize jitter, Low-Latency Engineering and Infrastructure explores operating systems, networking, time synchronization, feed handling, and hardware acceleration. The intent is not to fetishize nanoseconds but to give practitioners the vocabulary and techniques to be predictably fast where it matters, and intentionally slower where safety, auditability, or model quality benefits.

Finally, DevOps, Governance, and Operational Excellence completes the machine. CI/CD, containers, and infrastructure as code provide safe repetition. Observability and registries make models, data, and services traceable. Compliance and security are framed as design constraints that improve systems when embraced early. Post-trade operations, reconciliations, and continuity planning ensure that profitable systems are also accountable ones.

This book is written for three overlapping audiences. Quant researchers will find principled workflows and diagnostics that anticipate live trading. Software and systems engineers will find architectures, performance patterns, and reliability practices tailored to market constraints. Operators, risk managers, and compliance professionals will find controls and evidence trails integrated rather than bolted on. A working familiarity with probability, linear algebra, and programming (Python and some C++), as well as basic Linux and networking concepts, will help you move quickly; each chapter includes practical guidance to connect concepts to implementation.

Across chapters you will see concise identifiers (e.g., T-040 or T-221). These map concepts across the book and allow you to navigate prerequisites and dependencies without repeating material. The text favors design rationales over cookbook recipes, emphasizes trade-offs, and offers "good defaults" together with failure modes and escape hatches. Code snippets are minimal and illustrative; production code varies by organization, but the architectural patterns and testing strategies generalize.

You can read linearly to build a full system, or follow role-based tracks: researchers may focus on data, statistics, and backtesting before portfolio construction; engineers may emphasize architecture, low-latency, and DevOps; leaders may skim foundations and concentrate on blueprint, governance, and operations. Regardless of path, the invitation is the same: build machines that are not only fast and clever but also honest, observable, and resilient. Markets change; a well-designed trading machine changes with them.

Chapter 1

Market Foundations and Data Backbone

Before you architect engines, optimize latency, or tune models, you need to understand the machine you are wiring into: the market itself and the data it emits. This chapter peels back the abstractions quants often take for granted-what actually trades, where and against whom you trade, how an order really lives and dies, and how noisy, fractured feeds are engineered into a coherent historical record. By the end, you will see ticks, books, bars, and corporate actions not as raw inputs but as design constraints that quietly shape every algorithmic trading decision you make.

1.1 Financial Instruments and Market Structure

Algorithmic trading systems do not trade in the abstract. They trade specific *instruments*, on specific *venues*, against specific *counterparties*, under specific *rules*. This section gives you a concrete mental model of that ecosystem.

We will start with the question: *what* is actually being traded, in payoff and risk terms, rather than in legal or textbook categories. Then we zoom out: *where* these instruments trade, and *who* the other players are. Throughout, keep in mind that every concept here will later reappear as a field in your data model or as a constraint in your algorithms.

Instruments as Payoff Functions

At the most abstract level, a financial instrument is a contract that specifies a payoff as a function of future states of the world. For a given instrument i, we can write its payoff at time T as

$$\Pi_i(T) = f_i\big(S_1(T), S_2(T), \dots; \omega\big),$$

where $S_k(T)$ are underlying variables (prices, interest rates, indices, FX rates, default events, etc.) and ω captures contractual details (strike, notional, maturity, coupon, and so on).

For algorithmic trading, three aspects of f_i matter more than anything else:

- **Shape of the payoff**: linear or non-linear in the underlying.
- **Embedded leverage and margin**: how much exposure you control per unit of posted capital.
- **Path dependence**: whether only the final state matters, or the path taken to get there.

We will now walk through core asset classes with this lens.

Equities: Linear Ownership Claims

A *common stock* is an ownership claim on a firm. For most algorithmic trading purposes, the relevant payoff function for a one-share long position over a horizon ending at T is

$$\Pi_{equity}(T) = S(T) - S(0) + D(0, T),$$

where $S(t)$ is the stock price and $D(0, T)$ is the sum of cash dividends received between 0 and T.

Two key properties:

- **Linear payoff**: if the price goes up by \$1, your P&L goes up by \$1 per share, ignoring dividends. This linearity makes equities a natural base instrument in many strategies and an intuitive benchmark for risk.
- **No fixed maturity**: common stock is perpetual. Algorithmic strategies impose their own horizons (intraday, overnight, monthly) through their trading rules and risk management.

In many markets you can also *short* equities. A one-share short position has payoff

$$\Pi_{short\ equity}(T) = S(0) - S(T) - C_{borrow}(0, T),$$

where C_{borrow} captures stock borrow fees, rebates, and other financing costs. Shorting introduces:

- **Asymmetric risk**: your loss is unbounded above if $S(T) \to \infty$.
- **Operational frictions**: locate requirements, recalls, and hard-to-borrow constraints.

From a system design perspective, equities set the baseline: a relatively simple instrument with a direct market price, linear exposure, and well-understood microstructure.

Futures: Standardized, Levered Price Bets

A *futures contract* is an exchange-traded agreement to buy or sell an underlying asset at a future date for a price agreed today. Crucially, futures are *marked to market* daily: profits and losses are realized each day as the contract price moves.

For a long futures position with contract price $F(0)$ and futures price at time T of $F(T)$, ignoring daily mark-to-market and financing, the net payoff can be written as

$$\Pi_{fut}(T) = F(T) - F(0).$$

This is again linear in the underlying price, but two features distinguish futures from cash equities:

- **Embedded leverage**: you only post a margin (often a small fraction of notional). Controlling a notional of $1,000,000 might require $50,000–$100,000 of margin, so a 1% move in the underlying can be a 10–20% move in your account equity.

- **Expiry and roll**: each contract has a fixed expiration date. If your strategy wants continuous exposure, it must *roll* from a maturing contract into a later one. This creates predictable bursts of trading volume and specific calendar effects your system should be aware of.

Futures exist on many underlyings: equity indices, single stocks, interest rates, commodities, FX, and volatility indices. For your trading machine, the important unifying observation is that most futures P&L is *linear* in some economically meaningful underlying, with predictable margin and expiry mechanics.

Options: Non-Linear, Convex Payoffs

Options introduce curvature. A European call option on an underlying with price $S(T)$ at maturity, strike K, and premium C_0 (paid upfront) has payoff

$$\Pi_{call}(T) = \max(S(T) - K, 0) - C_0 e^{rT},$$

where r is a financing rate. A put option has

$$\Pi_{put}(T) = \max(K - S(T), 0) - P_0 e^{rT}.$$

Key properties from an algorithmic viewpoint:

- **Non-linearity**: small changes in S can have disproportionately large effects on option value, especially near the strike and as maturity approaches. Sensitivities (the "Greeks") become core risk metrics.

- **Asymmetric exposure**: buying options limits downside (premium paid) and gives unbounded upside (for calls) or limited upside (for puts). Selling options reverses that profile.

- **Path-insensitivity for European options**: only the terminal $S(T)$ matters for intrinsic value. American or exotic options can be path-dependent, but liquid listed options are often modeled as (approximately) European for short maturities.

In an options portfolio, your net exposure is not just a single linear factor but a vector of sensitivities (delta, gamma, vega, theta, etc.). Your trading machine must therefore represent not only prices and quantities but also model-based risk measures, and must track how trades reshape those measures over time.

FX and Fixed Income: Currencies and Time

Foreign exchange (FX). In spot FX, you always trade one currency against another. A EUR/USD quote of 1.1000 means 1 euro costs 1.1000 U.S. dollars. A long position in EUR/USD is simultaneously:

- Long EUR (you benefit if EUR appreciates).
- Short USD (you lose if USD strengthens).

Payoff over your horizon depends on the change in the *exchange rate* and on the *interest rate differential* between the two currencies, which influences forward rates and carry costs. For high-frequency strategies focused on short horizons, the rate differential plays a smaller role than intraday volatility and transaction costs; for medium-horizon carry or trend strategies, it becomes central.

Fixed income. Bonds and interest rate products exchange money over time. The simplest fixed rate bond pays coupons and returns principal at maturity. Its price is the discounted present value of those cash flows. From a trading standpoint, key dimensions include:

- **Interest rate risk**: captured by duration and convexity.
- **Credit risk**: probability of default or spread widening relative to benchmarks.
- **Curve structure**: yields at different maturities form a curve; many strategies are curve-relative (e.g., trading steepeners or flatteners) rather than absolute-level bets.

Many algorithmic strategies trade interest rate *futures* or swaps rather than individual bonds, because they are more standardized and liquid. Still, their payoffs are ultimately functions of the term structure of interest rates.

Instrument Landscape Diagram

To keep the preceding discussion visually anchored, the following figure lays out the main instrument types at the center, with venues and participant types around them, and arrows indicating order and information flows. We will refer back to this diagram throughout the section.

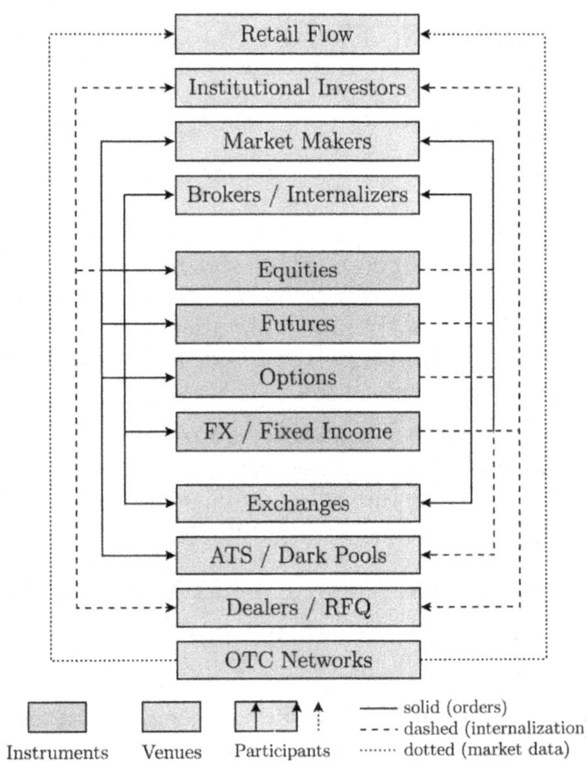

Instrument–market ecosystem: core asset classes in the center, surrounded by venues and participant types with order and information flows.

Venue Architectures: Where Trades Happen

With instruments in mind, we now ask: where do these contracts actually change hands? From an algorithmic trading perspective, the answer determines:

- What market data you see (full order book, quotes only, indicative prices).
- How you are allowed to interact (limit orders, RFQ, auctions).
- What latencies, fees, and regulatory constraints apply.

Centralized Order-Driven Exchanges

Many equities, equity index futures, and listed options trade on centralized *limit order book* (LOB) venues. The core idea:

- Participants submit *limit orders* to buy or sell at specified prices.
- The venue maintains an aggregate book of bid (buy) and ask (sell) orders, sorted by price and time.
- Trades occur when incoming orders cross existing quotes.

This structure generates rich *microstructure data*: order book states, trades, cancellations, and order additions. Your trading machine can see, and potentially react to, the full stack of liquidity at different price levels.

For system design, a limit order book market implies:

- Your execution algorithms can choose between *posting* liquidity (becoming part of the book) and *taking* liquidity (hitting existing quotes).

- Your data layer must represent a time-varying order book, often at multiple depth levels, across many venues.

Quote-Driven and RFQ Markets

Some instruments—especially in fixed income and certain derivatives—trade in more *quote-driven* or *request-for-quote* (RFQ) markets:

- Dealers or market makers quote bid and ask prices.
- Clients request quotes for a given size and side, potentially from multiple dealers.
- The client then chooses which quote to hit or lift.

From your system's perspective:

- The visible market is often *thinner*: you may see indicative quotes or trade prints but not a full book.
- Execution logic is more like negotiation: send RFQ, receive quotes, select counterparty.

This architecture leads to different data shapes and latencies. You often have snapshots of *best* quotes, not a continuous stream of order book updates.

Lit Markets, Dark Pools, and Internalization

Even for a single equity, liquidity is typically fragmented:

- **Primary exchanges** (lit): display pre-trade transparency; full or partial order book visible.
- **Alternative trading systems (ATS) and dark pools**: allow trading with limited pre-trade transparency.
- **Internalizers**: broker-dealers that fill client orders against their own or other clients' inventory, sometimes without routing to public venues if they can provide equal or better prices.

The functional implications for your algorithm:

- **Smart order routing (SOR)** becomes necessary: given multiple venues, you must decide where to send an order to achieve best execution according to specified criteria.
- Observed *tape prints* (public trades) may be only part of the full trading activity; some volume occurs off-exchange and later reports as off-book prints.

Your market model must therefore support:

- Multiple venues per instrument, each with its own microstructure and fees.
- Aggregation of liquidity across venues when simulating or executing a strategy.

Market Participants and Their Incentives

Instruments do not trade in a vacuum. Different participant types bring different objectives and constraints, which shape prices, spreads, and volatility.

Retail Order Flow

Retail traders—individual investors using broker platforms—often submit relatively small orders, with less aggressive timing and less sophisticated routing. In many jurisdictions, retail flow is:

- **Internalized** by brokers or sold to wholesalers.
- **Priced differently** from institutional flow because it is, on average, less informed.

For an algorithmic trader, this matters because:

- Retail-heavy periods (e.g., around certain news or social media events) can change liquidity patterns.
- Some venues or counterparties may specialize in interacting with retail flow, affecting fill quality.

Institutional Investors

Institutional investors (asset managers, pension funds, hedge funds) typically trade larger sizes with more attention to implementation costs. They might:

- Use execution algorithms (VWAP, TWAP, POV, implementation shortfall) to slice large orders.
- Be less sensitive to microsecond-level latency, but highly sensitive to market impact and slippage.

Your trading machine may operate as one of these institutional participants, or it may attempt to infer their behavior from the tape. In either case, understanding that much of observed volume reflects gradual execution of large orders helps interpret patterns in order flow and volatility.

Market Makers and Liquidity Providers

Market makers quote both bid and ask prices, intending to earn the bid–ask spread in exchange for providing liquidity. Their key characteristics:

- They manage inventories of instruments and dynamically adjust quotes to hedge risk.
- They are highly sensitive to adverse selection: the risk of being hit mostly when prices are about to move against them.

From a system design perspective:

- If you are building a market making strategy, your algorithms must rapidly update quotes, monitor inventory, and predict short-term price moves.
- If you are not making markets, market makers' behavior determines the spread you pay when crossing the spread and the depth available when posting orders.

Brokers and Internalizers

Brokers sit between end-clients and venues. They:

- Receive client orders.
- Perform regulatory and risk checks.
- Route orders to venues or fill them internally.

Internalizers or wholesalers may:

- Fill retail orders at or better than the national best bid and offer (NBBO).
- Aggregate flow from multiple brokers, providing liquidity and potentially profiting from the spread and from internal crossing.

For your trading machine, brokers are often the immediate counterparty: you send orders to them via APIs. Their internalization and routing policies affect your realized execution prices and the mapping from your high-level order to concrete interactions with exchanges and ATSs.

From Mental Model to Data and Constraints

The purpose of this section is not only conceptual clarity but also preparation for engineering. Each concept maps to concrete requirements in later chapters.

- **Instrument payoffs** (linear vs. non-linear, levered vs. unlevered) determine:
  - How you represent positions and exposures (delta, duration, vega, etc.).
  - How you simulate P&L under scenarios or in backtests.
- **Venue microstructure** (limit order book vs. RFQ, lit vs. dark) determines:
  - What market data schemas you need (books, quotes, indicative prices).
  - What order types you can use and how to model execution uncertainty.

- **Participant incentives** (retail, institutional, market maker) shape:
  - The statistical properties of order flow that your models will attempt to exploit or withstand.
  - The regimes in which your strategies may face different liquidity or volatility environments.

In the next sections, we will trace an order's full lifecycle through this ecosystem and then connect these market foundations to precise data models and engineering pipelines. As you design your trading machine, always return to the mental picture established here: specific contracts, traded on specific venues, against specific participants, under rules that systematically shape the data your algorithms see and the constraints they must respect.

1.2 Order Mechanics and Trade Lifecycle Overview

In the previous section we focused on *what* is traded and *where* it trades: the instruments, venues, and participants that make up the electronic marketplace. We now zoom in on a single, concrete question:

What happens, step by step, when your trading machine decides to buy or sell?

This section follows one order all the way from strategy intent to final settlement. At each stage, we highlight:

- the **business event** (what is happening economically),
- the **technical event** (what messages and states your system must handle), and
- the **data artifacts** (objects, identifiers, and timestamps you must store).

By the end, an order will no longer be a vague notion. It will be a precise sequence of states and messages that your code must produce, consume, and persist.

Bird's-Eye View of the Trade Lifecycle

Before diving into details, it is useful to have a visual overview that keeps the moving parts organized. Figure shows the main stages of the trade lifecycle as a left-to-right flow, with swimlanes for the major actors: your trading logic ("Trader"), the broker/venue, clearing, and your internal systems.

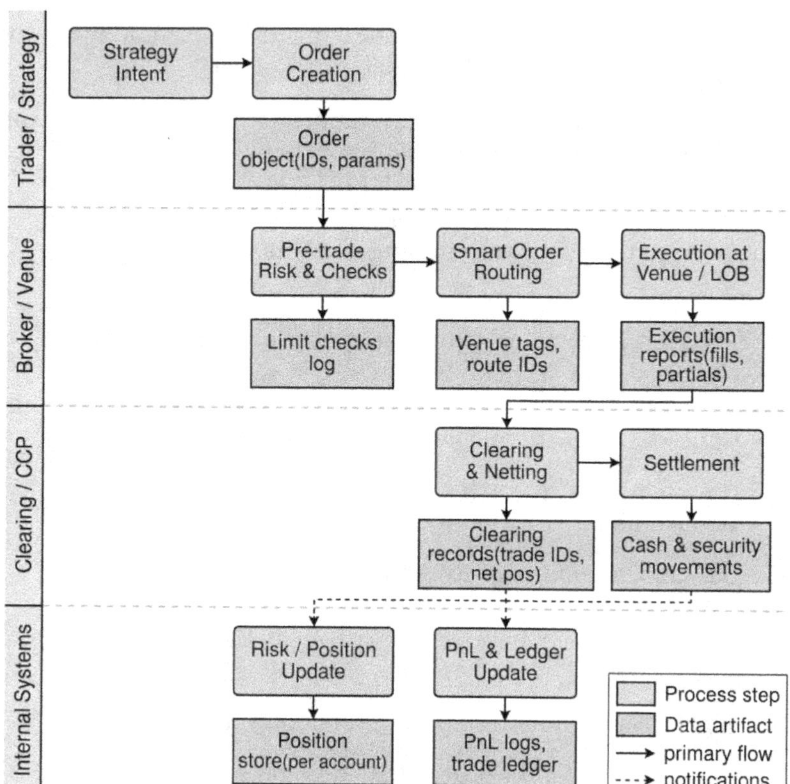

We now walk through these stages carefully, always linking the business story to concrete data states.

From Strategy Intent to Concrete Order

Every order in your system begins as some form of *intent*. An alpha model, risk overlay, or portfolio optimizer decides that you should change your exposure to a particular instrument.

Strategy intent. At this point, the information is often high-level:

- Instrument identifier (e.g., ticker for an equity, symbol/root and expiry for a future).
- Target position or trade size (e.g., "increase position by 10,000 shares" or "target 2% of portfolio in this asset").
- Time horizon or urgency (e.g., "complete by end of day" vs. "complete as quickly as possible").

This intent is *not* yet an order the market can understand. It is a request to the *execution layer* of your trading machine.

Order creation: turning intent into parameters.

The execution layer transforms intent into a concrete *order object*. This means:

- Choosing the **side**: buy or sell.
- Specifying the **quantity**: number of shares, contracts, or notional amount.
- Selecting an **order type** and key parameters:

- *Market order*: "Buy 10,000 shares at the prevailing market prices now."
- *Limit order*: "Buy 10,000 shares, but only at a price ≤ 100.50."
- *Stop or stop-limit*: orders that become active when the price crosses a trigger.

- *Iceberg / hidden*: only part of the size is visible in the order book at any time.
- *Pegged*: price is dynamically tied to some reference (e.g., bid, mid, or last).

- Choosing **time-in-force** (TIF): how long the order remains valid:

- *Day*: expires at end of session.
- *Good-till-cancelled (GTC)*.
- *Immediate-or-cancel (IOC)*: fill what you can immediately, cancel the rest.
- *Fill-or-kill (FOK)*: either filled in full immediately, or cancelled.

At this moment your system must instantiate a well-defined *order object* with fields such as:

- Internal order ID (unique within your system).
- Instrument ID (normalized across venues).
- Side, quantity, order type, limit price/stop price (if applicable), TIF.
- Account or strategy identifiers (who "owns" this order).
- Timestamps: creation time, send time, last update time.

This object becomes the canonical representation against which all later events (modifications, fills, cancels) will be reconciled.

Pre-Trade Checks and Broker Interaction

Once the order object is created, the next stage is to send it out of your house into the broker or venue landscape.

Risk and compliance checks.

Before an order is accepted into the market, it usually passes through multiple layers of pre-trade controls:

- **Your own risk layer** may:

- Check max order size per instrument.
- Enforce exposure and leverage limits per strategy or account.
- Block trades that would violate regulatory or internal constraints.

- **Broker risk systems** perform similar checks:

- Overall client credit and capital.
- Market-specific rules (e.g., price collars, short sale rules).

Each check produces events like "accepted", "rejected", or "modified" (for example, a broker may clip an order to a maximum size). These are communicated back as confirmations or rejections that:

- must be recorded in your *order state machine*, and
- often carry a reason code or text (useful for debugging and compliance).

From a data standpoint, pre-trade checks add:

- A log of risk check events with timestamps and result codes.
- Potentially, updated fields on the order object (e.g., reduced size).

Smart order routing.

In modern, fragmented markets, a single instrument may trade on many venues. Brokers (and sometimes buy-side firms) operate *smart order routers* (SOR) that decide:

- Which venue or combination of venues to route to.

- Whether to post liquidity or take it.
- How to slice a large parent order into smaller *child orders*.

Routing decisions depend on:

- Real-time quotes and order book depth across venues.
- Historical fill quality and fee structures.
- Regulatory and client preferences (e.g., avoid certain dark pools).

For your trading machine, routing introduces another layer of IDs and states:

- **Parent order ID**: the original order from your system.
- **Child order IDs**: per-venue orders created by the SOR.
- **Route identifiers**: records of each dispatch of size to a specific venue at a specific time.

If you do not have visibility into child orders (for example, when using a fully broker-managed algorithm), you still receive execution reports, but you will not see all internal routing details. Your system must be prepared for this opacity.

Interaction with the Order Book and Executions

Once routed, the order interacts with the market's microstructure.

Order matching and fills.

On a limit order book venue:

- A *marketable* order (e.g., a buy with a limit price at or above the best ask) will immediately execute against resting orders on the opposite side.
- A *non-marketable* limit order (buy with a limit price below the best ask) will rest in the book until,

- the market moves to it,
- it is cancelled or modified, or
- it expires (due to TIF).

Executions can be:

- **Partial fills**: only part of your quantity trades; the remainder stays open.
- **Multiple fills**: your order may be matched against several counterparties at slightly different prices or times.

Each fill generates an *execution report* (also called a fill or trade confirmation) that typically includes:

- Execution ID (unique per fill).
- Related order ID(s) and child/route IDs if applicable.
- Executed quantity and price.
- Execution time (exchange time and sometimes broker receipt time).
- Liquidity flag (e.g., whether you added or removed liquidity).
- Venue identifier.

Your order state machine must now evolve through states such as:

$$\text{NEW} \to \text{PARTIALLY\_FILLED} \to \text{FILLED}$$
$$\text{or} \quad \text{NEW} \to \text{REJECTED}$$
$$\text{or} \quad \text{NEW} \to \text{PARTIALLY\_FILLED} \to \text{CANCELLED}$$

These states are not just labels. They govern:

- How much remaining quantity is eligible for further trading.

- What your risk system considers as open exposure vs. completed trades.

Auctions and special mechanisms.

Not all executions occur via continuous matching. Many venues run opening, closing, or intraday auctions where:

- Orders accumulate in an auction book.
- A single uncrossing price is determined.
- All eligible trades execute at that auction price.

Auction executions produce fills just like continuous trading, but with:

- Distinct execution types (e.g., code for "auction trade").
- Different timing (at discrete auction events).

When designing your data model, make sure to capture execution type so that later analytics (for example, implementation shortfall calculations) can differentiate between auction and continuous fills.

Allocations, Clearing, and Settlement

Once fills occur at the venue, the economic exposure has shifted. But the legal and accounting processes continue downstream.

Allocations across accounts.

Large institutional orders are often placed on behalf of multiple funds or sub-accounts. In that case:

- A *block trade* is executed in the market.
- Post-trade, the broker or the buy-side OMS *allocates* the filled quantity across underlying accounts according to pre-specified rules (e.g., pro-rata to target sizes).

This creates:

- An allocation record per account, mapping the parent trade to child positions.
- Account-level trade IDs and quantities that your internal systems will book.

Even if you run a single account, it is useful to maintain an internal concept of allocations across strategies or models, so you can attribute P&L correctly.

Clearing and netting.

After trade execution, the clearinghouse or bilateral clearing process:

- Validates both sides of the trade.
- Nets offsetting trades (e.g., buy and sell of the same instrument on the same day).
- Determines final positions and margin requirements.

Clearing generates its own data artifacts:

- *Clearing confirmations* with:
- Trade IDs (often different from your internal or venue IDs).
- Final settled quantities and prices.
- Fees and margin figures.
- *Net position records* at the clearing level.

Your system must reconcile these with:

- The sum of your execution reports.
- Your internal positions as of that date.

Discrepancies must be investigated—these can signal missing trades, incorrect allocations, or mapping errors between identifiers.

Settlement: cash and securities move.

On the settlement date (e.g., T+2 for many equities), the following occurs:

- Cash leaves or enters your custody account.
- Securities move into or out of your custody account.

Settlement data includes:

- Settlement date and value date.
- Cash amount and currency.
- Quantity of securities delivered or received.
- Fees, taxes, or commissions charged.

At this point, the trade is no longer just an exposure; it has become a realized change to your asset and cash balances. Your general ledger and P&L systems must incorporate these movements.

Internal States: Positions, Risk, and P&L

While the outside world is performing clearing and settlement, your internal systems must maintain an accurate, time-resolved view of what you own and what you owe.

Position records.

A *position* is your net quantity of an instrument in a given account. Positions change when:

- Trades are executed (fills).
- Corporate actions occur (beyond the scope of this section, but important later).

- Transfers or manual adjustments are made.

Your position store should track, at minimum:

- Instrument ID and account.
- Current quantity (net long or short).
- Average cost or other cost basis representation.
- Timestamps of last update.

For many strategies, positions are also maintained at:

- Strategy-level (how much each model "owns").
- Aggregated views (sector, country, asset class).

Risk and limits.

As executions come in, your risk engine recalculates:

- Exposure metrics (e.g., gross, net, and factor exposures).
- Leverage and margin utilization.
- Sensitivities (e.g., deltas, durations) where relevant.

These risk states, in turn, may trigger:

- Automatic throttling of further orders.
- Forced position reductions or hedges.

The key point is that the *order lifecycle and the risk lifecycle are intertwined.* Your system must react to trade events in near real time, not just at end of day.

P&L and trade ledger.

Finally, every execution and settlement event must flow into your P&L and accounting ledger. This includes:

- **Realized P&L**: profit or loss locked in when you close or reduce positions.
- **Unrealized P&L**: mark-to-market gains or losses on open positions.
- **Transaction costs**: commissions, fees, taxes, and slippage relative to benchmarks.

Your trade ledger becomes the authoritative history of:

- Every order and fill.
- How trades map to positions and P&L.
- Which strategy or account was responsible.

This ledger is essential for:

- Strategy evaluation and backtesting validation.
- Regulatory reporting and audits.
- Debugging and understanding anomalous outcomes.

Why the Lifecycle Model Matters for Engineering

It is tempting, when designing an algorithmic trading system, to think primarily in terms of alpha models and order submission APIs. The trade lifecycle reminds us that:

- An "order" is not a single event but a *state machine* that:
- accumulates risk checks, routes, child orders, partial fills, cancels, and amendments,
- produces a trail of identifiers and timestamps.
- Each stage of the lifecycle introduces *distinct data objects*:

- Order objects, execution reports, allocation records, clearing confirmations, settlement records, position updates, P&L entries.

- Consistency across these objects is not optional:

- Your backtests will only be meaningful if they can be mapped onto realistic order and execution behavior.

- Your live system's risk and P&L will only be trustworthy if all these events reconcile.

In the next section, we will shift focus from the lifecycle of a single order to the *market data* that feeds your algorithms and the *corporate actions* that reshape historical series. Keep the lifecycle picture in mind: every tick, quote, and bar will eventually be linked to orders, fills, and positions as your trading machine turns data into decisions and decisions into trades.

1.3 Market Data Modeling and Corporate Actions

In the previous sections, we built up two complementary pictures of the market:

- *What* is traded and *where* it trades (instruments and market structure).

- How a single *order* moves through the ecosystem from intent to settlement.

We now step back and ask a different, equally central question:

> *What does the market look like as data to your trading machine, and how does that data change over time as issuers restructure their capital?*

Your algorithms never see the market directly. They see time-stamped records: trades, quotes, order book updates, corporate action notices, and reference data from vendors. This section defines the canonical data shapes your system must understand—ticks, order books, and bars—and then explains how corporate actions and reference data reshape both historical price series and live feeds.

Throughout, we will emphasize two themes:

1. **Shape and semantics**: *exactly* what each record means, and what it does *not* mean.
2. **Stability and evolution**: how those records must be adjusted or reinterpreted when an issuer changes its capital structure or when instruments roll.

Ticks: The Atomic Events

The most granular view of market data is the *tick*: an event that occurs at a specific time and changes the visible state of the market.

For most electronic venues, there are two fundamental tick types:

- **Trade ticks** (also called prints): indicate that a trade occurred.
- **Quote or book-update ticks**: indicate that a standing order was added, modified, or removed, changing the bid/ask.

Trade Ticks

A trade tick tells you that an actual transfer of shares/contracts took place between counterparties at a particular price and size.

At a minimum, a trade tick record should contain:

- timestamp: when, in exchange time, the trade occurred.
- instrument_id: which instrument traded (normalized symbol).
- price: execution price.

- size: quantity traded.
- trade_id: unique identifier for this print on this venue.
- side_indicator: often a flag like "buyer-initiated" or "seller-initiated" (derived by comparing trade price to prevailing quotes).
- venue: which exchange or internalizer printed the trade.

Trades are the raw material for:

- Volume calculations.
- Realized volatility estimates.
- Slippage and transaction cost analysis.

Quote and Book-Update Ticks

Quote ticks represent changes to the best bid/ask, or deeper changes in the limit order book. The spectrum ranges from:

- **Top-of-book feeds**: only best bid/ask and sizes.
- **Level-2 feeds**: bids and asks at multiple price levels, often aggregated across participants.
- **Full depth feeds**: every visible order in the book.

A typical quote tick at top-of-book might contain:

- timestamp
- instrument_id
- bid_price, bid_size
- ask_price, ask_size
- quote_condition (e.g., regular, crossed, locked, indicative)

For order book deltas, each tick might represent a single modification:

- action: add, modify, cancel.
- price_level: price at which the order book changed.
- size_change: how much size was added or removed.
- order_id (for full-depth, order-by-order feeds).

These ticks let you reconstruct the evolving supply and demand landscape and simulate the interaction of your own orders with that landscape.

Order Books: Structured Views of Liquidity

Ticks carry individual events. For strategy logic and backtesting, however, you often want structured *snapshots* of the order book: "what did the market look like at time t?"

Order Book Snapshot Representation

An order book snapshot at time t can be conceived as two sorted lists:

$$\begin{aligned}\text{Bids}(t) &= \{(p_{b,1}, q_{b,1}), (p_{b,2}, q_{b,2}), \dots\},\\ \text{Asks}(t) &= \{(p_{a,1}, q_{a,1}), (p_{a,2}, q_{a,2}), \dots\},\end{aligned}$$

with prices sorted $p_{b,1} > p_{b,2} > \dots$ and $p_{a,1} < p_{a,2} < \dots$.
A snapshot object for the top N levels should minimally include:

- timestamp
- instrument_id
- Arrays of bid_price[k], bid_size[k] for $k = 1 \dots N$
- Arrays of ask_price[k], ask_size[k] for $k = 1 \dots N$
- venue or aggregation flag

Two main ways to build snapshots:

1. **Exchange-provided snapshots**: some feeds deliver them directly at fixed intervals or on each change.
2. **Reconstructed snapshots**: you consume deltas (add/modify/cancel) and maintain your own in-memory book, occasionally persisting snapshots.

Book Deltas and Compression

Full snapshots at high frequency are large and redundant. Many systems instead store *deltas*:

- At time t_1: full snapshot.
- Between t_1 and t_2: a stream of book updates.
- At t_2: either another snapshot or just continued deltas.

Replaying deltas is essential for:

- High-fidelity backtests of intraday execution algorithms.
- Simulation of order matching (e.g., a limit order resting in the book).

From a modeling standpoint, this means your data schema for books must support:

- Efficient linkage between snapshots and deltas.
- Correct, deterministic reconstruction for a given time window.

Bars: Time-Aggregated Views

Ticks and books are detailed but unwieldy. For many alpha models and risk systems, you instead want *bars*: aggregated summaries over fixed time or event windows.

Time Bars

The most familiar bars are time-based, for example, 1-minute or 1-day OHLCV bars:

- **Open**: first trade price in the interval.
- **High**: maximum trade price in the interval.
- **Low**: minimum trade price in the interval.
- **Close**: last trade price in the interval.
- **Volume**: sum of traded size in the interval.

Bar records should also contain:

- `bar_start_time` and `bar_end_time`
- `instrument_id`
- `num_trades` (optional but often useful)
- A `bar_type` field (e.g., "trades", "quotes").

These bars are convenient for:

- Factor construction (momentum, volatility, liquidity measures).
- Charting and diagnostics.
- Coarser backtests where microsecond timing is not critical.

Quote-Driven Bars

In some contexts, especially for illiquid instruments or in quote-driven markets, few trades occur. Trade-driven bars may then be misleading (e.g., bars with zero volume and a stale last price). An alternative is to define bars from quotes:

- **Mid-price bars**: compute open/high/low/close based on mid-price (bid + ask)/2.
- **Bid/ask bars**: track the evolution of the bid and ask separately.

The choice between trade-driven and quote-driven bars is not just aesthetic. It affects:

- Your perception of volatility and liquidity.
- The behavior of indicators (e.g., moving averages) used in strategies.

It is therefore important that each bar series includes metadata indicating:

- Its construction method (trade, mid, bid, ask).
- Its time zone and calendar (exchange-local vs. UTC, trading days).

Volume and Event-Driven Bars

Time is not the only way to aggregate. For strategies sensitive to order flow, *volume bars* or *event bars* can be more appropriate:

- **Volume bars**: each bar contains approximately the same traded volume (e.g., 10,000 shares), regardless of how long that takes in clock time.
- **Trade-count bars**: each bar aggregates a fixed number of trades.

These constructions aim to normalize bars in terms of "information content" rather than clock time. Your data model for bars should thus allow:

- Non-uniform time intervals.
- Explicit recording of the aggregation criterion (volume, trades, time).

Normalization Choices and Time

Across ticks, books, and bars, you must make systematic normalization choices. Two are particularly important:

Time Zones and Calendars

Market data streams come time-stamped in *exchange local time*. For multi-venue or multi-asset strategies, you typically normalize to a single canonical time, often UTC, while preserving the original timestamps as additional fields.

Your schema should clearly distinguish:

- `timestamp_exchange`: as reported by the venue.
- `timestamp_utc`: your normalized timestamp.
- `receive_timestamp`: when your system actually received the event (useful for latency measurement).

Similarly, you must attach each instrument to a *trading calendar*:

- Which days are holidays or half days.
- What the continuous trading hours and auction periods are.

Bars and derived metrics should be defined with respect to these calendars to avoid mixing trading and non-trading intervals.

On-Book vs. Off-Book Trades

Not all trades in the tape are the outcome of continuous limit order book matching:

- **On-book** trades: direct results of matching visible orders.
- **Off-book** or reported trades: negotiated trades, internal crosses, block trades, or dark pool executions reported with a delay.

Depending on your use case:

- You may want to include off-book trades in daily volume but not in intraday execution simulations.
- You may want to exclude certain trade conditions (e.g., late prints, corrections) from high-frequency models.

This requires that each trade tick carries condition codes, and your schema has room for:

- trade_condition flags.
- A normalized classification (e.g., regular, auction, off-book, late, corrected).

Corporate Actions: When the Instrument Changes Underneath You

So far, we have assumed that an instrument's identity is stable and that prices can be compared directly over time. In reality, issuers routinely change their capital structure through *corporate actions*. If you ignore these, your historical price series will contain artificial discontinuities that can break strategies and backtests.

Types of Corporate Actions

Common corporate actions that affect price series include:

- **Stock splits and reverse splits**: change the number of shares outstanding and the per-share price by a known ratio (e.g., 2-for-1, 1-for-10).
- **Cash dividends**: periodic cash payouts to shareholders.
- **Stock dividends and bonus issues**: additional shares issued to existing shareholders, often expressed as a percentage.

- **Spin-offs**: part of the company is separated into a new entity; existing shareholders receive shares of the new entity.
- **Rights issues**: existing shareholders receive rights to buy new shares, typically at a discount.
- **Symbol changes, mergers, and delistings**: the identity of the instrument itself changes or disappears.

Each action is characterized by several key dates:

- **Announcement date**: when the action is announced.
- **Record date**: holders on this date are entitled to the benefit.
- **Ex-date**: the first day the instrument trades without the upcoming entitlement; prices usually adjust on or just before this date.
- **Payment or effective date**: when cash or shares are actually delivered.

Your trading machine needs clean, timely data on these events and a consistent way to incorporate them into both live and historical data.

Adjusting Price Histories

Corporate actions distort raw prices. For example, in a 2-for-1 split:

- Every share becomes two shares.
- The price roughly halves (ignoring small frictions).

If you look at a raw daily price chart, it will show a large apparent drop—misleading for trend or volatility analysis. To address this, data providers and trading systems maintain *adjusted price series*.

Price-Only Adjusted Series

One common approach is to adjust only the price (and often volume), not the total return:

- For splits, you rescale historical prices and volumes by the split ratio so that the chart looks continuous.
- For certain other actions (like stock dividends), similar multiplicative factors are applied.

For example, suppose a stock trades at $100 on day $t-1$, executes a 2-for-1 split overnight, and opens at $50 on day t. A price-only adjusted series would:

- Divide all pre-split prices by 2, so the $100 becomes $50.
- Multiply all pre-split volumes by 2, so that turnover in currency units is preserved.

The benefits:

- Visual continuity: charts and moving averages do not show artificial jumps.
- Volatility measures are not contaminated by mechanical price halving.

However, cash dividends and many non-proportional corporate actions still create discontinuities under this scheme.

Total-Return Adjusted Series

For research on long-horizon factors, you often prefer a *total-return* view that assumes all dividends are reinvested back into the stock. In a total-return series:

- Both splits and cash dividends result in backward adjustments.

- A dividend of $1 on a $50 stock leads to a small proportional downward adjustment of prior prices so that the ex-dividend drop disappears from the series.

Conceptually, you define an adjustment factor A_t that accumulates all past corporate actions, and then define an adjusted price $\tilde{P}_t$ as

$$\tilde{P}_t = P_t \times A_t.$$

When a dividend or split occurs, you update A_t for all t before the event so that the time series of $\tilde{P}_t$ is smooth. This makes:

- Long-run return calculations consistent with a buy-and-hold investor reinvesting payouts.
- Factor backtests more faithful to investor experiences.

Unadjusted Series

Sometimes you deliberately want *unadjusted* raw prices:

- To precisely match what traders saw and could trade at on a given day.
- For execution simulations or replays of intraday behavior.

In these contexts, you cannot silently shift historical prices, because you would be backtesting on a world that never existed. Instead, you:

- Keep raw ticks and bars unchanged.
- Carry corporate action events alongside them as separate series.

This highlights a key design principle: your data model should support *multiple parallel views* of the same instrument:

- Raw (unadjusted) view.
- Split-adjusted view.

- Total-return view (if needed).

Each view is derived from the same underlying raw data plus corporate action metadata, but serves different downstream consumers.

Corporate Actions in Live Feeds

So far we have discussed how corporate actions reshape *historical* series. They also affect *live* trading:

- On ex-dividend dates, prices may adjust at the open as the entitlement changes.
- Around splits, tick sizes and typical spreads can change, influencing execution costs.
- Around symbol changes, your symbol mapping and identifier resolution must be correct or you will stop receiving data or send orders to the wrong place.

In a live system, you need:

- A feed of upcoming corporate actions with sufficient lead time.
- Logic in your instrument master to:
  - Update tick sizes, lot sizes, and other trading parameters.
  - Flip primary identifiers if symbols change.
  - Apply scaling factors to positions if necessary (e.g., in spin-offs).
- Consistent alignment between live price feeds and the adjustment scheme used in monitoring dashboards (e.g., your intraday P&L should not jump solely because a split adjustment was applied).

Reference Data: The Glue Around Prices

Market data (trades, quotes, bars) tells you *how* instruments trade. Reference data tells you *what* those instruments are and how they relate to each other.

Core reference data fields include:

- Identifiers: exchange tickers, ISIN, CUSIP, internal IDs.
- Instrument attributes: asset class, currency, tick size, lot size, contract multiplier, expiry date.
- Listing and delisting dates.
- Corporate action history and future schedule.
- Mappings to indices, sectors, and other classifications.

Good reference data management ensures that:

- Your bars and ticks can always be joined to the correct instrument, even after symbol changes.
- Your risk and P&L calculations use correct multipliers and contracts specs.
- Your backtests are reproducible across vendors and over time, despite changes in vendor codes or corporate structures.

Putting It Together: Data Shapes as System Contracts

By this point, you can think of tick, book, bar, corporate action, and reference data records as *contracts* between your data layer and the rest of the trading machine:

- Ticks and books: fine-grained, event-level view suitable for execution modeling and high-frequency alpha.

- Bars: aggregated, human- and model-friendly summaries at various horizons.
- Corporate actions and reference data: context that tells you when, how, and why the numerical series should be scaled, linked, or retired.

Downstream systems—from alpha research to real-time risk—depend on these contracts being:

- **Explicit**: fields and semantics clearly documented.
- **Consistent**: the same instrument and time period always map to the same adjusted values given a chosen convention.
- **Versioned**: changes in corporate action interpretation or vendor feeds are traceable.

In the next section, we will move from defining these data shapes to the engineering pipelines that ingest, normalize, check, and store them at scale. The concepts introduced here—ticks, books, bars, corporate action-adjusted series, and reference data—will become the building blocks of those pipelines and the objects that your backtesters and live trading engines consume.

1.4 Data Engineering Pipelines and Quality

The previous sections defined *what* the market looks like as data: ticks, order books, bars, corporate actions, and reference data. We now turn to the engineering question:

> *How do we turn raw, messy vendor feeds into trustworthy datasets that strategies, backtests, and live trading engines can safely consume?*

The answer is an end-to-end data pipeline that ingests heterogeneous feeds, transforms and normalizes them (ETL), checks and repairs quality issues, and records enough metadata and lineage that you can always answer:

- Where did this data come from?
- How was it transformed?
- Can I reproduce it, or roll back if necessary?

This section will proceed from a high-level pipeline view down to concrete mechanisms for quality and lineage.

A High-Level View of the Market Data Pipeline

Figure provides a visual scaffold for the pipeline we will discuss: raw feeds enter on the left, are processed through ETL and quality checks in the middle, stored in layered data stores, and flow out to research and live trading systems on the right.

High-level market data pipeline: raw vendor feeds flow through parsing/normalization, quality checks, and enrichment into curated stores consumed by research and live trading, with metadata and lineage recorded alongside.

We now use this diagram as a map while we examine each stage in more detail.

Ingest: Receiving Raw, Heterogeneous Feeds

Your starting point is a collection of vendor and broker feeds. These may include:

- Real-time market data (ticks, quotes, order book events).
- End-of-day bars and reference data snapshots.
- Corporate action announcements and instrument master data.

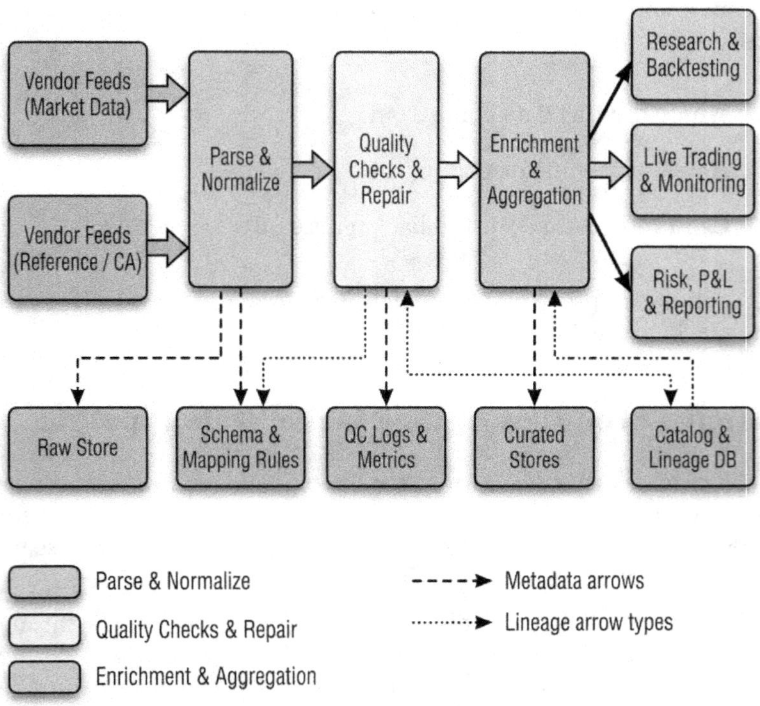

The key characteristics of raw feeds:

- **Heterogeneous protocols**: FIX, proprietary binary, CSV/TSV, JSON over HTTP, SFTP drops, message queues, etc.
- **Different schemas**: field names, units, and encodings differ between vendors.
- **Inconsistent quality**: clock skew, dropped messages, late corrections, and misclassified trades.

The ingest layer has three main responsibilities:

- **Capture**: reliably receive all events, with minimal loss.
- **Persist**: write an immutable copy of the raw feed to a *raw store*, ideally append-only and time-partitioned.
- **Tag with metadata**: capture source identifiers, connection status, and receiver timestamps.

A best practice is to treat raw data as a *write-once* asset: you never overwrite it, and you never attempt to "fix" it in place. Instead, you build cleaned and enriched datasets on top, always able to go back to the raw source when necessary.

ETL: Parsing, Normalization, and Basic Enrichment

Once data is safely ingested and stored, the next step is ETL (Extract, Transform, Load). For market data, ETL typically includes:

Parsing and Schema Mapping

Each feed is parsed into a well-defined internal schema:

- Extract and type-cast fields (e.g., convert strings to numeric, handle missing values).
- Map vendor-specific field names to canonical names (e.g., SECID, RIC, Symbol all to instrument_id_vendor plus an internal instrument_id).
- Normalize units (e.g., price in currency units, not "cents" or "ticks"; volume in shares or contracts).

At this stage you also separate different logical streams:

- Trades vs. quotes vs. book updates.
- Reference data vs. corporate actions.
- Per-venue vs. consolidated data.

Your *schema repository*—a set of formal definitions for each data type—is essential documentation and code for this step. It should be machine-readable (YAML, JSON, or similar) and version-controlled, so changes in field definitions are tracked over time.

Time Normalization

As discussed earlier, each event arrives with a venue timestamp. ETL adds:

- A normalized `timestamp_utc`.
- A `receive_timestamp` when your system saw the message.

Normalizing time enables:

- Cross-venue ordering of events.
- Latency measurement and monitoring.

Care must be taken in handling daylight savings and historical time-zone changes; delegating this to a robust library is strongly recommended.

Basic Enrichment

Even early in the pipeline, you can join useful reference data:

- Map vendor instrument codes to an internal `instrument_id`.
- Attach trading calendar information (e.g., is this within regular trading hours?).
- Attach contract specifications (e.g., multiplier for futures).

This enrichment makes downstream logic simpler and reduces repeated lookups at query time.

Quality Checks: Detecting and Repairing Problems

Once data is syntactically valid and normalized, you must ask: *Is it plausible?* Data quality problems can silently propagate into bad decisions if not caught early.

We can categorize common issues and corresponding checks.

Gaps and Missing Data

Gaps occur when:

- Whole intervals have no trades or quotes when there should be activity.
- Entire days or instruments are missing due to upstream outages or ingest failures.

Checks include:

- **Heartbeat checks**: ensure that each active instrument receives at least some data over expected intervals during trading hours.
- **Coverage checks**: for end-of-day bars and reference data, verify that all expected instruments are present.

Repair strategies:

- Mark missing intervals explicitly and exclude them from certain analytics.
- Re-request data from vendors where possible.
- In limited cases, fill small intra-bar gaps with last-known values for continuity, while flagging imputed regions.

Duplicates and Out-of-Order Events

Duplicates can occur when connections drop and are replayed, or when multiple feeds overlap. Out-of-order events arise from network delays or clock skew.

Checks:

- Enforce `trade_id` uniqueness per instrument and venue.
- Detect non-monotonic sequences of event timestamps.

Repairs:

- Deduplicate based on unique IDs where available.
- Resort events by `timestamp_utc` for storage, but preserve original timestamps and out-of-order flags for transparency.

Outliers and Bad Prices

Some ticks will be clearly wrong:

- Trade prices far from prevailing quotes.
- Negative prices or volumes.
- Spikes that exceed plausible ranges given historical volatility.

Checks:

- Range checks on price and volume (non-negative, within plausible bounds).
- Cross-validation with order book: trades should typically occur within the current bid–ask spread or just outside it.
- Statistical filters: identify returns that exceed some large multiple of recent volatility.

Repairs:

- Flag suspicious records with a quality code (do not erase them silently).
- Exclude flagged records from certain derived datasets (e.g., bar construction) while keeping them in raw archives.

- For corporate actions where large price changes are expected (e.g., splits), ensure your checks are aware of ex-dates to avoid false alarms.

Clock Skew and Latency Anomalies

In low-latency trading, the difference between venue timestamps and your receive timestamps matters:

- If the venue clock drifts, event times may appear shifted.
- If network connections stall, messages may arrive in bursts, distorting apparent order flow.

Checks:

- Monitor distribution of (receive_timestamp – timestamp_exchange).
- Raise alerts when this latency exceeds thresholds or changes regime.

Repairs:

- Mainly operational: adjust infrastructure or switch to backup feeds.
- For research datasets, document latency characteristics so that backtests do not assume unrealistic information timing.

Quality Metrics and Dashboards

Quality checks feed into metrics such as:

- Percentage of missing bars per instrument per day.
- Number of outlier trades detected and flagged.
- Average and 99th-percentile latency by venue.
- Schema or mapping errors encountered during ETL.

These metrics should be:

- Stored in a *QC log store* (as indicated in Figure).
- Exposed via dashboards to the trading and data engineering teams.
- Tied to alerts when thresholds are breached.

The goal is to treat data quality as a first-class operational concern, on par with system uptime.

Enrichment and Curated Storage Layers

After ETL and quality checks, you build the datasets that strategists and live systems actually use. These curated layers sit between raw feeds and end-users.

Canonical Event Stores

At the lowest curated level, you maintain canonical stores of:

- Trade ticks (cleaned and normalized).
- Quote and order book events.
- Corporate actions and reference data.

These are typically stored in time-series optimized formats:

- Columnar storage (e.g., Parquet) for efficient range scans in research.
- Specialized time-series databases or key-value stores for low-latency access in live trading.

Key design points:

- Partitioning by date and instrument universe.
- Indexing on `instrument_id` and `timestamp_utc`.

- Compression tuned to the sparsity and distribution of events.

Derived Data: Bars, Features, and Aggregates

On top of event stores, you compute:

- OHLCV bars at various frequencies and constructions (trade, quote, volume bars).
- Order book snapshots at regular intervals (e.g., every second) or event-driven.
- Factor inputs and statistical features (e.g., rolling volatility, spreads, order flow imbalance).

These derived datasets:

- Should be versioned by their construction parameters (e.g., bar length, inclusion rules for off-book trades).
- May be materialized (stored) or computed on demand, depending on cost and usage.

Joining Corporate Actions and Reference Data

At this layer, you integrate corporate actions and reference data to produce:

- Adjusted price series (split- or total-return-adjusted) alongside raw series.
- Historical instrument mapping tables (how identifiers evolved over time).
- Attribute-enriched datasets (each bar tagged with sector, currency, tick size, etc.).

This enriched view enables cross-sectional and time-series research without repeatedly performing complex joins.

Metadata, Catalog, and Lineage

As datasets proliferate, it becomes essential to know what each table or file actually represents. This is the role of metadata and lineage.

Metadata and Cataloging

For each dataset (raw or curated), maintain:

- **Descriptive metadata**:
  - Human-readable name and description.
  - Data type (ticks, bars, reference).
  - Instrument universe and date range.
- **Technical metadata**:
  - Schema (field names, types, units).
  - Storage location and partitioning scheme.
  - Data volume and update frequency.
- **Quality metadata**:
  - Known limitations or caveats (e.g., missing venues, partial history).
  - Aggregate quality metrics (e.g., percentage of missing days).

A *data catalog* is a centralized service or repository where this metadata is stored and queryable—the "directory" of your trading data universe.

Lineage: From Output Back to Sources

Data lineage answers: *Which sources and transformations produced this dataset or even this individual value?*

At a coarse level, for each dataset you should record:

- Input datasets and vendors.
- ETL jobs and code versions used.
- Time of last successful build.

At a finer level, you can attach lineage to:

- Individual partitions (e.g., daily files).
- Specific computation runs (e.g., factor model builds).

Lineage is invaluable when:

- A vendor later reports a correction: you can identify all derived datasets that must be recomputed.
- You want to reproduce an old backtest exactly, years later: you can re-run it on the same data versions and transformation code.
- You investigate unexpected strategy behavior: you can determine whether data changes or bugs in processing played a role.

Serving Research and Live Trading Safely

The right-hand side of Figure shows the consumers of curated data: research and backtesting, live trading, and risk/P&L.

Research and Backtesting

Researchers need:

- High-throughput, flexible access to large historical datasets.
- Clear documentation of adjustment conventions and universes.
- The ability to fix a data snapshot for a given experiment (i.e., avoid accidental mixing of updated and old data).

The pipeline supports this by:

- Providing stable, versioned datasets for backtesting.
- Exposing metadata and lineage so researchers can select the appropriate level of adjustment and quality.

Live Trading and Monitoring

Live systems need:

- Low-latency access to current market data and reference data.
- Immediate reflection of certain reference changes (e.g., symbol changes, tick size updates).
- Robustness to transient data quality issues (e.g., briefly inconsistent quotes).

Here, your pipeline must support:

- Streaming interfaces from curated event stores into trading engines.
- Real-time or near-real-time QC checks with safe fallbacks (e.g., dropping obviously bad ticks while raising alerts).

Risk, P&L, and Reporting

Risk and reporting systems depend on:

- Consistent integration of market data, corporate actions, and trade/position data (from earlier lifecycle sections).
- Reliable historical series for stress testing and scenario analysis.

The same curated and metadata-rich datasets power these systems, enabling:

- Daily reconciliation between front-office views and official books and records.
- Transparent audits of how reported numbers were derived.

Design Principles and Trade-Offs

To close, it is useful to summarize the design principles that should guide your market data pipeline:

- **Raw data is immutable**: never overwrite vendor feeds; build clean layers on top.
- **Schemas are explicit and versioned**: field definitions live in code and documentation, not in people's heads.
- **Quality is measured, not assumed**: every dataset is accompanied by QC metrics and flags.
- **Transformations are reproducible**: ETL jobs are deterministic and version-controlled, with lineage recorded.
- **Multiple views coexist**: raw, adjusted, and enriched datasets serve different needs; do not try to force a single "one-size-fits-all" representation.

Your algorithmic trading machine lives and dies by the quality of its data backbone. Elegant alpha models and sophisticated execution logic will fail if fed inconsistent, incomplete, or poorly documented data. By building robust pipelines, systematic quality checks, and rich metadata from the start, you transform raw market noise into a reliable substrate on which the rest of the architecture can safely operate.

Chapter 2

Quantitative Methods and Statistical Foundations

Most trading systems fail not because their ideas are bad, but because their math is sloppy. This chapter arms you with the quantitative habits that separate research from roulette: treating markets as noisy probability spaces, modeling time-varying risk, and validating signals in a way that survives contact with live capital. You will not become a mathematician-you will become dangerous enough with probability, statistics, time series, and optimization to build machines that earn your trust (and keep it).

2.1 Probability, Distributions, and Inference

Algorithmic trading systems operate in an environment where nothing is certain and almost everything that matters is noisy: prices, volumes, news responses, slippage, and even the apparent performance of our own strategies. In this section we formalize that uncertainty using probability, build up the idea of random variables and distributions, and then show how to estimate and test the quantities we care about in practice: expected returns, volatilities, correlations, and Sharpe ratios.

Our goal is not to turn you into a pure mathematician, but to give you a language and toolkit. Once you see markets as probabilistic systems rather than a sequence of anecdotes, concepts like "alpha", "risk", and "statistical significance" become concrete and measurable.

Probability as the Language of Market Uncertainty

Outcomes, events, and probabilities

Every trading decision is made before the outcome is known. Suppose your strategy takes a long position in a stock for one day. Tomorrow's close relative to today's close might be up $+1.2\%$, down -0.7%, or something else entirely. We model this by:

- A *sample space* Ω: the set of all possible outcomes. For a one-day return, a natural choice is

  $$\Omega = \{r \in \mathbb{R} : -1 < r < \infty\},$$

  since a return cannot be less than -100%, but can in principle be arbitrarily large on the upside.
- An *event* A: a subset of Ω we care about, such as "strategy loses money",

  $$A = \{r \in \Omega : r < 0\}.$$
- A *probability* function $P(\cdot)$: assigns to each event A a number $P(A) \in [0, 1]$, interpreted as the long-run frequency with which A occurs if we could repeat the trading setup many times.

For example, if over a large sample we see that on 45% of days the daily return is negative, we might approximate

$$P(\text{loss tomorrow}) \approx 0.45.$$

This is already useful. Once you can attach probabilities to events such as "day ends with a loss" or "drawdown exceeds 10% this month", you can speak precisely about risk instead of relying on vague adjectives like "often" or "rarely".

Conditional probability and Bayes' rule

Trading almost never happens in a vacuum. We care about probabilities *conditional* on current information: regime labels, volatility state, signals, and so on.

If A is an event (e.g., "loss tomorrow") and B is another event (e.g., "today's realized volatility is above its 90th percentile"), the *conditional probability* of A given B is

$$P(A \mid B) = \frac{P(A \cap B)}{P(B)},$$

provided $P(B) > 0$.

In words: the chance of a loss tomorrow *given* that we are currently in a high-volatility state equals the chance that *both* a loss happens and volatility is high, divided by the chance that volatility is high at all.

Conditional probabilities let us encode ideas like:

- "The win rate of this mean-reversion strategy is 60% *when volatility is low*, but only 48% when volatility is high."
- "The probability that our stop-loss is hit is much higher if we enter a position shortly before a macro announcement."

Bayes' rule in trading terms.

Bayes' rule simply reverses conditioning:

$$P(B \mid A) = \frac{P(A \mid B)P(B)}{P(A)}.$$

In trading language, think of B as "market is in a mean-reverting regime" and A as "our signal fired today". Bayes' rule lets you update your belief about the regime probability after observing the signal.

You might estimate $P(A \mid B)$, the chance of a signal in a mean-reverting regime, from historical data. You might also have a prior $P(B)$ (e.g., mean-reverting regime 30% of the time). After observing the signal, Bayes' rule gives you $P(B \mid A)$, the updated regime probability. This is the probabilistic backbone behind many regime-switching and Bayesian strategy-combination models.

Random Variables and Expectations

So far we have spoken about events like "loss" or "stop-loss hit". To do serious work in quantitative finance, we need to handle numerical quantities: returns, P&L in dollars, realized volatility, drawdowns, and more. These are modeled as *random variables*.

Random variables

A *random variable* X is a function that assigns a real number to each outcome in Ω. Formally, $X : \Omega \to \mathbb{R}$. Practically, you can think of it as a numeric quantity whose realized value is uncertain.

Common examples:

- R: one-day return of a strategy.
- V: realized volatility over the next week.
- N: number of trades executed by a strategy in a given day.

All of the familiar financial statistics—mean return, variance, covariance, Sharpe ratio—are functions of one or more random variables.

Expectation: average outcomes

The *expectation* or *expected value* of a random variable X, denoted $E[X]$, is its long-run average value across many repetitions of the same setup.

If X is *discrete*, taking values $x_1, x_2, \ldots$ with probabilities $P(X = x_i)$, then

$$E[X] = \sum_i x_i P(X = x_i).$$

If X is *continuous*, with probability density function $f_X(x)$, then

$$E[X] = \int_{-\infty}^{\infty} x f_X(x)\, dx.$$

In trading terms:

- The expected daily return of a strategy, $E[R]$, is its theoretical average daily return across many hypothetical realizations of the future.
- The expected P&L in dollars, $E[\text{P\&L}]$, tells us whether the strategy makes money on average.

Variance, standard deviation, and covariance

Risk is not just about bad events; it is about variability. Two central measures are:

Variance and standard deviation.

The *variance* of X is

$$\text{Var}(X) = E\big[(X - E[X])^2\big].$$

The *standard deviation* is

$$\sigma_X = \sqrt{\text{Var}(X)}.$$

In markets, σ_R for returns R is what we usually call *volatility*. High volatility means returns are widely spread around their mean; low volatility means they are tightly clustered.

Covariance and correlation.

Given two random variables X and Y (e.g., returns of two different assets),

$$\text{Cov}(X, Y) = E\big[(X - E[X])(Y - E[Y])\big]$$

measures how they move together. The *correlation* is a scale-free version:

$$\rho_{XY} = \frac{\text{Cov}(X, Y)}{\sigma_X \sigma_Y}.$$

Correlation is central to portfolio construction: combining uncorrelated or negatively correlated strategies can reduce overall risk without necessarily sacrificing expected return.

Distributions Used in Finance

Once we have random variables, we need a way to describe how their values are spread out. This is what the *distribution* of a random variable captures.

Discrete distributions: Bernoulli, binomial, and Poisson

Bernoulli: single trade outcome.

A Bernoulli random variable X takes value 1 with probability p and 0 with probability $1 - p$. For a trading strategy that either wins or loses a fixed amount on each trade, we can use a Bernoulli to model "hit" vs. "miss".

- Let $X = 1$ if a trade is profitable, 0 otherwise.
- Then $p = P(X = 1)$ is the *hit rate* (win rate).
- We have $E[X] = p$ and $\mathrm{Var}(X) = p(1 - p)$.

Binomial: number of winners in n trades.

If we execute n trades, each modeled as independent Bernoulli with win probability p, the total number of winners K follows a binomial distribution:

$$P(K = k) = \binom{n}{k} p^k (1 - p)^{n-k}, \quad k = 0, \dots, n.$$

This is useful when you ask: "Given an assumed win rate of p, how surprising is it that I saw only k winners in n trades?" That is a first step towards hypothesis testing of hit rates.

Poisson: event counts in time.

A Poisson random variable with parameter $\lambda > 0$ models the count of events in a fixed time interval when events occur randomly but at an average rate λ. In markets, Poisson and related processes are used to model:

- Number of trades arriving per second in a limit order book.
- Number of marketable orders hitting your quotes.

- Number of large price jumps in a week.

For a Poisson(λ) variable N,

$$E[N] = \lambda, \quad \text{Var}(N) = \lambda.$$

Continuous distributions: normal, t, and lognormal

Normal (Gaussian) distribution.

The normal distribution $N(\mu, \sigma^2)$ with mean μ and variance σ^2 is ubiquitous in statistics and historically in finance. If $X \sim N(\mu, \sigma^2)$, its density is

$$f_X(x) = \frac{1}{\sqrt{2\pi}\sigma} \exp\left(-\frac{(x-\mu)^2}{2\sigma^2}\right).$$

Why is it so popular?

- It is fully characterized by two parameters, μ and σ^2.
- Linear combinations of jointly normal variables are also normal.
- Sums of many small, independent effects tend to look approximately normal (central limit theorem).

In basic portfolio theory, returns are often *assumed* to be normal to make math and optimization tractable. However, actual financial returns usually exhibit:

- *Heavy tails*: more extreme events than the normal distribution predicts.
- *Skewness*: asymmetry between large gains and large losses.

Thus, normality is often a convenient approximation, but you should remain aware of its limitations, especially when assessing tail risk.

Student's t distribution: heavier tails.

When returns have fatter tails than normal, the Student's t distribution with ν degrees of freedom is a natural alternative. It resembles the normal distribution but with heavier tails, particularly for small ν. As $\nu \to \infty$, the t-distribution converges to a normal.

In practice, t-distributions appear when we account for uncertainty in the variance estimate, and they form the basis of many confidence intervals and tests for means (e.g., Sharpe ratios for finite samples).

Lognormal distribution: modeling prices.

Instead of modeling prices P_t directly as normal, we often model $\log P_t$ as normal. If $\log P_T$ is normally distributed, then P_T is *lognormal*: always positive and multiplicative in nature. This aligns with the fact that returns compound over time. Many continuous-time models (e.g., geometric Brownian motion) imply lognormal prices.

From Distributions to Estimation

So far we have discussed theoretical objects: true means, true variances, true distributions. In reality we never see the full distribution; we only observe a finite sample of data: daily returns over the last three years, trade-level P&L, etc. *Estimation* is about using this sample to infer properties of the underlying distribution.

Sample mean and variance

Suppose we observe n returns $r_1, r_2, \ldots, r_n$ from a strategy. The *sample mean* is

$$\bar{r} = \frac{1}{n} \sum_{i=1}^{n} r_i.$$

We use $\bar{r}$ as an estimator of the true expected return $\mu = E[R]$.

The *sample variance* is

$$s^2 = \frac{1}{n-1} \sum_{i=1}^{n} (r_i - \bar{r})^2,$$

and the *sample standard deviation* is $s = \sqrt{s^2}$. We use s as an estimator of the true volatility σ.

The factor $1/(n-1)$ (rather than $1/n$) corrects for the fact that we have already used the sample to estimate $\bar{r}$; it makes s^2 an *unbiased* estimator of σ^2 under mild assumptions.

Sharpe ratio as an estimator of risk-adjusted return

The *Sharpe ratio* is a central quantity in quantitative trading. For returns r_t in excess of a risk-free rate,

$$\text{Sharpe} = \frac{E[r_t]}{\sqrt{\text{Var}(r_t)}} = \frac{\mu}{\sigma}.$$

In finite samples we estimate it with

$$\hat{S} = \frac{\bar{r}}{s}.$$

A higher Sharpe suggests more expected return per unit of risk. But remember: $\hat{S}$ is a random quantity computed from noisy data; it itself has a distribution. That means we can (and should) ask whether an observed Sharpe is statistically distinguishable from zero, and how much it might be inflated by luck.

Concept Map: From Probability to Inference

Right after introducing random variables, it is helpful to visualize how the main concepts in this section relate to one another. Figure presents a concept map linking basic probability, random variables, distributions, and inference tasks, with brief trading annotations.

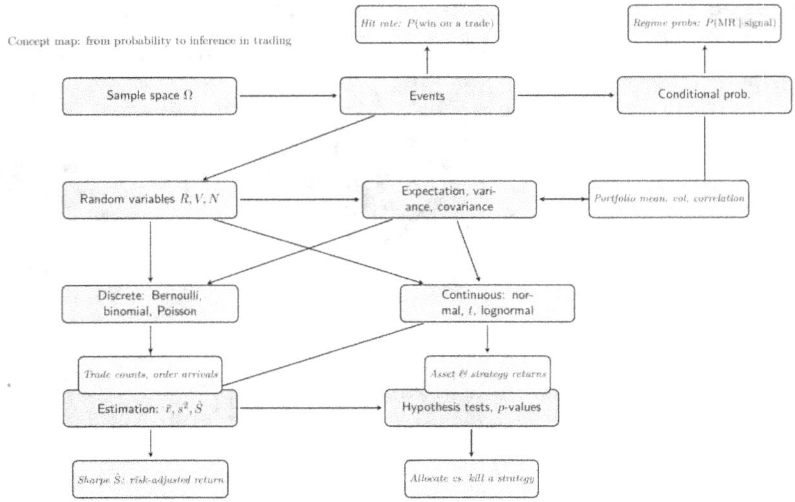

Inference: From Samples to Decisions

Estimation gives us point values like $\bar{r}$ or $\hat{S}$. But these numbers are themselves uncertain. We need tools to quantify and act on that uncertainty. This is the role of *statistical inference*: confidence intervals and hypothesis tests.

Sampling variability and confidence intervals

Imagine two strategies, A and B, each with 250 daily returns (about one trading year):

- Strategy A: $\bar{r}_A = 0.08\%$ per day, $s_A = 1.0\%$.
- Strategy B: $\bar{r}_B = 0.10\%$ per day, $s_B = 1.5\%$.

Is B really better than A? The observed difference in means is only 0.02% per day. That could easily be noise.

A *confidence interval* for the true mean μ gives a range of plausible values based on the sample. Under mild assumptions, an approximate

95% confidence interval for the mean return is

$$\bar{r} \pm 1.96 \cdot \frac{s}{\sqrt{n}}.$$

If Strategy A has a confidence interval $[0.04\%, 0.12\%]$ and Strategy B has $[0.01\%, 0.19\%]$, the intervals overlap heavily; we cannot confidently say that B's mean is higher, even though its sample mean is.

This matters for capital allocation. If you ignore sampling variability, you may over-allocate to strategies whose observed performance was simply lucky.

Hypothesis testing: is there alpha?

Hypothesis testing formalizes questions like "is this edge real?" as a statistical experiment.

Testing mean return.

We typically start with a *null hypothesis*:

$$H_0 : \mu = 0 \quad \text{(no alpha)}$$

against an alternative

$$H_1 : \mu > 0 \quad \text{(positive alpha).}$$

Given n observed returns $r_1, \ldots, r_n$, we compute the *test statistic*

$$T = \frac{\bar{r} - 0}{s/\sqrt{n}}.$$

Under H_0 and mild assumptions, T approximately follows a Student's t distribution with $n - 1$ degrees of freedom. Intuitively, T measures how many standard errors $\bar{r}$ is away from zero.

The *p-value* is the probability, under H_0, of observing a test statistic at least as extreme as the one you got. If the p-value is small (e.g., below 5%), the observed mean would be quite unlikely if $\mu = 0$, so you may decide to reject H_0 in favor of H_1.

Type I and Type II errors.

Two types of mistakes are possible:

- *Type I error*: reject H_0 when it is actually true (you think you found alpha, but there is none). The probability of this under your testing rule is the *significance level*, often 5%.
- *Type II error*: fail to reject H_0 when it is false (you miss a real alpha).

In a research pipeline that tries many ideas, Type I errors are especially dangerous: they correspond to overfitted strategies that look great in backtest but fail live. Later in this chapter we will discuss multiple-testing adjustments and overfitting defenses. For now, the key takeaway is that hypothesis tests quantify the risk of being fooled by randomness, but they do not eliminate it.

Testing volatility and correlation

The same hypothesis-testing framework extends to other quantities:

- **Volatility changes.** Test whether volatility has changed between two periods (e.g., pre- and post-regime change) using tests for equality of variances.
- **Correlation changes.** Test whether the correlation between two assets or strategies has shifted, which impacts diversification benefits and risk models.

In each case, you:

- Specify a null hypothesis (e.g., "volatility is unchanged").
- Choose a test statistic sensitive to the hypothesized change.
- Compute a p-value under the null.
- Decide whether the evidence is strong enough to act (e.g., adjust risk limits, rebalance portfolios).

How Much Data Do You Need?

A recurring practical question is: "How much data do I need before trusting an edge?" The answer depends on:

- The signal's true Sharpe ratio (unknown).
- The frequency of observations (daily vs. intraday).
- The acceptable risk of Type I and Type II errors.

Roughly speaking, the standard error of the Sharpe ratio estimate shrinks like $1/\sqrt{n}$. Doubling your sample length reduces uncertainty by only about 30%. This is why short backtests (e.g., a few months of intraday data) are almost always too noisy to rely on for capital-intensive decisions.

The quantitative machinery developed in this section—probability, distributions, expectation, and inference—provides the language to compute, rather than guess, how uncertain your estimates are. In later sections we will extend these ideas to time series (where independence across observations is no longer a good assumption) and to more complex models of volatility and correlation. At every stage, the same principles apply: specify randomness clearly, connect it to financial quantities of interest, estimate carefully, and test rigorously before you deploy real capital.

2.2 Time Series Fundamentals and Volatility Modeling

In the previous section we treated returns as random variables drawn from some distribution and developed tools for expectation, variance, and inference. Implicitly, we pretended these observations were *exchangeable*: their order did not matter. For many problems in algorithmic trading, that is not enough. Markets are explicitly *time-ordered* systems. The state today depends on what happened yesterday; tomorrow's risk depends on today's volatility.

This section upgrades our probabilistic view to a *time-aware* one. We will:

- Distinguish price levels from returns and log-returns.
- Define stationarity and the basic autocorrelation tools used to diagnose temporal structure.

- Introduce AR/MA/ARMA models as simple baselines for predictable components in returns.
- Show why volatility is time-varying and develop ARCH/GARCH models to forecast it for trading and risk management.

Throughout, keep in mind the practical goal: turning past data into forecasts of future returns and volatility that can drive position sizing, risk limits, and execution logic.

From Prices to Returns

Let P_t denote the price of an asset (or portfolio) at time t. In a typical trading dataset, t might be a day, an hour, or a minute.

Why we almost never model prices directly

Prices are typically nonstationary: they drift upwards or downwards over long horizons, and their scale changes over time (an index that was at 100 can later be at 5000). Many statistical tools assume that the underlying process has a constant mean and variance over time. That assumption fails badly for prices.

Instead, we model *returns*, which are approximately stationary over moderate horizons and behave more like the random variables discussed earlier.

Simple and log returns

The *simple* (or arithmetic) return from $t-1$ to t is

$$R_t = \frac{P_t - P_{t-1}}{P_{t-1}}.$$

The *log* return is

$$r_t = \log\left(\frac{P_t}{P_{t-1}}\right) = \log P_t - \log P_{t-1}.$$

For typical daily or intraday changes where $|R_t|$ is small, we have $r_t \approx R_t$. Log returns have two convenient properties:

- They *add* over time: $r_{t,t+k} = r_{t+1} + \cdots + r_{t+k}$.
- They correspond to modeling prices as always-positive lognormal variables.

For time series modeling we can work with either R_t or r_t. We will use r_t as the generic notation for "return."

Stationarity: When Time Series Models Make Sense

When we speak about the "distribution" of a random variable, we imagine a stable pattern. For time series, the analogous assumption is *stationarity*.

Weak stationarity

A time series $\{X_t\}$ is (weakly) stationary if:

- The mean is constant over time: $E[X_t] = \mu$ for all t.
- The variance is constant: $\text{Var}(X_t) = \sigma^2$ for all t.
- The covariance between two times depends only on the lag, not on absolute time:

$$\text{Cov}(X_t, X_{t+k}) = \gamma(k) \quad \text{for all } t.$$

Intuitively, the statistical behavior of a stationary series does not change as you slide along the time axis. There may be dependence across time, but the rules of the game are stable.

Prices vs. returns.

- Prices P_t usually have a nonconstant mean and variance: they trend, and their scale grows with time. They are nonstationary.
- Returns r_t are often closer to stationary: their mean and variance fluctuate much less over time (though volatility can still change).

This is why almost all financial time series models are specified for returns or log-price changes, not raw prices.

Autocorrelation and partial autocorrelation

Stationarity does not mean independence. Consecutive returns can be correlated: think of short-term mean reversion or momentum.

The *autocovariance function* at lag k is

$$\gamma(k) = \mathrm{Cov}(X_t, X_{t+k}),$$

and the *autocorrelation function* (ACF) is

$$\rho(k) = \frac{\gamma(k)}{\gamma(0)}.$$

Empirically, we estimate $\rho(k)$ from sample data and plot it against k. The ACF tells us how strongly the series is linearly related to past values at different lags.

The *partial autocorrelation function* (PACF) measures the correlation between X_t and X_{t+k} once we remove the linear influence of intermediate lags $1, \ldots, k-1$. It is useful for identifying which lag terms belong in an autoregressive model.

Trading interpretation.

- Significant positive $\rho(1)$ can indicate short-term momentum: positive returns tend to be followed by positive returns.
- Significant negative $\rho(1)$ can indicate mean reversion: positive returns tend to be followed by negative returns.
- Persistent autocorrelations at multiple lags can suggest microstructure effects, delayed information diffusion, or slowly decaying impact.

These patterns are often tiny at daily horizons but can be meaningful at intraday or tick levels where frictions and order flow mechanisms dominate.

AR, MA, and ARMA Models for Returns

Autocorrelation suggests we can predict part of tomorrow's return using past returns. The simplest way to formalize this is through linear time series models.

Autoregressive (AR) models

An autoregressive process of order p, AR(p), is defined by

$$r_t = \phi_1 r_{t-1} + \phi_2 r_{t-2} + \cdots + \phi_p r_{t-p} + \varepsilon_t,$$

where ε_t is white noise: independent, zero-mean, constant-variance shocks.

- The coefficients ϕ_i capture how past returns feed into the current return.
- Stationarity requires restrictions on the ϕ_i (roots of the characteristic polynomial lie outside the unit circle), but common software handles this for you.

AR(1) intuition.

For AR(1):

$$r_t = \phi r_{t-1} + \varepsilon_t.$$

- If $\phi > 0$ but small, we have mild positive serial correlation: short-term momentum.
- If $\phi < 0$, we have mean reversion: positive returns tend to be followed by negative returns.
- If $\phi = 0$, we fall back to independent shocks: no linear predictability.

AR models serve as baseline predictive models for returns and as residual generators for more complex models such as GARCH.

Moving average (MA) models

A moving average process of order q, MA(q), is

$$r_t = \varepsilon_t + \theta_1 \varepsilon_{t-1} + \theta_2 \varepsilon_{t-2} + \cdots + \theta_q \varepsilon_{t-q}.$$

Instead of relating r_t directly to past returns, MA models relate r_t to past shocks.

MA components can arise from temporary liquidity imbalances, inventory effects, or the way quotes and trades reflect information with a delay. They can capture short-lived transients in returns that AR models may not represent as simply.

ARMA: combining AR and MA

The ARMA(p, q) model combines the two:

$$r_t = \phi_1 r_{t-1} + \cdots + \phi_p r_{t-p} + \varepsilon_t + \theta_1 \varepsilon_{t-1} + \cdots + \theta_q \varepsilon_{t-q}.$$

ARMA models are the workhorse for modeling the conditional mean of stationary time series. In financial returns, their role is usually modest:

- At daily horizons, ϕ_i and θ_j are often small; linear predictability in mean is limited.
- At intraday or tick horizons, ARMA structures can be stronger due to microstructure effects.

Even when the mean is nearly unpredictable, ARMA models are valuable as a *filtering* step: we remove any small mean structure and study the residuals, which then feed into volatility models.

Volatility: The Heartbeat of Risk

So far we have treated volatility as constant (or at least not explicitly time-varying). Real markets are clearly not like that. Periods of calm alternate with bursts of turbulence; high volatility tends to cluster in time.

Evidence for time-varying volatility

If you plot daily returns for an index or liquid stock, you will typically see:

- Periods where returns are small and quiet.
- Periods where returns swing wildly.

- These periods are not randomly scattered; big moves tend to follow big moves.

Mathematically, while raw returns r_t show little autocorrelation, functions of returns like r_t^2 or $|r_t|$ often have strong and persistent autocorrelation. This is *volatility clustering*.

Volatility clustering is crucial for risk management and trading:

- A strategy that sizes positions ignoring volatility clustering will be over-levered in turbulent times and under-levered in calm times.
- Risk limits expressed in terms of "max daily loss" or "VaR" must adapt to changing volatility.

Rolling Volatility and GARCH: A Visual Overview

Before introducing formal volatility models, it is helpful to visualize prices, returns, rolling volatility, and a GARCH-based volatility estimate on the same time axis. Figure shows such a multi-panel plot using simulated data that mimics key stylized facts: nonstationary prices, near-stationary returns, and clustered volatility.

This figure highlights three key ideas:

- Prices are nonstationary, drifting over time.
- Returns are roughly stationary in mean, but their dispersion changes.
- Volatility can be modeled and forecast as a time-varying process, responsive to recent shocks.

We now formalize that last point with ARCH and GARCH models.

ARCH and GARCH: Modeling Conditional Volatility

In an AR or ARMA model, the conditional mean $E[r_t \mid \mathcal{F}_{t-1}]$ depends on the past information set $\mathcal{F}_{t-1}$, but the variance is constant. To cap-

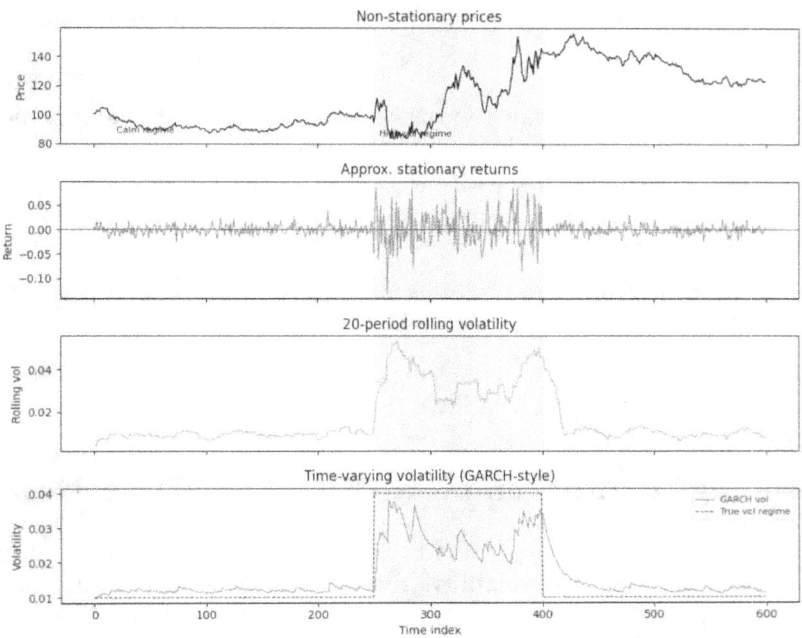

Figure 2.1: Illustrative multi-panel time series: (1) nonstationary prices, (2) approximately stationary returns, (3) rolling volatility, and (4) a GARCH-style volatility estimate tracking a changing volatility regime.

ture volatility clustering, we extend the model so that the *conditional variance* also depends on past data.

ARCH: Autoregressive Conditional Heteroskedasticity

An ARCH(q) model posits that

$$r_t = \sigma_t \varepsilon_t,$$

where:

- ε_t is white noise with zero mean and unit variance (often assumed i.i.d. standard normal or t-distributed).

- σ_t^2 is the *conditional variance* at time t, defined by

  $$\sigma_t^2 = \alpha_0 + \alpha_1 r_{t-1}^2 + \alpha_2 r_{t-2}^2 + \cdots + \alpha_q r_{t-q}^2,$$

  with $\alpha_0 > 0$ and $\alpha_i \geq 0$ for stability and positivity.

Key ideas:

- Large squared returns in the recent past increase today's variance.
- Volatility "remembers" recent shocks but only through a finite number of lags.

ARCH models capture volatility clustering because a big move (large r_{t-1}^2) increases σ_t^2, making big moves more likely today, which in turn feed forward.

GARCH: Adding persistence with lagged variance

Empirically, volatility is highly persistent: high-vol regimes can last weeks or months. Capturing this with an ARCH(q) model might require many lags. The Generalized ARCH, or GARCH, model adds lagged variance terms directly.

A GARCH(1,1) model—the most widely used specification in finance—is:

$$r_t = \sigma_t \varepsilon_t,$$

$$\sigma_t^2 = \omega + \alpha r_{t-1}^2 + \beta \sigma_{t-1}^2,$$

with $\omega > 0$, $\alpha \geq 0$, $\beta \geq 0$, and $\alpha + \beta < 1$ for stationarity.

Interpretation:

- ω is the long-run variance level.
- α controls how strongly recent squared returns affect volatility (short-run shock response).
- β controls how persistent volatility is (how slowly it decays back to normal after a shock).

If $\alpha + \beta$ is close to 1, volatility is very persistent; a volatility spike has a long half-life.

Combining mean and volatility models

In practice, we often combine a mean model and a volatility model. For example, an AR(1)-GARCH(1,1) model:

$$r_t = \mu + \phi(r_{t-1} - \mu) + \sigma_t \varepsilon_t,$$
$$\sigma_t^2 = \omega + \alpha r_{t-1}^2 + \beta \sigma_{t-1}^2.$$

This decomposes the return into:

- A predictable component in the mean (often small in liquid markets).
- A predictable, time-varying volatility component that responds to recent shocks.

Using Volatility Forecasts in Trading Systems

Volatility models are not academic curiosities; they are core components of algorithmic trading and risk engines.

Dynamic position sizing and volatility targeting

Suppose your strategy targets a constant risk level, e.g., a daily volatility of 1% for the portfolio. Let $\hat{\sigma}_t$ be your forecast of tomorrow's return volatility from a GARCH or related model.

If your current position size corresponds to a volatility of 2% (twice your target), you can scale down exposure by about a factor of 2. More generally, volatility targeting uses the rule

$$\text{position size}_t \propto \frac{\text{target volatility}}{\hat{\sigma}_t}.$$

This stabilizes the risk of the strategy over time and can improve the performance of risk-adjusted portfolios, especially when combined across multiple signals.

Risk-parity and portfolio volatility control

In a multi-asset portfolio, volatility forecasts feed into:

- **Risk-parity construction:** allocate capital so each asset or strategy contributes a desired fraction of total risk, using forecast volatilities and correlations.
- **Dynamic leverage:** increase overall leverage in low-vol regimes and reduce it in high-vol regimes, within risk limits.

Here, the covariance matrix of returns is typically modeled as a function of time, of which GARCH-style models for individual assets are building blocks.

Execution and intraday risk management

At intraday horizons, volatility forecasts help:

- Adjust limit prices and order sizes to current microstructure risk.
- Set tighter limits on slippage and temporary impact during high-volatility periods.
- Trigger defensive actions (e.g., reduce exposure or widen spreads) when volatility exceeds thresholds.

Even simple rolling volatility estimates, when updated frequently, can materially improve execution quality in an event-driven trading system.

Diagnostics and Model Discipline

As with any model, ARMA-GARCH pipelines must be checked against data to avoid overfitting and misguided confidence.

Residual checks

After fitting a time series model, inspect the *residuals*:

- For the mean model (AR/ARMA), residuals should have negligible autocorrelation if the model captured the linear structure.
- For the volatility model, standardized residuals $\hat{\varepsilon}_t = r_t/\hat{\sigma}_t$ should look like white noise with roughly constant variance.

If significant autocorrelation remains, your model is missing structure; if volatility models leave clear patterns in $r_t^2/\hat{\sigma}_t^2$, they are mis-specified.

Ljung-Box and information criteria

The Ljung-Box test is a formal way to check whether a group of autocorrelations is jointly zero. It is commonly applied to residuals to test whether a model has adequately whitened them.

When comparing alternative ARMA orders or volatility specifications, information criteria like AIC or BIC provide a balance between fit and parsimony. They penalize unnecessary parameters, helping to avoid overfitting noise.

This section has extended our earlier probabilistic foundations into the time domain:

- We moved from price levels to returns, which are closer to stationary and suitable for modeling.
- We introduced stationarity, autocorrelation, and AR/MA/ARMA models as baselines for return dynamics.
- We emphasized that while mean returns are often weakly predictable, volatility is strongly time-varying and clustered.
- We developed ARCH and GARCH models as practical tools to forecast conditional volatility and described how those forecasts feed into position sizing, risk-parity, and execution.

In the next section we will confront a sobering fact: even well-specified time series models can tempt us into overfitting and spurious alphas if we are careless. We will turn to statistical pitfalls and defenses that keep the quant research process honest in the presence of multiple testing, nonstationarity, and time-dependent data.

2.3 Statistical Pitfalls and Overfitting Defense

By now we have a powerful toolkit. We can model returns as random variables, describe their distributions, build time-series models for mean and volatility, and compute Sharpe ratios, confidence intervals, and p-values. It is tempting to believe that with enough math and code, the backtest will tell us the truth.

It will not, unless we are extremely disciplined.

This section focuses on a different kind of skill: *not fooling yourself*. Overfitting, data leakage, and misuse of validation procedures can manufacture impressive-looking alphas that collapse the moment they hit live markets. The goal here is to develop systematic defenses so that statistical rigor becomes a competitive advantage, not an afterthought.

We will proceed in four steps:

- Explain what overfitting means in trading terms.
- Catalog common statistical pitfalls: multiple testing, look-ahead and leakage, data snooping, survivorship bias.
- Introduce time-aware validation schemes: rolling and walk-forward evaluation, and the notion of an embargo period.
- Tie these together with a visual summary and a simple research checklist.

What Overfitting Really Means in Trading

Overfitting occurs when a model (or trading rule) is tuned so closely to past noise that its apparent performance in-sample is not representative of its true performance out-of-sample.

Two viewpoints on overfitting

Conceptual viewpoint.

Suppose you test hundreds of variations of a mean-reversion signal: different lookback windows, thresholds, stop-loss levels, and universes. You keep the one with the highest historical Sharpe ratio. Even if there is *no true edge* in any of them, some will look very good just by chance.

In this sense, overfitting is "confusing noise for signal" because you searched too aggressively for patterns.

Geometric viewpoint.

Picture each historical return path as a jagged curve in a high-dimensional space (one dimension per time step). A very flexible model—say, a deep tree-based learner or a signal with many knobs—can "bend" itself to get very close to that specific curve. It hugs the noise. But when you roll forward in time, the future curve bends differently. The model, tailored to yesterday's noise, no longer fits.

This geometric picture is helpful: the more degrees of freedom a strategy has, the easier it is to approximate any particular backtest path, and the more suspicious you should be of spectacular in-sample performance.

Indicators of overfitting in backtests

Red flags that often indicate overfitting include:

- Extremely high Sharpe ratios (e.g., > 3 annualized) on modest data samples without a compelling economic story.
- Strategies that only work on narrowly defined universes or small time windows, failing immediately outside them.
- Large drops in performance when you make small, reasonable changes to the implementation (execution assumptions, transaction costs, rebalancing schedules).

The rest of this section is about designing your research pipeline to systematically reduce the chances of these scenarios.

Multiple Testing and the Lure of Many Ideas

In a modern quant environment you can generate thousands of candidate signals and model variations quickly. That efficiency is a double-edged sword.

The multiple-testing problem

Recall from earlier: a standard hypothesis test at the 5% significance level allows a 5% probability of a Type I error—declaring an effect where none exists. If you test just one signal, that might be acceptable. If you test 100 *independent* signals, even if *none* have true alpha, you expect about 5 of them to look "significant" purely by luck.

In trading terms:

- A naive research process that keeps everything with p-value < 0.05 will accumulate many fake alphas when the number of trials is large.
- The more flexible your models and the more hyperparameters you tune, the more implicit tests you are running, even if you do not formalize them as separate hypothesis tests.

Practical defenses for multiple testing

You do not need to perform formal Bonferroni or Benjamini-Hochberg adjustments for every feature search to gain large benefits. A few practical heuristics already improve robustness:

Use more conservative thresholds.

Instead of treating p-values < 0.05 as "significant", tighten the bar in a research setting that tries many ideas—e.g., require p-values < 0.01 or even < 0.001 before treating something as a serious candidate.

Penalize model complexity.

Complex models fit noise more easily. Favor simpler signals and models:

- Prefer fewer parameters when two models show similar performance.
- Regularize aggressively (e.g., shrink coefficients toward zero).
- Require stronger statistical evidence for complex models than for simple ones.

Pre-register parts of your research plan.

Before looking at the data (or at least, before seeing formal backtest results), jot down:

- The main hypothesis (e.g., "3-5 day mean reversion in large-cap U.S. equities").

- The core signal construction, rough parameter ranges, and primary performance metric.

You are not locked in, but this practice reduces retrospective storytelling and discourages p-hacking.

Independent confirmation sets.

Reserve a substantial portion of data as a *holdout* that you do not touch during idea exploration or parameter tuning. Only at the end do you compute performance on this untouched data. Many ideas that looked promising in exploratory analysis will fail this harsher test, and that is good.

Leakage and Look-Ahead Bias

Even with perfect multiple-testing discipline, you can still fool yourself if information from the future "leaks" into your training or signal construction.

What is leakage?

Leakage occurs when you inadvertently use data that would not have been available at the decision time, or when your training and test sets overlap in subtle ways.

Common examples:

- Using end-of-day prices to simulate orders placed "at the open" without modeling the gap.
- Including delisted or future constituents when building a universe (survivorship bias).
- Computing features that aggregate over a window that extends into the future relative to the prediction timestamp.
- Using overlapping windows for targets in a way that causes your train and test sets to share the same realized outcomes.

Leakage generally inflates backtest performance because you are granting the strategy partial foresight that it cannot have in reality.

Look-ahead bias in signal construction

Look-ahead bias is a particularly insidious form of leakage where you use future information when you should be using only current or past data. Typical cases:

- Using quarterly fundamental data at the quarter's end date instead of at the actual publication date when it became known to the market.
- Training a model on a dataset where labels depend on prices at $t+1$ but features are computed from windows that include data beyond t.
- Rebalancing a portfolio based on information that was only finalized after the supposed trade time (e.g., index membership changes).

The defense is simple in principle but demanding in practice: every piece of data used by your model must be time-stamped and must respect causality. When you simulate a decision at time t, only data with timestamps $\leq t$ may be used.

Data Snooping and Survivorship Bias

Data snooping: reusing the same backtest too often

Data snooping occurs when you use the same data repeatedly for idea generation, model selection, and evaluation. Even if each individual test is honest, the cumulative effect is that you gradually tune your process to the idiosyncrasies of that dataset.

Symptoms:

- Endless cycles of "tweak, re-run backtest, tweak again" on the same historical period.
- Over-reliance on one particular crisis or bull market as evidence that the strategy is robust.

Mitigations:

- Use multiple, disjoint time periods for evaluation (e.g., pre-2008, 2009-2015, 2016-2021).
- Rotate which period you treat as your "primary" validation set across research projects.
- Periodically freeze a dataset as a long-term holdout: once you have evaluated strategies on it, do not keep iterating with that same set as your playground.

Survivorship bias

Survivorship bias arises when you construct your universe based only on assets that are *currently* alive, ignoring those that went bankrupt, delisted, or otherwise disappeared.

In equities, for example, using today's index constituents to backtest over the last 20 years artificially increases backtest performance because it excludes firms that failed and dropped out. Many long-short or fundamental signals look better under survivorship bias than they really are.

Defenses:

- Use point-in-time universes: reconstruct past membership lists as of each historical date.
- Include delisted securities and model their exit events (e.g., bankruptcy, acquisition) explicitly in your P&L.

Time-Aware Validation: Why IID Cross-Validation Fails

In standard machine learning with iid data, random train/test splits and K-fold cross-validation are routine. For time series, these procedures can be disastrously misleading.

The problem with random splits in time series

When you randomly assign days to train and test sets, you mix the past and future. The model can effectively "peek" ahead because patterns from later regimes leak into the training set and inform predictions about earlier regimes in the test set.

Consequences:

- You underestimate the impact of regime shifts and structural breaks.
- You overestimate how well the model will generalize to genuinely unseen future periods.

Therefore, your validation must respect the arrow of time.

Rolling and walk-forward validation

Two common time-aware validation schemes are:

Rolling (or expanding) window.

You fit the model on a window of past data and test it on the next block, then roll forward:

- Train on period 1, test on period 2.
- Train on period 1–2, test on period 3.
- Train on period 1–3, test on period 4.
- ...

This mimics how you would operate in live trading: at each point, you use only data up to that time.

Walk-forward optimization.

When tuning hyperparameters (e.g., lookbacks, thresholds), you can:

- Within each training window, split into an internal train and validation segment.
- Use the internal validation to select hyperparameters.
- Evaluate the chosen model on the subsequent out-of-sample test segment.

You then roll this entire procedure forward. This is essentially nested cross-validation adapted to time.

Label overlap and the need for an embargo

In many strategies, targets (labels) for adjacent timestamps overlap. For example:

- You predict a 5-day return, $R_{t,t+5}$, using features at time t.
- The label for time t uses prices up to $t+5$; the label for time $t+1$ uses prices up to $t+6$, and so on.

If you arbitrarily cut your dataset into training and test sets, the training set might contain labels that depend on prices used in test labels (or vice versa). This creates a subtle information leak.

To avoid this, we introduce an *embargo* period: a buffer of time between the train and test segments during which no observations are used for either.

- If your label horizon is H days, a simple rule is to insert an embargo of at least H days between train and test windows.
- More generally, the embargo length should cover the longest horizon over which your labels and features overlap.

Visual Summary: Naive vs. Walk-Forward and Embargoed Splits

Figure summarizes three splitting schemes on a single timeline:

- Naive random cross-validation that mixes past and future.
- Proper walk-forward splits without embargo.
- Walk-forward splits with an embargo period to prevent label overlap leakage.

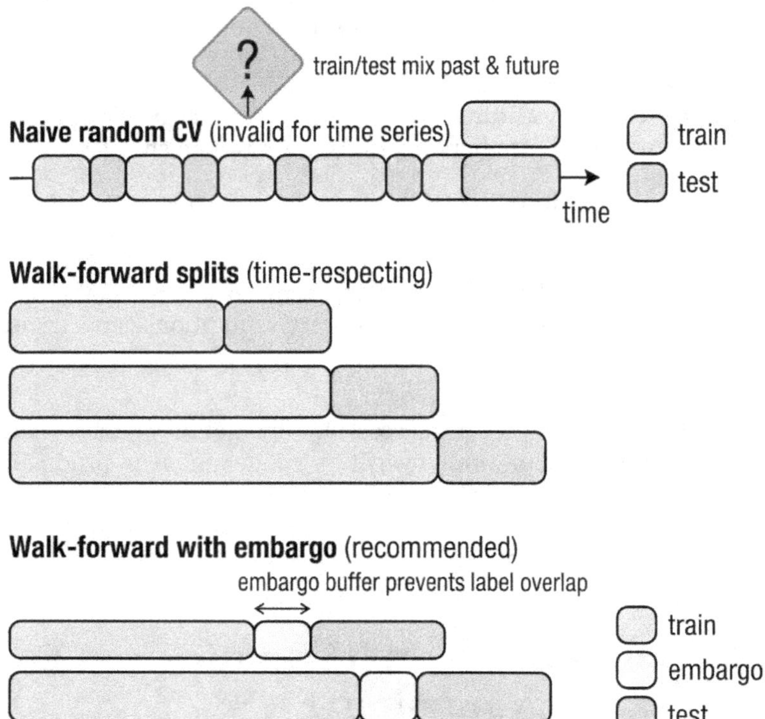

A Minimal Overfitting Defense Checklist

Bringing these ideas together, you can think of your research process as an *algorithm* for producing strategies, not just a sequence of ad hoc steps. A minimally robust algorithm should include:

- **Causal data handling.** Ensure every input respects time ordering; avoid look-ahead by construction.
- **Point-in-time universes.** Construct asset universes and features using only information available at each historical date; include delisted assets.

- **Multiple-testing awareness.** Track how many ideas and variations you have tried; use stricter thresholds and favor simpler models.
- **Time-aware validation.** Use rolling or walk-forward schemes with appropriate embargo periods, not random shuffles.
- **Holdout evaluation.** Maintain at least one untouched dataset slice for final performance assessment of mature strategies.
- **Robustness checks.** Stress-test strategies across subperiods, parameter perturbations, execution assumptions, and transaction cost scenarios.

None of these steps guarantee success, but together they greatly reduce the rate at which you promote overfit or fragile alphas to production. In a competitive environment where many participants are willing to delude themselves with "good-looking" backtests, internalizing these defenses is itself a durable edge.

2.4 Optimization Mathematics and Convex Programming

In the preceding sections we learned how to describe uncertainty (probability and distributions), how to model time dependence (ARMA, GARCH), and how to defend ourselves against statistical illusions (overfitting and leakage). Those tools give us *estimates*: expected returns, volatilities, covariances, and sometimes scenario-dependent forecasts.

This section is about turning those estimates into *decisions*. Once you know (or believe you know) expected returns and risks, you still need a systematic way to answer questions such as:

- How should I allocate capital across strategies or assets?
- How should I trade today to move from my current portfolio to a target one while controlling costs and risk?

- How do I enforce constraints: maximum leverage, long-only, sector caps, turnover limits, risk budgets?

The mathematical framework that ties all of this together is *optimization*. In particular, we will focus on *convex optimization*, which is both expressive enough for most portfolio and execution problems, and tractable enough for real-time implementation.

We proceed in stages:

- Briefly refresh core linear algebra and calculus in portfolio language.
- Introduce the general optimization viewpoint.
- Define convex sets and convex functions, and explain why convexity is so valuable.
- Present the Karush-Kuhn-Tucker (KKT) conditions and their economic interpretation.
- Specialize to quadratic programs (QPs), the workhorse class behind many portfolio and execution problems.

Linear Algebra Refresher in Portfolio Language

Vectors and portfolios

A vector in $\mathbb{R}^n$ is simply an ordered list of n numbers:

$$w = (w_1, w_2, \ldots, w_n)^\top.$$

In a portfolio context:

- w can represent *weights* in n assets: w_i is the fraction of capital invested in asset i.
- Alternatively, w can represent *position sizes* (e.g., number of shares, or dollar exposure) for each asset.

If r is a vector of random asset returns

$$r = (r_1, r_2, \ldots, r_n)^\top,$$

then the portfolio return is the linear combination

$$r_p = w^\top r = \sum_{i=1}^{n} w_i r_i.$$

This simple linear form is the basis of most optimization problems in portfolio management.

Matrices, covariance, and risk

A matrix is a rectangular array of numbers. In our context, the most important matrix is the covariance matrix of asset returns:

$$\Sigma \in \mathbb{R}^{n\times n}, \quad \Sigma_{ij} = \text{Cov}(r_i, r_j).$$

Given weights w, the *variance* of the portfolio return is

$$\text{Var}(r_p) = \text{Var}(w^\top r) = w^\top \Sigma w.$$

A few key properties:

- Σ is *symmetric*: $\Sigma_{ij} = \Sigma_{ji}$.
- Σ is (under mild conditions) *positive semidefinite*: for all x,

  $$x^\top \Sigma x \geq 0.$$

  Intuitively, any weighted combination of returns has nonnegative variance.

This quadratic form $w^\top \Sigma w$ will reappear as the canonical measure of risk in mean-variance portfolio optimization.

Norms: size of a vector

A norm is a function that measures the “size” of a vector. The most common are:

- ℓ_2 (Euclidean) norm:

$$\|w\|_2 = \sqrt{\sum_{i=1}^{n} w_i^2}.$$

- ℓ_1 norm:

$$\|w\|_1 = \sum_{i=1}^{n} |w_i|.$$

In trading applications:

- $\|w\|_2$ can be used as a proxy for “concentration” of positions or for regularization (shrinking weights toward zero).
- $\|w\|_1$ often appears in turnover and transaction cost models, since the total traded volume between two portfolios $w^{(0)}$ and $w^{(1)}$ is proportional to $\|w^{(1)} - w^{(0)}\|_1$.

Gradients, Hessians, and First-Order Thinking

Optimization is about minimizing or maximizing some objective function $f(w)$. To reason about how f changes when we tweak w, we need derivatives.

Gradient: direction of steepest change

For a differentiable scalar function $f : \mathbb{R}^n \to \mathbb{R}$, the *gradient* $\nabla f(w)$ is the vector of partial derivatives:

$$\nabla f(w) = \begin{pmatrix} \frac{\partial f}{\partial w_1}(w) \\ \vdots \\ \frac{\partial f}{\partial w_n}(w) \end{pmatrix}.$$

Intuition:

- $\nabla f(w)$ points in the direction of steepest *increase* of f at w.
- $-\nabla f(w)$ points in the direction of steepest *decrease*.

In a simple mean-variance objective

$$f(w) = -\mu^\top w + \frac{\lambda}{2} w^\top \Sigma w,$$

where μ is the expected return vector and $\lambda > 0$ is a risk aversion parameter, the gradient is

$$\nabla f(w) = -\mu + \lambda \Sigma w.$$

This gives a clean economic interpretation:

- The $-\mu$ term says "increase weights where expected returns are higher".
- The $\lambda \Sigma w$ term says "decrease weights where they contribute more to portfolio variance".

Hessian: curvature of the objective

The *Hessian* of f is the matrix of second derivatives:

$$\nabla^2 f(w) = \left[\frac{\partial^2 f}{\partial w_i \partial w_j}(w) \right]_{i,j}.$$

It captures the curvature of f:

- If $\nabla^2 f(w)$ is positive semidefinite for all w, f is convex (bowl-shaped).
- If it is positive definite, f is strictly convex: there is a unique global minimizer.

For the quadratic form $f(w) = \frac{1}{2}w^\top Qw + c^\top w$, the Hessian is simply

$$\nabla^2 f(w) = Q.$$

When Q is positive semidefinite, f is convex.

Optimization Viewpoint: Objectives and Constraints

Most portfolio and execution decisions can be phrased as:

$$\begin{aligned} &\text{minimize or maximize } f(w) \\ &\text{subject to constraints } g_i(w) \le 0, \quad h_j(w) = 0. \end{aligned}$$

Objectives in trading problems

Common objective forms include:

- **Maximize expected return minus a risk penalty:**

$$\max_w \; \mu^\top w - \frac{\lambda}{2} w^\top \Sigma w.$$

- **Minimize risk for a given return target:**

$$\min_w \; w^\top \Sigma w \quad \text{s.t. } \mu^\top w \ge R_{target}.$$

- **Minimize tracking error to a benchmark:**

$$\min_w \; (w - w^{bench})^\top \Sigma (w - w^{bench}).$$

- **Minimize transaction costs plus risk when rebalancing:**

$$\min_{w} \underbrace{\kappa\|w - w^{(0)}\|_1}_{\text{linear costs}} + \underbrace{\frac{\gamma}{2}\|w - w^{(0)}\|_2^2}_{\text{quadratic impact}} + \underbrace{\frac{\lambda}{2} w^\top \Sigma w}_{\text{risk}}.$$

Each of these is a function of the decision vector w, often combining linear and quadratic terms.

Constraints in trading problems

Typical constraints can be written as:

- **Budget / fully invested:**

$$\mathbf{1}^\top w = 1$$

  where **1** is the vector of ones.

- **Leverage limit:**

$$\|w\|_1 \leq L_{max}.$$

- **Long-only:**

$$w_i \geq 0 \quad \forall i.$$

- **Position and group limits:**

$$w_i \leq u_i \quad \forall i, \quad a_k^\top w \leq b_k \quad \text{for sector/industry groups.}$$

- **Turnover constraint:**

$$\|w - w^{(0)}\|_1 \leq \tau_{max}.$$

Most of these are *linear* (equalities or inequalities in w) or involve norms that keep the problem convex.

Convex Sets, Convex Functions, and Why They Matter

Convex sets

A set $C \subset \mathbb{R}^n$ is convex if for any two points $x, y \in C$ and any $\theta \in [0, 1]$, the convex combination

$$\theta x + (1 - \theta)y \in C.$$

Geometrically, if you take any two feasible portfolios in a convex set, any mix between them is also feasible. Many natural constraint sets in portfolio management are convex: hyperplanes ($\mathbf{1}^\top w = 1$), halfspaces ($a^\top w \leq b$), boxes ($l_i \leq w_i \leq u_i$), and norm balls ($\|w\|_1 \leq L$, $\|w\|_2 \leq L$).

Convex functions

A function $f : C \to \mathbb{R}$ is convex on a convex set C if for all $x, y \in C$ and $\theta \in [0, 1]$,

$$f(\theta x + (1 - \theta)y) \leq \theta f(x) + (1 - \theta)f(y).$$

Intuitively, the graph of a convex function lies below the straight line joining any two points on the graph. A few key facts relevant to trading:

- Linear functions $f(w) = c^\top w$ are both convex and concave.
- Quadratic forms $f(w) = \frac{1}{2}w^\top Qw + c^\top w$ are convex if Q is positive semidefinite (this includes variance and many penalty terms).
- Norms are convex functions (e.g., $\|w\|_1$, $\|w\|_2$).

Why convexity is gold

Convexity gives two critical guarantees:

- **Local minima are global minima.** For convex problems, any point where the gradient (or subgradient) satisfies certain optimality conditions is *guaranteed* to be the best solution over the entire feasible region.

- **Algorithms are reliable.** Many efficient numerical methods (gradient descent, interior-point methods, proximal algorithms) are designed specifically for convex problems and have strong convergence guarantees.

For an algorithmic trading system that must rebalance portfolios frequently and reliably, this robustness is invaluable. You do not want a solver that occasionally gets stuck in bad local minima.

KKT Conditions: Optimality with Constraints

When constraints are present, optimality is more subtle than "set the gradient to zero". The *Karush-Kuhn-Tucker* (KKT) conditions generalize this idea.

General constrained problem

Consider the problem:

$$\min_{w} \; f(w)$$

subject to

$$g_i(w) \leq 0, \quad i = 1, \ldots, m; \quad h_j(w) = 0, \quad j = 1, \ldots, p,$$

where f and g_i are convex and h_j are affine (linear + constant). This is a convex optimization problem.

Lagrangian and multipliers

We form the *Lagrangian*:

$$\mathcal{L}(w, \lambda, \nu) = f(w) + \sum_{i=1}^{m} \lambda_i g_i(w) + \sum_{j=1}^{p} \nu_j h_j(w),$$

where:

- $\lambda_i \geq 0$ are Lagrange multipliers for inequality constraints.
- ν_j are multipliers for equality constraints.

The idea is that at the optimum, relaxing or tightening a constraint has an associated "shadow price" given by its multiplier.

KKT conditions

Under mild regularity conditions, a point $w^\star$ is optimal if and only if there exist multipliers $\lambda^\star, \nu^\star$ such that:

- **Primal feasibility:**

$$g_i(w^\star) \leq 0, \quad h_j(w^\star) = 0.$$

- **Dual feasibility:**

$$\lambda_i^\star \geq 0 \quad \forall i.$$

- **Complementary slackness:**

$$\lambda_i^\star g_i(w^\star) = 0 \quad \forall i.$$

  This means: if a constraint is not binding ($g_i(w^\star) < 0$), its multiplier is zero ($\lambda_i^\star = 0$); only active constraints have positive shadow prices.

- **Stationarity:**

$$\nabla f(w^\star) + \sum_{i=1}^{m} \lambda_i^\star \nabla g_i(w^\star) + \sum_{j=1}^{p} \nu_j^\star \nabla h_j(w^\star) = 0.$$

Economic interpretation.

In a portfolio optimization:

- The gradient $\nabla f(w^\star)$ represents the marginal change in objective (e.g., risk-adjusted return) when slightly changing weights.

- The terms $\lambda_i^\star \nabla g_i(w^\star)$ adjust this for binding constraints (like leverage or risk limits). A nonzero $\lambda_i^\star$ tells you that relaxing that constraint would improve the objective.

For example, if a leverage constraint $\|w\|_1 \leq L_{max}$ is binding and has a large multiplier, it means "if I were allowed a bit more leverage, I could significantly improve my objective". This is exactly the shadow price of the leverage constraint.

Quadratic Programming: The Workhorse Engine

A *quadratic program* (QP) is an optimization problem with a quadratic objective and linear constraints:

$$\min_{w} \frac{1}{2} w^\top Q w + c^\top w$$

subject to

$$Aw \leq b, \quad A_{eq} w = b_{eq},$$

where:

- Q is a symmetric positive semidefinite matrix.
- c is a vector.
- A, A_{eq} are matrices; b, b_{eq} are vectors.

Because $Q \succeq 0$ and the constraints are linear, QPs are convex and can be solved efficiently and reliably, even at large scale.

Mean-variance portfolio as a QP

The canonical Markowitz problem,

$$\min_{w} \frac{\lambda}{2} w^\top \Sigma w - \mu^\top w$$

subject to

$$\mathbf{1}^\top w = 1, \quad w \in \mathcal{C},$$

is a QP with:

- $Q = \lambda\Sigma$,
- $c = -\mu$,
- equality constraint $\mathbf{1}^\top w = 1$,
- additional linear constraints encoded in $\mathcal{C}$ (e.g., $w \geq 0$ for long-only, sector limits, leverage caps).

Solving this QP gives the portfolio that balances expected return against risk according to λ, within the allowed constraint set.

Volatility targeting and regularization

Suppose you have an alpha forecast $\hat{\mu}$ and you want a portfolio that aligns with it while controlling risk and turnover from your current portfolio $w^{(0)}$. Consider:

$$\min_w \; -\hat{\mu}^\top w + \frac{\lambda}{2} w^\top \Sigma w + \frac{\eta}{2} \|w - w^{(0)}\|_2^2$$

subject to

$$\mathbf{1}^\top w = 1, \quad \|w\|_1 \leq L_{max}.$$

Here:

- The first term encourages alignment with predicted alpha.
- The second term penalizes risk.
- The third term is an ℓ_2-regularization that discourages large moves away from the current portfolio (a soft turnover penalty).

This objective is a quadratic function of w; the constraints are linear and an ℓ_1-norm bound, which can be expressed with linear inequalities by introducing auxiliary variables. The result is again a QP.

Execution and quadratic costs

In execution models, slippage and temporary impact are often modeled as increasing more than linearly with trade size. A simple form is:

$$\text{cost}(x) = a^\top |x| + \frac{1}{2} x^\top B x,$$

where:

- x is the vector of trade sizes (shares to buy/sell).
- a models linear costs (bid-ask spread, fees).
- B is a positive semidefinite matrix capturing quadratic impact (larger trades push prices more, correlated across assets).

If you want to trade from current holdings $h^{(0)}$ to target holdings h, with $x = h - h^{(0)}$, you can set up:

$$\min_h \frac{1}{2}(h - h^{(0)})^\top B (h - h^{(0)}) + a^\top |h - h^{(0)}|$$

subject to:

- risk or exposure constraints on h,
- market and liquidity constraints (e.g., max participation rates).

This is again a QP (with linearized absolute values) and can be embedded into an event-driven trading system to determine optimal child orders.

Numerical and Engineering Considerations

In a production algorithmic trading machine, optimization is a live component, not a one-off calculation. A few practical aspects matter:

Conditioning and scaling

The covariance matrix Σ or cost matrix Q can be ill-conditioned (eigenvalues spanning many orders of magnitude), which can slow down solvers or produce numerically unstable solutions. Remedies include:

- Shrinkage estimators for Σ to avoid extremely small or noisy eigenvalues.
- Scaling variables so that constraints and objective terms have comparable magnitudes.
- Adding small ridge terms (e.g., ϵI) to Q to improve conditioning.

Solver choice and latency

For batch, overnight optimization (e.g., daily portfolio rebalancing), interior-point methods or high-accuracy commercial QP solvers are suitable. For intraday or high-frequency adjustments, you may need:

- Faster, approximate methods (e.g., projected gradient descent, coordinate descent).
- Warm-starting from the previous solution w^{prev} to exploit temporal continuity.

The choice is an engineering trade-off between optimality guarantees, speed, and robustness.

Robustness and model risk

The optimization problem is only as good as its inputs (μ, Σ, a, B, etc.), which are estimated with noise and subject to regime changes. It is therefore prudent to:

- Stress-test solutions under perturbed inputs (e.g., amplify volatilities, shift correlations).

- Incorporate robustness directly (e.g., add penalties on large position or leverage changes).
- Combine optimization outputs with hard risk limits and heuristics in the execution layer.

In this section we have:

- Recast basic linear algebra and calculus in portfolio terms: weights as vectors, covariance as a positive semidefinite matrix, risk as a quadratic form, gradients as risk-return trade-off indicators, and Hessians as curvature.
- Framed trading problems as optimization problems with clear objectives and constraints.
- Introduced convex sets and convex functions, explaining why they make optimization reliable and tractable.
- Presented the KKT conditions as the unifying language for constrained optimality, with shadow prices that have clear economic meaning.
- Specialized to quadratic programming, showing how mean-variance portfolios, volatility targeting, regularization, and quadratic execution costs can all be expressed and solved within this framework.

Together with the probabilistic and time-series tools developed earlier, convex optimization is the mathematical engine that turns statistical forecasts into concrete, implementable decisions in an algorithmic trading machine.

Chapter 3

Architecture and Software Engineering for Trading Systems

A profitable model is not a trading system. In this chapter, we cross the bridge from research notebooks to live markets: choosing the right languages for each component, structuring services and APIs so they can evolve, enforcing reliability through tests and version control, and finally wiring everything into a coherent end-to-end architecture. By the end, you'll see exactly how individual strategies plug into a larger machine that can survive real-world latency, failures, and change.

3.1 Programming Languages and Vectorized Computing

In the previous chapter we treated a trading system as an engineered machine: a set of services that ingest market data, generate signals, manage portfolios and risk, and route orders to venues. In this section we move one level down and ask a very practical question:

What should we write this machine in?

Modern trading platforms are rarely written in a single language. Instead, they use a small, carefully chosen set of runtimes, each optimized for a different part of the problem:

- Python, together with libraries like NumPy and pandas, for research, data analysis, and much of the batch and near-real-time logic.
- Modern C++ for the latency- and throughput-critical components in the live trading path.

The goal of this section is to explain *why* this division of labor works so well, and *how* to connect these layers so that research code can flow into production without constant rewrites.

Python as the Research Workbench

Python has become the dominant language of quantitative research because it optimizes for the scarcest resource in a research group: human time.

Why Python?

Python offers:

- **Expressiveness:** Strategy ideas can be written in a few lines of code that closely resemble the underlying math.
- **Ecosystem:** There are mature libraries for numerical computing, statistics, optimization, machine learning, and visualization.
- **Interactivity:** Notebooks and interactive shells make it easy to explore data and iterate rapidly.

For example, computing daily returns from a price series in pure Python might look like this:

```
prices = [100.0, 101.5, 100.0, 102.0]
returns = []
```

```
for i in range(1, len(prices)):
    r = (prices[i] / prices[i - 1]) - 1.0
    returns.append(r)
```

This code is readable, but it runs in the standard Python interpreter and executes the loop one iteration at a time. On small lists this is fine; on tens of millions of points—which is common when you work with tick or intraday bar data across many symbols—this becomes too slow.

The solution in the Python world is vectorization, via NumPy and pandas.

Python's Limits in Live Trading

Understanding Python's limits will motivate the multi-language architecture we will build later.

Single-threaded performance. The reference CPython interpreter has a Global Interpreter Lock (GIL), which ensures that only one thread executes Python bytecode at a time. While you can achieve parallelism via multiple processes or C extensions that release the GIL, raw multi-threaded Python code does not scale linearly on multi-core machines.

Interpreter overhead. Each loop iteration in pure Python involves significant overhead: type checking, bytecode dispatch, and dynamic attribute lookups. This overhead dominates when you have to apply simple arithmetic to large arrays of numbers.

Latency nondeterminism. For live trading, particularly intraday or high-frequency trading, you care about microsecond- and millisecond-level latencies and predictable response times. The Python runtime introduces extra variability (e.g., garbage collection pauses, dynamic dispatch), which makes it challenging to meet tight latency budgets in critical paths like order handling.

These limitations do *not* make Python a poor choice overall: they simply mean Python must be used thoughtfully, in the right layer of the system. For most research tasks and offline processing, Python is ideal. For some real-time tasks, we must reach for lower-level languages or use Python as a controller around optimized native code.

Vectorized Computing with NumPy and pandas

Vectorization is the main technique that allows Python-based research code to scale to large datasets. Intuitively, *vectorization means "do many operations at once in optimized native code, instead of looping item by item in Python."*

NumPy Arrays: Moving Loops into C

NumPy introduces the ndarray, a contiguous, typed block of memory that stores numeric data efficiently. When you perform arithmetic on arrays, NumPy implements the loop in compiled C (or C++/Fortran), not in Python.

Consider again our return computation, this time with NumPy:

```
import numpy as np

prices = np.array([100.0, 101.5, 100.0, 102.0])
returns = prices[1:] / prices[:-1] - 1.0
```

Conceptually, we are still computing $(p_t/p_{t-1}) - 1$ for each time step, but the inner loop runs in optimized C, operating on the whole array slice. Python simply orchestrates a few high-level operations.

This change in perspective is crucial: *you write code in terms of whole arrays (vectors) and columns, and let numeric libraries handle the low-level iteration and memory access.*

pandas DataFrames: Tabular Time Series

pandas builds on NumPy to provide labeled, tabular data structures such as the DataFrame. This is particularly suited to trading data, which is naturally organized in tables:

- Rows: timestamps.
- Columns: symbols, prices, volumes, factors, signals, positions, and so on.

Here is an example of computing log returns and a moving volatility estimate for multiple symbols:

```
import pandas as pd
```

```
import numpy as np

# price_df: rows = timestamps, columns = symbols
price_df = pd.DataFrame(
    {
        "AAPL": [100.0, 101.0, 100.5, 102.0],
        "MSFT": [50.0, 49.5, 50.5, 51.0],
    }
)

log_returns = np.log(price_df / price_df.shift(1))
rolling_vol = log_returns.rolling(window=3).std()
```

Several important ideas appear here:

- **Broadcasting and alignment:** The division price_df / price_df.shift(1) is applied element-wise across the entire table, with rows aligned by timestamp and columns by symbol.
- **Rolling windows:** The rolling(window=3).std() call computes, for each symbol, the standard deviation over a trailing 3-row window—again implemented in optimized C code.
- **Columnar operations:** All calculations work simultaneously across all symbols, which is exactly what we want for cross-sectional strategies.

Typical Vectorization Patterns in Trading

Most trading-related transforms can be written in a small number of vectorization patterns. Mastering these patterns makes your research code both fast and easy to read.

Returns and differences. Arithmetic on shifted arrays for price or volume changes:

```
returns = prices.pct_change() # (p_t / p_{t-1}) - 1
spread_change = spread.diff() # s_t - s_{t-1}
```

Normalization and scaling. Subtracting means, dividing by standard deviations, or applying robust scaling:

```
# Cross-sectional z-score at each date
zscore = (factor_df - factor_df.mean(axis=1)[:, None]) / \
        factor_df.std(axis=1)[:, None]
```

Group-by operations. Aggregating by sector, industry, or portfolio:

```
# Assume df has columns: ['timestamp', 'symbol', 'sector', 'weight', 'return']
grouped = df.groupby(['timestamp', 'sector'])
sector_return = (grouped['weight'] * grouped['return']).sum()
```

Rolling and expanding windows. Moving averages, volatilities, and maximum drawdowns:

```
ma_20 = price_df.rolling(20).mean()
vol_60 = return_df.rolling(60).std()
```

In each case, what would otherwise be an explicit `for` loop in Python becomes one or two vectorized operations applied to whole arrays or columns. This design is not just syntactic sugar; it is a key performance and reliability technique.

From Naive Loops to Vectorized Pipelines

To see the performance and clarity benefits of vectorization in a more realistic context, consider a toy intraday strategy:

- You have mid-quote prices for 1,000 symbols at 1-minute intervals.
- You compute a 30-minute moving average and a 120-minute moving average.
- You generate a signal when the short average crosses the long average.

A naive implementation might loop over timestamps and symbols explicitly. A vectorized implementation expresses the entire logic in a small number of operations:

```
short_ma = price_df.rolling(window=30).mean()
long_ma = price_df.rolling(window=120).mean()

signal = (short_ma > long_ma).astype(int) - (short_ma < long_ma).astype(int)
```

Here, signal is a DataFrame with the same shape as price_df, containing $+1$ for long, -1 for short, and 0 for neutral. The entire pipeline—rolling means, comparisons, and signal encoding—is expressed with handful of high-level, vectorized operations. Under the hood, the heavy lifting uses efficient, cache-friendly loops in C.

This style of code has three practical advantages:

- **Performance:** It scales to millions of rows and thousands of columns on a single machine.
- **Correctness:** Fewer explicit loops and indices means fewer off-by-one and alignment bugs.
- **Portability:** The same vectorized transforms can often be reused (or reimplemented) in other languages and environments, including C++ and database engines.

Where Modern C++ Belongs in the Stack

While NumPy and pandas can handle large batch computations and many forms of near-real-time analytics, certain parts of a trading system demand tighter control over performance, memory, and concurrency than Python can provide. This is where modern C++ (C++11 and beyond) plays a crucial role.

Latency- and Throughput-Critical Components

In a typical production trading stack, C++ is used for:

- **Market data handlers:** Parsing, normalizing, and distributing high-volume data feeds from exchanges and brokers.
- **Execution adaptors and OMS/EMS cores:** Managing order lifecycles, routing logic, and low-latency communication with venues.
- **Real-time risk checks:** Performing pre-trade checks and limit enforcement in the hot path before orders leave the system.

These components often need to handle:

- Hundreds of thousands to millions of messages per second.
- Single-digit microsecond processing budgets per message.
- Predictable latency, even under bursty loads.

Such requirements favor a compiled, statically typed language with fine-grained control over memory layouts, cache usage, and concurrency—all strengths of modern C++.

Modern C++ Features that Matter for Trading

Modern C++ includes language and library features that are particularly valuable when building trading systems:

RAII (Resource Acquisition Is Initialization). RAII ties the lifecycle of resources (e.g., network sockets, file handles, locks) to object lifetimes. As objects go out of scope, their destructors automatically release resources. This pattern yields deterministic cleanup, which simplifies error handling in complex systems.

Move semantics. C++11 introduced move semantics, which allow efficient transfer of ownership of resources without copying. This reduces unnecessary allocations and copies when passing messages through queues, which is common in event-driven architectures.

Templates and generic programming. Templates enable the creation of generic components (e.g., message queues, order books, numerical routines) that can be specialized for different types without sacrificing performance. The compiler generates optimized code for each instantiation.

Concurrency primitives. The standard library and many frameworks provide threads, atomics, lock-free data structures, and asynchronous I/O. These tools allow building high-throughput, multi-core aware services.

Used carefully, these features support the two core engineering goals in trading systems: low latency and predictable behavior.

Interfacing Python and C++

To leverage both ecosystems, you must connect Python-based research logic and C++-based production services cleanly. There are two broad patterns:

- **In-process bindings:** Python code calls directly into C++ functions compiled as shared libraries.
- **Out-of-process services:** Python and C++ components communicate over well-defined APIs (e.g., REST, gRPC, or message queues).

In-Process Bindings: Extending Python with C++

In-process bindings are useful when you have a performance-critical numeric kernel that you want to reuse in both research and production without duplicating code. For example:

- A custom options pricing engine.
- A fast implementation of a path-dependent risk measure.
- A low-level data structure, such as an order book or a specialized time-series container.

Libraries such as `pybind11`, Cython, or the Python C API allow you to expose C++ functions and classes as Python modules. From the Python side, they look like ordinary functions; the heavy computation, however, runs in compiled C++ and can release the GIL.

The workflow typically looks like this:

- Prototype and test the algorithm in pure Python/NumPy.
- Identify performance bottlenecks via profiling.
- Re-implement the hot paths in C++ and expose them to Python.
- Replace the Python implementation with a call into the C++ extension.

The rest of your research code—data loading, pre- and post-processing, plotting—remains in Python, while the critical inner loop is now as fast and deterministic as a native C++ implementation.

Out-of-Process Services: Microservices and APIs

For many live trading components, especially those dealing with network I/O and stateful interactions with exchanges, running Python and C++ in the same process is not desirable. Instead, components communicate over the network (or IPC) via APIs and message buses.

A typical division might be:

- **Python layer:** Strategy research, signal generation in backtests, batch analytics jobs, and perhaps some low-frequency or latency-tolerant live strategies.
- **C++ services:** Market data gateways, risk engines, and OMS/EMS cores that handle real-time message flow.

The boundary between these worlds is defined by explicit interfaces—for example:

- A *signal API* where strategies publish target positions or orders.
- An *order management API* where an external client (which might be written in Python) submits orders and subscribes to fills and state updates.

Python code interacts with these services via client libraries or HTTP/gRPC calls. This architecture has several benefits:

- **Language independence:** Strategy logic can be written in Python, R, or any other language that can speak the API.
- **Isolation and robustness:** A Python process crash does not take down the OMS. Services can be scaled and deployed independently.
- **Clear responsibility boundaries:** The C++ layer focuses on performance and correctness in the hot path; the Python layer focuses on research agility.

The price you pay is the overhead of serialization and network communication. For high-frequency trading, you might keep more logic in-process in C++ to avoid this; for medium- and low-frequency strategies, the flexibility of a service-oriented split usually outweighs the extra latency.

Putting It Together: A Layered Language Stack

To keep these roles and interfaces in mind, it is useful to think of the overall trading system as a set of layers, each with a dominant language and responsibility.

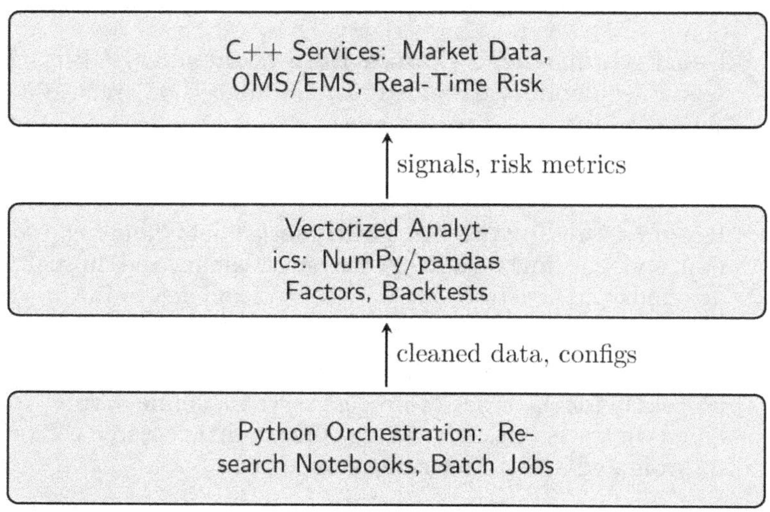

At the bottom, Python orchestrates data loading, cleaning, and experimentation. The central tier uses vectorized NumPy and pandas code to compute factors, run backtests, and analyze portfolio behavior. At the top, C++ services implement the live data and execution machinery that must operate with tight latency constraints.

In a mature platform, the interfaces between these layers are stable and well-documented. For example:

- The research environment saves factor and signal time series to a standardized format that both Python and C++ tools can read.
- The live C++ system exposes APIs that are mirrored in a simulated environment, which Python backtests can call.

Design Principles for Productivity and Performance

- **Use Python where human time is most valuable.** Research, exploratory data analysis, and high-level orchestration should prioritize clarity and ease of change. Vectorized libraries (NumPy, pandas) bridge much of the performance gap.
- **Reserve C++ for the hot path.** Market data handling, execution, and real-time risk checks face strict latency and throughput demands and benefit from C++'s control and determinism.
- **Design clear interfaces between layers.** Whether via in-process bindings or out-of-process services, define narrow, well-typed contracts (e.g., messages, APIs) so that research code can be promoted without rewriting core logic.
- **Think in vectors and tables, not scalars and loops.** Express strategy logic as operations on entire series or matrices. This mental model will make your code faster, more concise, and easier to port across languages.

In the next section we will build on this language stack and introduce architecture patterns, APIs, and serialization formats that allow these components to interact as a coherent trading platform.

3.2 Architecture Patterns, APIs, and Serialization

In the previous section we divided the trading stack by *language*: Python and vectorized libraries for research and analytics, C++ for latency-critical services, with clear interfaces in between. We now zoom out from languages to *architecture*.

Even with the best choice of languages, a trading platform can become fragile if its components are tangled: strategy code directly opening broker sockets, risk logic buried inside a spreadsheet, or portfolio calculations duplicated in multiple scripts. Such systems are hard to evolve: adding a new venue or risk check means rewriting large sections of code.

The goal of this section is to show how clean architecture patterns, explicit APIs, and disciplined serialization choices let you grow a trading system from a single strategy to a portfolio of strategies and venues *without* a constant cycle of rewrites.

We will proceed in four steps:

1. Introduce architecture patterns suited to trading systems.
2. Present a concrete service-oriented layout of a trading platform.
3. Insert a diagram of the core services and their API connections.
4. Discuss API design and serialization formats, and how they support evolution over time.

From Monoliths to Structured Systems

A common starting point for a new trader is a monolithic application: one process (often a notebook or script) that pulls market data, computes signals, manages positions, and sends orders. This is fine for learning, but it does not scale in complexity.

The problem is not size per se, but *entanglement*. When strategy logic is mixed with networking code, file I/O, and user interface elements, any change in one area risks breaking others. To avoid this, we need architectural patterns that enforce separation of concerns.

Three patterns are particularly helpful in trading:

- **Layered architecture** for clear dependency direction.
- **Hexagonal (ports-and-adapters) architecture** to isolate domain logic from infrastructure.
- **Event-driven design** where high-frequency, time-ordered data flows dominate.

Layered Architecture: Controlling Dependencies

In a layered architecture, the system is arranged in concentric zones of responsibility. Dependencies are allowed to flow in only one direction (typically from outer layers into inner ones), never in cycles. A minimal layering for trading might be:

- **Presentation / Interface layer:** Dashboards, CLI tools, monitoring, and user controls.
- **Application / Orchestration layer:** Strategy runners, schedulers, and workflow logic (e.g., "run overnight rebalance").
- **Domain layer:** Core trading concepts—orders, positions, risk checks, pricing models.
- **Infrastructure layer:** Databases, message brokers, exchange gateways, external APIs.

The domain layer is central: it encodes what trading *means* for your platform. It should depend on no external detail. Your order object should not know whether it will be stored in PostgreSQL or sent via FIX.

Layering matters because it gives you a disciplined rule: *domain logic never calls into GUI code or directly opens sockets*. Instead, it depends on abstract interfaces. Infrastructure is plugged in around it.

Hexagonal Architecture: Ports and Adapters

Hexagonal (or ports-and-adapters) architecture refines layering by focusing explicitly on how the domain interacts with the outside world. The core idea:

- The domain exposes *ports*: abstract interfaces such as "submit order", "fetch historical prices", "run risk check".
- Concrete *adapters* implement these ports for specific technologies: one adapter for Broker A via FIX, another for Broker B via REST, another for a simulation engine in your backtester.

Your strategy engine, portfolio service, and risk engine live in the hexagon's center. They depend only on port interfaces. When you need to connect to a new venue, you write a new adapter without changing the strategies.

This is especially powerful in trading because:

- Venues and brokers change over time; you want to swap them without rewriting core logic.
- You need both live adapters and simulation adapters for the same ports, so that backtests and production share the same domain code.

Event-Driven Design: Streams of Market Data and Orders

Market data and order flows are naturally modeled as events over time:

- Quotes, trades, order book updates, reference data changes.
- Order submissions, acknowledgments, partial fills, cancels, rejections.

In an event-driven architecture, components produce and consume such events via queues or message buses. Each service focuses on its reaction to events:

- A *data service* ingests exchange feeds and publishes normalized market data events.

- A *strategy service* subscribes to market data events, updates its internal state, and emits signal or order events.
- An *OMS/EMS service* consumes order events, talks to exchanges, and emits execution events.
- A *risk service* monitors positions and orders, emitting risk warnings or constraints.

This design aligns with backtesting as well: the same events can be recorded to disk and replayed later into the same services, helping you test new versions deterministically.

Core Trading Services as Collaborating Components

Building on these patterns, a modern trading platform is best viewed as a set of collaborating services, each with a bounded responsibility:

- **Data service** (or market data gateway).
- **Strategy service** (strategy engine).
- **Portfolio service**.
- **Risk service**.
- **OMS/EMS** (Order Management / Execution Management System).

We will use this decomposition repeatedly in the rest of the book, so it is worth understanding each one conceptually:

Data service. Connects to exchanges, brokers, and reference data providers; normalizes and cleans data; persists it to storage (e.g., Parquet files or a time-series database); and publishes real-time feeds to subscribers.

Strategy service. Encapsulates a strategy's logic. It consumes normalized data and configuration, computes signals or desired positions, and sends *intent* messages (e.g., "go long 5,000 shares of AAPL") rather than raw broker-specific orders.

Portfolio service. Maintains a golden record of positions, P&L, and exposures; aggregates across strategies; and provides portfolio-level views and constraints. It is typically the single source of truth for current holdings.

Risk service. Enforces risk limits before and after trades. Given proposed orders and current portfolio state, it can approve, modify, or reject trades and can also signal back to strategies (e.g., "reduce risk in this sector").

OMS/EMS service. Manages the lifecycle of orders, routes them to venues, and handles acknowledgments, cancels, and fills. It encapsulates exchange connectivity details and ensures consistent state transitions for orders.

To see how these fit together, it is helpful to visualize the services and their primary communication channels.

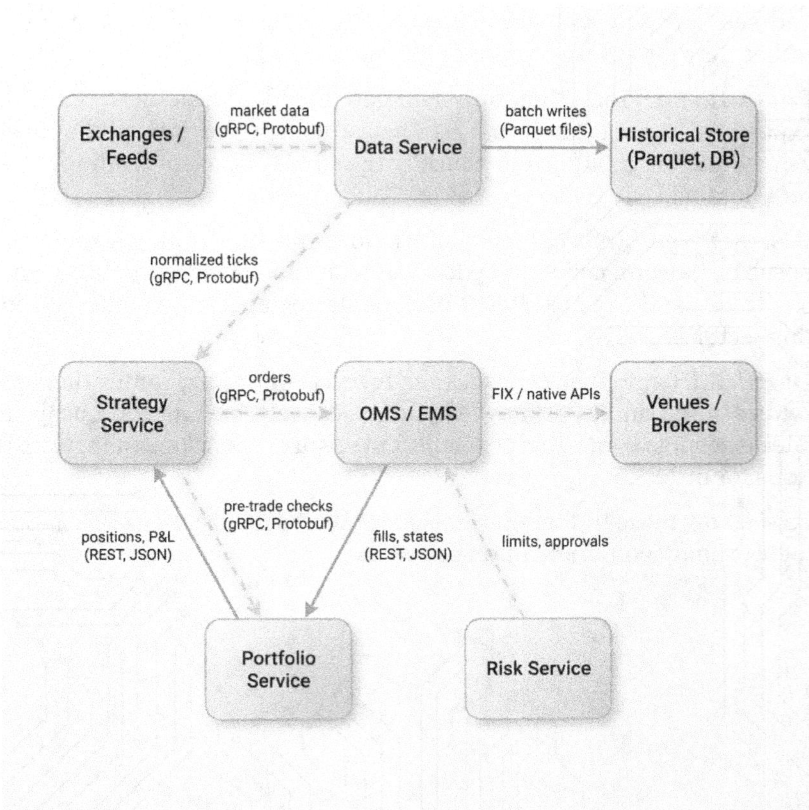

In this diagram:

- Solid arrows represent REST-style request/response APIs carrying JSON or batch formats like Parquet.
- Dashed arrows represent streaming or RPC-style APIs (e.g., gRPC) carrying compact, schema-defined messages (e.g., Protobuf).
- The historical store holds large datasets (often in columnar formats such as Parquet) consumed by research and backtesting.

This high-level structure reflects the architectural principles we discussed: separated domains, clear responsibility boundaries, and explicit, technology-agnostic ports between them.

API Design: Boundaries, Resources, and Interactions

With services outlined, we must define how they talk to one another. An API is more than a collection of endpoints; it is the *contract* that keeps your system coherent as it grows.

Three design questions are central:

1. What are the main *resources* we expose?
2. Should interactions be *synchronous* (request/response) or *asynchronous* (events/streams)?
3. What transport protocols fit best: *REST* over HTTP or *gRPC*-style RPC?

Choosing Resource Boundaries

Resources are the nouns of your system. In trading, common resources include:

- **Orders** (/orders): create, amend, cancel, query status.
- **Positions** (/positions): current exposures by instrument, account, or strategy.
- **Signals** (/signals): strategy outputs, target positions, or factor values.
- **Risk checks** (/risk/check): evaluate whether a proposed action breaches limits.

Defining clear resource boundaries helps in several ways:

- *Consistency:* All strategies interact with the OMS via the same order resource, regardless of underlying broker.

- *Traceability:* You can reconstruct a trading day by replaying API calls and responses.
- *Evolution:* Adding, say, a new `order_type` field is a matter of evolving the `/orders` resource schema.

Synchronous vs Asynchronous Interactions

Some interactions naturally fit a synchronous request/response pattern:

- **Place order:** A strategy sends a request and needs a quick acknowledgment: accepted, rejected, or queued.
- **Query position:** A monitoring tool requests the current position state and receives a snapshot.
- **Run risk check:** Before sending an order, the strategy calls a risk API and waits for an approval or reason for rejection.

Others are better modeled as streams or subscriptions:

- **Market data:** Strategies subscribe to symbol streams; data arrives continuously.
- **Fills and order updates:** Clients subscribe to order events; fills, cancels, and rejections are pushed as they occur.
- **Risk alerts:** The risk service broadcasts alerts or throttling instructions.

A common pattern is to combine both:

- Use synchronous APIs for point queries and commands (REST or unary gRPC calls).
- Use streaming APIs or message buses for continuous event flows (gRPC streams, Kafka topics, etc.).

REST vs gRPC in Trading Systems

REST (HTTP with JSON) and gRPC (binary RPC with Protobuf or similar) each have a role.

REST + JSON. Advantages:

- Human-readable and easy to debug with simple tools.
- Widely supported across languages and frameworks.
- Well-suited to low-frequency, latency-tolerant operations: configuration, queries, reporting.

Typical uses in trading:

- Querying positions, P&L, or risk summaries from the portfolio or risk service.
- Administrative tasks: starting/stopping strategies, fetching logs, updating configuration.
- Integration with external systems (e.g., reporting dashboards, compliance tools).

gRPC + Protobuf (or similar RPC stacks). Advantages:

- Compact binary encoding and efficient serialization.
- Strongly-typed interfaces defined in language-agnostic IDL files.
- Built-in support for streaming and bi-directional RPC.

Typical uses:

- Real-time market data delivery from data services to strategy engines.
- Low-latency order submission and execution updates between strategies and OMS.

- High-throughput, internal service-to-service calls within a data center.

In practice, many platforms use both: REST/JSON for control-plane and reporting functions, and gRPC/Protobuf for data-plane, latency-sensitive flows. The service diagram above reflects this split via solid (REST) and dashed (gRPC) arrows.

Serialization Formats: JSON, Protobuf, and Parquet

Serialization is the process of converting in-memory objects into byte streams for transport or storage. Your choice of format affects performance, debuggability, and schema evolution. We focus on three families:

- **JSON** for human-readable messages and external APIs.
- **Protobuf/Avro-style schemas** for compact, strongly-typed internal messaging.
- **Parquet** for analytical storage of large historical datasets.

JSON: Human-Friendly, but Verbose

JSON is text-based and self-describing: keys and structure are visible. For example:

```
{
  "order_id": "A123",
  "symbol": "AAPL",
  "side": "BUY",
  "qty": 5000,
  "order_type": "LIMIT",
  "limit_price": 175.25
}
```

Pros:

- Easy to inspect in logs and debugging tools.
- Flexible and widely supported.

- Good for low-frequency control and monitoring.

Cons:

- Verbose: large messages increase bandwidth and storage usage.
- Weak typing: everything is text; consumers must parse and validate types.
- Slower to parse than binary formats, especially at high throughput.

In trading systems, JSON is well-suited for REST APIs that are used by humans or external systems, where ease of understanding outweighs throughput concerns.

Protobuf/Avro: Compact and Strongly Typed

Protobuf, Avro, and similar schema-based formats define messages with explicit types. For example, in Protobuf's interface definition language you might write:

```
message Order {
  string order_id = 1;
  string symbol = 2;
  enum Side { BUY = 0; SELL = 1; }
  Side side = 3;
  int32 qty = 4;
  double limit_px = 5;
}
```

The compiler generates strongly-typed classes for multiple languages (C++, Python, Java, etc.). Messages are encoded in a compact binary format.

Pros:

- Efficient encoding and decoding, suitable for high-volume streams.
- Strong typing: fields have well-defined types and defaults.
- Versioning support: you can add new optional fields while keeping old consumers working.

Cons:

- Not human-readable without tooling.
- Requires schema management and code generation as part of your build.

In trading, Protobuf-style formats are ideal for internal event streams: market data, order and execution events, risk messages, and inter-service communication where performance and correctness are critical.

Parquet: Columnar Storage for Analytics

Parquet is a columnar storage format optimized for analytical workloads over large datasets. Instead of storing rows one by one, Parquet stores each column contiguously, with compression and encoding tuned to the data type.

This is particularly important when working with:

- Years of tick or bar data across thousands of instruments.
- Factor and signal histories used in cross-sectional analysis.
- Execution logs and order books for market microstructure research.

Advantages of columnar formats like Parquet:

- **I/O efficiency:** Analytical queries often touch only a subset of columns (e.g., timestamp, symbol, price); irrelevant columns can be skipped.
- **Compression:** Similar values stored together compress well, reducing storage and improving cache locality.
- **Interoperability:** Many tools (Spark, pandas, SQL engines) can read and write Parquet directly.

Your data service can write normalized data, factors, and execution logs into Parquet files partitioned by date, symbol, or exchange. Research and backtesting code then scan these files efficiently.

Schema Evolution and Backward Compatibility

Over time, your APIs and messages will change. New fields are added, old ones deprecated, sometimes entire resources are refactored. Poorly managed, this can break running strategies.

To keep systems evolvable, follow a few key practices:

- **Version your APIs.** Include explicit version numbers in URLs (e.g., /v1/orders) or in RPC service definitions. Avoid making breaking changes to existing versions; instead, introduce new ones.
- **Prefer additive changes.** Add new optional fields with sensible defaults rather than deleting or renaming existing fields. Schema-based formats like Protobuf are designed to support this.
- **Avoid "stringly typed" payloads.** Do not pack complex data into opaque strings (e.g., JSON blobs inside JSON fields). This prevents static analysis and makes downstream systems brittle.
- **Maintain clear contracts.** Document which fields are required, which are optional, and what their semantics are. Align logs and monitoring with these contracts, so you can detect when clients misuse the API.

For a trading organization, backward compatibility is not only a convenience but a risk control. You want to know that a strategy running against /v1/orders behaves the same way next week as it did last month, unless you deliberately migrate it to /v2/orders.

How Clean Architecture Enables Evolution

By now, several themes should be visible:

- **Architecture patterns** (layered, hexagonal, event-driven) help you keep domain logic independent from volatile infrastructure details.

- **Service boundaries** (data, strategy, portfolio, risk, OMS/EMS) reflect real trading responsibilities and support separate scaling and deployment.
- **APIs and serialization** (REST/JSON, gRPC/Protobuf, Parquet) provide clear, typed contracts for communication and storage, balancing debuggability and performance.

Together, these choices allow a trading platform to evolve:

- You can add new strategies that simply plug into existing ports (signal, order, risk, data) without touching the OMS implementation.
- You can introduce a new venue adapter or change a broker without altering strategy code.
- You can extend messages and APIs to support new order types or risk checks while keeping legacy clients running.

In the next section, we will discuss the engineering practices—testing, version control, and secure coding—that keep such an architecture reliable under real-world stresses and failures.

3.3 Testing, Version Control, and Secure Coding

In the previous sections we clarified *what* our trading system looks like—a collection of services with clear APIs—and *how* we implement them using a mix of Python, vectorized libraries, and modern C++. We now turn to a different, but equally important, question:

How do we keep this machine correct, auditable, and safe as it changes over time?

The answer lies in three disciplines that are sometimes treated as afterthoughts, but in a capital-at-risk environment must be viewed as first-class engineering concerns:

- A structured approach to **testing**.
- Professional use of **version control** (Git).
- Conscious **secure coding** and secrets management.

Together, these turn a fragile prototype into a platform on which you can run real money and sleep at night.

The Testing Pyramid for Trading Systems

Testing is about more than "does my backtest run." It is about building enough confidence in your code that you can deploy changes without fear. To make this tractable, we organize tests in a pyramid:

- Many fast, small *unit tests* at the base.
- Fewer, slower *integration tests* in the middle.
- A small number of *end-to-end tests* at the top.

Each level focuses on different questions and different failure modes.

Unit Tests: Verifying Small Pieces in Isolation

Unit tests check small, deterministic pieces of logic in isolation. In trading systems, typical units include:

- A signal function that takes prices and returns indicators.
- A position update routine that adjusts quantities after fills.
- A risk rule that caps exposure by sector or instrument.
- A function that maps strategy intents ("target 10% weight") to concrete orders.

A good unit test has the following properties:

- **No external dependencies:** No network calls, databases, or random API keys. You pass in inputs and assert on outputs.

- **Fast:** Milliseconds to run, so you can execute the entire test suite frequently.

- **Deterministic:** Same inputs always produce the same outputs. Any randomness in the underlying logic is controlled via fixed seeds.

For example, consider a function that converts a series of prices into returns:

```
import numpy as np

def compute_returns(prices):
    return prices[1:] / prices[:-1] - 1.0

def test_compute_returns_simple_case():
    prices = np.array([100.0, 110.0, 99.0])
    expected = np.array([0.10, -0.10])
    np.testing.assert_allclose(compute_returns(prices), expected, rtol=1e-8)
```

This test is trivial, but it locks in expected behavior and prevents later refactors from silently breaking the basic math.

In C++, unit tests can verify order-state transitions, risk calculations, or any other core routines:

```
TEST(OrderStateMachine, FillMovesToFilled) {
    Order o("AAPL", Side::Buy, 100);
    o.onAck();
    o.onFill(100);
    EXPECT_EQ(o.state(), OrderState::Filled);
}
```

Well-designed unit tests help you refactor with confidence, because they tell you quickly if an apparently local change has altered fundamental behavior.

Integration Tests: Verifying Interactions Between Services

Unit tests cannot catch errors that only appear when components collaborate. For that, you need integration tests that exercise a few services together. In the trading context, examples include:

- Strategy engine $\leftrightarrow$ OMS: does a signal actually produce the correct order messages?
- OMS $\leftrightarrow$ risk service: are risk checks invoked before orders are sent to venues, and are rejections handled correctly?
- OMS $\leftrightarrow$ portfolio service: are fills reflected in positions and P&L correctly?

Integration tests are more realistic than unit tests, but also slower and more complex. To keep them manageable:

- Use **test doubles** (mocks or fakes) for third-party systems: simulate an exchange, rather than connecting to a real one.
- Control all external inputs: feed in known streams of market data and order events.
- Assert on clear, observable outcomes: final positions, number of orders sent, risk flags raised, etc.

For instance, an integration test might:

- Start a test instance of the strategy service and OMS.
- Feed in a small sequence of prices that should trigger a buy signal.
- Verify that exactly one buy order with the expected size is submitted to the (mocked) exchange adapter.
- Verify that, after a simulated fill, the portfolio service reports the correct position.

The key idea is that you exercise the actual collaboration patterns defined by your APIs, using the real network stack or IPC, not in-process shortcuts.

End-to-End Tests: Simulating Full Trading Sessions

At the top of the pyramid are end-to-end tests that simulate full trading sessions, from data ingestion to trade booking. These are the closest thing to a dress rehearsal for production.

A typical end-to-end test scenario might:

- Start all core services: data, strategy, portfolio, risk, OMS/EMS.
- Replay a day of historical market data from Parquet files through the data service.
- Allow strategies to run and generate orders.
- Use a simulated exchange that fills orders based on historical trades.
- Capture and compare final positions, P&L, and risk metrics against known-good baselines.

The most important property here is *determinism*: you should be able to run the same end-to-end test multiple times and obtain the same results. To achieve this:

- Use recorded data streams (ticks, bars, and events) rather than live feeds.
- Fix all random seeds and ensure no components depend on wall-clock timing for logic (only for scheduling).
- Record all external inputs (e.g., simulated exchange responses) so they can be replayed verbatim.

End-to-end tests are slower and fewer in number, but they are invaluable for catching regression bugs that only surface when the full machine is running.

Replays and Historical Bug Reproduction

One of the most powerful testing tools in trading systems is the *replay*. When a bug or anomaly occurs in production—an unexpected position, a mispriced order, a risk rule firing—you want to be able to reproduce it offline.

This requires:

- Logging or capturing **all relevant event streams**: incoming market data, strategy outputs, submitted orders, exchange responses, risk decisions.
- Including **code and configuration versions** in those logs (we will return to this under version control).
- Having a **replay harness** that can feed these captured events back into the system (or a subset of services) in the same order and timing.

With a replay harness, you can:

- Reproduce the exact conditions that led to a bug.
- Attach debuggers and extensive logging without impacting live trading.
- Validate that a proposed fix actually resolves the bug and does not introduce new problems.

Replays also enable *scenario testing*: you can construct synthetic sequences of events—for example, an exchange disconnect followed by a reconnect, or a volatility spike with rapid price movements—and verify system behavior in these stress conditions.

Version Control as a Risk Management Tool

Version control, particularly Git, is often introduced as a collaboration or backup tool. In trading systems, it has an additional, critical role: *risk management*. At any later date, you must be able to answer:

> "Exactly which code and configuration were live on day D, and how did they differ from day $D - 1$?"

Without a disciplined Git workflow, you cannot answer this question confidently, which complicates debugging, compliance, and post-mortems.

Fundamental Practices in Git

At minimum, adopt the following practices:

Use feature branches. Do not commit directly to the main branch. Instead:

- Create a branch per change or feature (e.g., `feature/new-vol-targeting`).
- Develop and test there.
- Merge back into `main` (or `master`) only via pull requests, after review and passing tests.

Write meaningful commit messages. A commit message like "fix stuff" is useless months later. A good message concisely explains:

- What was changed.
- Why it was changed (the motivation or bug reference).

Avoid committing secrets and generated artifacts. API keys, passwords, and certificates must *never* be committed. Large binary data (e.g., historical price files) and build outputs should also be excluded via `.gitignore`.

Releases, Tags, and Deployments

To connect code commits to deployed strategies, you should:

- **Tag releases:** When you prepare a deployment, create an annotated Git tag (e.g., strategy-v1.3.0). This marks a specific commit as a released version.
- **Record deployment metadata:** For each trading day, record which tags (versions) of each service and strategy were deployed. This can be automated via deployment scripts that write to a central registry or log.
- **Embed version info into binaries and logs:** Services can expose an endpoint (e.g., /version) or startup log line showing the Git commit hash and tag. This makes it easy to correlate runtime behavior with source code.

When a production issue occurs, you can then:

- Look up the deployed version tags and commit hashes for affected services.
- Check Git history to see what changed since the last known-good version.
- Run replays or tests against the exact code that was live.

This traceability is invaluable both for engineering and for regulatory or client reporting.

Collaboration and Code Review

Even if you are a solo quant today, adopting a collaboration-friendly workflow will pay off as your system grows.

- Use **pull requests** to review changes, even if you review your own code by taking a break and re-reading with a fresh eye.
- In team settings, establish **code review guidelines** that emphasize correctness, clarity, and risk implications, not just style.
- Require that all tests pass (unit, integration, and key end-to-end cases) before merging.

In trading, small code changes can have large financial impacts. Code review is one of the few systematic defenses against subtle bugs and unintended behavior.

Secure Coding and Secrets Management

Trading systems connect to real-money accounts and valuable data sources. A security failure can lead not just to downtime, but to financial loss or regulatory exposure. Secure coding is therefore not optional.

We will highlight a few core practices adapted to the trading context.

Handling Secrets and Credentials

API keys, passwords, and certificates are the keys to your brokerage accounts, data feeds, and internal systems. Mishandling them is one of the most common security errors.

Never hardcode secrets. Do not embed secrets directly in source code, configuration files committed to Git, or scripts. Instead:

- Use environment variables, secret management services (e.g., a vault), or encrypted configuration stores.
- Ensure that your code reads secrets at runtime from these sources.

Use least privilege. Give each service only the credentials and permissions it actually needs:

- A read-only analytics job should not have write access to live trading accounts.
- A monitoring dashboard should access aggregated views, not raw client-level secrets.

If an individual service is compromised, this limits the potential damage.

Validating External Inputs

Trading systems consume a lot of external data:

- Market data feeds and reference data.
- Requests from user interfaces or client APIs.
- Messages from other internal services.

Even if you control the other services, you must treat all external inputs as potentially malformed. Defensive steps include:

- **Schema validation:** For JSON or Protobuf messages, validate that required fields are present and of the correct type and range.
- **Length and rate limits:** Enforce maximum message sizes and request rates to avoid denial-of-service (DoS) issues.
- **Sanitizing free-form text:** For any unstructured inputs (logs, comments, labels), sanitize or escape content before using it in logs, databases, or UIs to reduce injection risks.

For example, if your system exposes a REST endpoint to place orders, it should:

- Reject orders with nonsensical sizes (e.g., negative or unreasonably large quantities).
- Validate symbols against a whitelist or reference data set.
- Enforce basic sanity checks on prices (e.g., non-negative, within a multiple of recent prices).

These checks not only improve security but also protect against operational mistakes and erroneous upstream data.

Secure Communications and Storage

Trading data and credentials in transit and at rest must be protected:

- Use **TLS/HTTPS** for all external and most internal service-to-service communications, especially where credentials or client-related data are involved.
- Store sensitive data (API keys, client identifiers) in encrypted form, with strict access controls.
- Limit direct access to production databases; provide read-only replicas or controlled APIs for research and reporting.

Although not every system requires bank-grade security, adopting baseline practices early will prevent painful retrofits later.

Bringing It Together: Discipline as an Edge

Testing, version control, and secure coding can feel orthogonal to alpha research, but in practice they are complementary:

- **Testing** turns your trading ideas into reliable components that survive refactors and scale to multiple strategies and markets.
- **Version control** gives you a precise history of what was live when, enabling confident iteration and accurate post-mortems.
- **Secure coding** protects your capital, your data, and your reputation from avoidable failures.

Most importantly, these practices *accelerate* research over time. When you trust your backtesting and deployment pipeline, you can move faster, test more ideas, and react quickly to market changes without being paralyzed by operational risk.

In the next section, we will assemble the entire chapter's concepts into an end-to-end blueprint of a modern trading platform, and show how strategies move from research notebooks, through these engineering safeguards, into robust production deployment.

3.4 End-to-End System Blueprint and Core Services

Up to this point in the chapter we have examined the building blocks of a professional trading platform:

- A language stack that combines Python, vectorized libraries, and C++.
- Architectural patterns that separate domain logic from infrastructure.
- APIs and serialization formats that connect services cleanly.
- Testing, version control, and security practices that keep changes safe.

We now assemble these ideas into a single, coherent blueprint: an *algorithmic trading machine* that runs from data ingestion all the way to exchange execution, and back again through portfolio and risk feedback.

This section has three goals:

- Present a high-level blueprint of the main zones of the system.
- Describe each core service and the signal and order flows between them.
- Walk through how a new strategy moves from research to production within this architecture.

A High-Level Blueprint of the Trading Machine

At the highest level, a modern trading platform can be viewed as four connected zones:

- **Data ingestion and storage.**

- **Strategy engine and signal bus.**
- **Portfolio and risk services.**
- **OMS/EMS and external venues.**

Information flows predominantly from left to right: raw data enters, is transformed into signals and orders, and is then executed in the market. Control and feedback signals flow in both directions: risk constraints, portfolio targets, and execution quality metrics loop back to strategies and operators.

Figure shows this blueprint in schematic form.

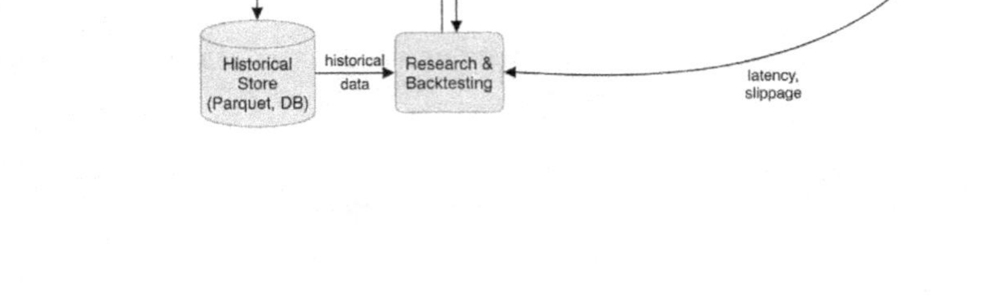

The rest of this section will unpack each zone, show how services within and across zones interact, and explain how the engineering practices from earlier sections fit into this picture.

Data Ingestion, Normalization, and Storage

Every trading decision begins with data. The data zone consists of two main components:

- **Ingestion and normalization service.**
- **Historical storage and retrieval.**

Ingestion and Normalization Service

This service receives raw feeds from exchanges, brokers, and data vendors. Its responsibilities include:

- **Parsing:** Decoding binary or textual feed formats into internal messages (often Protobuf or similar).
- **Normalization:** Standardizing field names, units (e.g., price scales), and identifiers (mapping vendor-specific symbols to canonical instruments).
- **Quality checks:** Filtering obviously bad ticks, enforcing monotonic timestamps where possible, and flagging anomalies.
- **Fan-out:** Publishing normalized data to downstream consumers: live strategy engines, monitoring tools, and the historical store.

For low-latency feeds, this service is typically written in C++ and uses an event-driven design. It is squarely in the "hot path" described earlier: a natural candidate for the C++ layer in the language stack.

Historical Storage and Retrieval

The ingestion service also writes data into a long-term store, often in columnar formats such as Parquet, partitioned by date and symbol. This store supports:

- Backtesting and research (via Python/pandas, Spark, or SQL engines).
- Post-trade analysis, TCA (transaction cost analysis), and compliance reporting.

Because this is batch-oriented and I/O-bound rather than latency-critical, much of the ETL (Extract-Transform-Load) pipeline can live in Python, using vectorized transforms to handle large datasets efficiently. Here, the layered architecture keeps domain definitions (e.g., what a "trade" or "order book snapshot" is) independent from the particular storage technology.

Strategy Engine and Signal Bus

The strategy zone transforms normalized data into trading *intent*: signals, target positions, and orders. It usually has two main layers:

- **Research and backtesting environment.**
- **Live strategy engine and signal bus.**

Research and Backtesting Environment

This environment is where most Python and vectorized computing lives. It uses historical data from the store to:

- Explore new factors and models.
- Run backtests that simulate the behavior of strategies under various assumptions.

- Analyze performance, risk, and robustness (drawdowns, turnover, capacity, etc.).

Critically, the research environment should share as much code as possible with the production domain layer. Hexagonal architecture helps here:

- The *core strategy logic* (signal calculation, portfolio optimization) is implemented in a technology-agnostic way.
- Adapters connect this core logic to either the backtesting harness (which replays historical data and simulates fills) or the live signal bus (which connects to real-time feeds and the OMS).

This reduces "model risk drift" between backtest and live trading: the same strategy code sees different adapters but identical domain interfaces.

Live Strategy Engine and Signal Bus

In production, strategy instances subscribe to real-time feeds from the data service and publish outputs to a *signal bus*. Depending on latency requirements and volume:

- Lower-frequency or overnight strategies may run entirely in Python processes, consuming data via gRPC or WebSocket and publishing orders over REST or gRPC.
- Higher-frequency strategies may run in C++ or a mixed stack, with critical path components implemented in native code and orchestrated by a lean control layer.

The signal bus is a logical concept: it may be implemented as a message queue, a set of topics in a streaming platform, or a bidirectional gRPC service. Its key properties are:

- **Loose coupling:** Strategies send signals or intents to the bus, not directly to the OMS or risk engines.

- **Standardized messages:** All strategies express their outputs in a common schema (e.g., target weights or order requests), making downstream processing uniform.
- **Observability:** Signals on the bus can be logged and monitored, enabling post-hoc analysis and replays.

By centralizing signal publication, you avoid each strategy reinventing connectivity, risk checks, and logging. This is a direct application of the ports-and-adapters pattern: strategies talk to abstract ports, and different adapters deliver those intents to OMS or simulation environments.

Portfolio and Risk Services

Between strategy outputs and raw order submission stand the *portfolio* and *risk* services. They provide a firm-wide view of positions and constraints, and ensure that any proposed trade is viewed in context.

Portfolio Service: The Golden Record of Positions

The portfolio service maintains authoritative state for:

- Positions by instrument, account, and strategy.
- Cash balances and margin usage.
- Daily and intraday P&L, realized and unrealized.
- Aggregated exposures by sector, factor, region, and other dimensions.

It consumes fills and order-state events from the OMS and updates internal ledgers accordingly. It also serves data back to:

- Strategies, so that they can make decisions based on current holdings and P&L.
- Risk engines, so that risk calculations have accurate inputs.

- Dashboards and reporting tools.

From an architectural standpoint:

- The portfolio service implements a set of well-defined APIs (often REST/JSON) for queries and snapshots, and sometimes gRPC or message-based feeds for streaming updates.
- Internally it may use a database optimized for time-series and ledger-like operations.

Testing and version control are crucial here: mistakes in how fills are applied or how P&L is computed can propagate silently unless guarded by unit and integration tests that simulate fills, corporate actions, and roll adjustments.

Risk Service: Enforcing Limits and Providing Feedback

The risk service enforces the firm's risk policies at multiple levels:

- **Pre-trade risk:** Before an order is routed, check whether it violates limits (per-instrument size caps, sector exposures, leverage limits, etc.).
- **Intraday monitoring:** While strategies are live, monitor exposures, drawdowns, and stress test results, issuing alerts or throttling instructions.
- **Post-trade analysis:** After the fact, evaluate whether actual exposures matched intended ones, and measure realized risk.

In the end-to-end blueprint, the risk service sits between strategy intents and OMS actions:

- Strategies send proposed trades to the signal bus, which forwards them to risk as well as to the portfolio service.
- Risk evaluates the proposals in light of current portfolio state and firm-wide constraints.

- Risk either approves the trades, possibly with adjusted sizes, or rejects them with reasons.
- The OMS only routes orders that pass risk checks.

Risk also sends feedback *back* to strategies and operators:

- Limits and throttling signals (e.g., *"max gross leverage reduced for today"*).
- Early warnings based on scenario analyses or stress events.

This feedback loop is represented by the dashed arrows in Figure. It is a key example of control-flow that runs counter to the primary data flow.

OMS/EMS and External Venues

At the rightmost end of the blueprint lies the OMS/EMS (Order Management / Execution Management System) and its adapters to external venues and brokers.

Order Management and State Machines

The OMS is responsible for the life cycle of orders within your system:

- Accepting validated order requests from strategies (via the portfolio/risk layer).
- Assigning internal identifiers and mapping to external venue formats.
- Tracking state transitions: New, Acknowledged, Partially Filled, Filled, Canceled, Rejected, etc.
- Handling cancels, amendments, and complex order types.

Under the hood, each order can be modeled as a state machine; C++ is commonly used here for deterministic, low-latency behavior. Unit tests verify that all legal transitions occur as expected and illegal transitions are prevented (e.g., you cannot amend a fully filled order).

The OMS publishes order-state events and fills back to:

- The portfolio service, for position and P&L updates.
- Strategy instances, for real-time awareness of execution.
- Logging and monitoring systems, for observability.

Execution Management and Venue Connectivity

The EMS focuses on *how* orders are executed:

- Choosing venues and routes (smart order routing).
- Splitting large parent orders into smaller child orders over time (execution algorithms).
- Managing exchange-specific features and throttling.

Execution adapters implement the ports-and-adapters pattern at the market edge:

- For each venue or broker, there is an adapter that understands its protocol (FIX, native binary, REST).
- The core OMS/EMS logic talks only to abstract interfaces (e.g., `send_child_order`, `cancel_order`), not directly to sockets or protocol-specific details.

This makes it much easier to add or replace venues without touching core execution logic. It also allows the same OMS/EMS to be used in simulation, with adapters that replay historical order books instead of sending real orders.

Feedback Loops and Control Paths

While the main data and order flow moves left-to-right, robust trading systems are defined by their feedback loops.

Portfolio and Risk Feedback to Strategies

As highlighted earlier:

- Portfolio service feeds current positions, exposures, and realized P&L back to strategies.
- Risk service communicates updated limits, alerts, and recommended de-risking actions.

Strategies that incorporate this information are more robust: they can adapt position sizes to available risk budgets, respect global constraints, and avoid unintentional concentration.

From an engineering perspective, these feedback paths are implemented via APIs (REST for snapshots, streaming RPC or message topics for updates). Tests must cover not only the straight-through path (signal $\rightarrow$ order $\rightarrow$ fill), but also how strategies react when risk tightens limits mid-session or when positions deviate from targets due to partial fills.

Execution Quality Feedback to Research

Another important loop connects execution and research:

- The OMS/EMS and venues produce detailed execution logs: timestamps, venues, prices, sizes, and order book context.
- These logs are stored historically (often in the same Parquet-based store as market data).
- Research tools analyze slippage, market impact, and execution reliability.

This allows you to adjust both strategies and execution algorithms in response to real-world behavior. For example:

- If a strategy systematically experiences higher slippage in small-cap names, you might revise its turnover targets or execution style.
- If a venue consistently rejects certain order types, you might adjust routing or adapter behavior.

These analyses heavily reuse the vectorized computing and data engineering stack introduced earlier, showing again how language and architecture choices support the full lifecycle.

From Research Idea to Production Strategy

To make this blueprint concrete, consider the journey of a new strategy:

- **Idea and prototyping.** A researcher works in Python, using `pandas` and historical data from the store to compute factors and simulate P&L. Early code is exploratory but quickly evolves into a clear, testable core model.
- **Backtesting and evaluation.** The strategy is wired into the backtesting harness, which uses adapters compatible with the production domain interfaces. Vectorized computations and event-driven backtests simulate fills and P&L across years of data.
- **Hardening and tests.** As the strategy matures, its core components (signal functions, sizing logic, risk overlays) are covered by unit tests. Integration tests verify interactions with simulated OMS and risk services. Version control tags mark stable backtest configurations.
- **Staging in the live system.** The strategy is deployed to a staging environment where it consumes *live* normalized data via the signal bus but operates in "paper" mode: orders are routed to a simulated exchange, not to real venues. End-to-end tests and replays are used to validate behavior.

- **Production rollout.** Once confidence is sufficient, configuration is switched so that the strategy's orders are sent through the real OMS/EMS to brokers. All changes are tracked in Git, and deployment scripts record which version is live.
- **Monitoring and iteration.** Portfolio and risk services track exposures; execution logs flow back to research. If behavior diverges from expectations, logs and stored events allow detailed investigation and targeted improvements.

At every step, the blueprint's structure provides guardrails:

- The strategy engine never talks directly to brokers; it talks to ports implemented by OMS and risk services.
- The same domain objects (orders, positions, fills) have consistent definitions across research, backtesting, and production.
- Tests and replays span from small, fast units up to full sessions with recorded data.

This end-to-end blueprint is more than a diagram; it is a way of thinking about your trading platform as a set of cooperating, well-defined services:

- The **data** zone transforms raw feeds into normalized, reusable datasets.
- The **strategy** zone turns data into intents via a signal bus, with shared code between research and production.
- The **portfolio and risk** zone contextualizes trades within the firm's balance sheet and constraints.
- The **OMS/EMS** zone turns validated orders into real executions and detailed logs.

Layered languages, clean architecture patterns, thoughtful APIs, robust tests, and secure coding all converge here. Together, they allow you to build an algorithmic trading machine that is not only fast and sophisticated, but also understandable, auditable, and resilient—a platform on which serious capital can be deployed with confidence.

Chapter 4

Strategy Research, Backtesting, and Machine Learning

Algorithmic trading edge is rarely found in a clever model alone-it emerges when disciplined research, realistic simulation, and machine learning all reinforce each other. In this chapter you will learn how to turn vague trading ideas into testable hypotheses, transform noisy market data into informative features, train and interrogate predictive models, and then subject your strategies to unforgiving, microstructure-aware backtests and walk-forward validations that tell you whether the edge you see on paper is likely to survive in live trading.

4.1 Research Workflow and Feature Engineering

In the previous chapter we treated strategies mostly at the conceptual level: economic intuition, signal ideas, and high-level system architecture. In this section we descend into the research "factory floor" and specify how an idea becomes a clean, testable dataset that can feed both machine learning models and a backtester.

Our goal is a disciplined, repeatable workflow. A good research workflow has three properties:

- **Hypothesis-driven:** every computation is traceable back to an economic or behavioral hypothesis.
- **Time-respecting:** nothing in the research process leaks information from the future into the past.
- **Reproducible:** given the same inputs and code, you obtain the same feature matrix, labels, and backtest.

We will walk through the full research loop:

- Formulate a precise trading hypothesis.
- Map that hypothesis to required data and labels.
- Ingest, clean, and align raw market data.
- Engineer cross-sectional and time-series features.
- Normalize, winsorize, and tag regimes.
- Assemble train/test sets that are ready for modeling and backtesting.

Throughout, keep in mind the end products: a feature matrix X and a label vector (or matrix) y, built in a way that a backtester can interpret correctly.

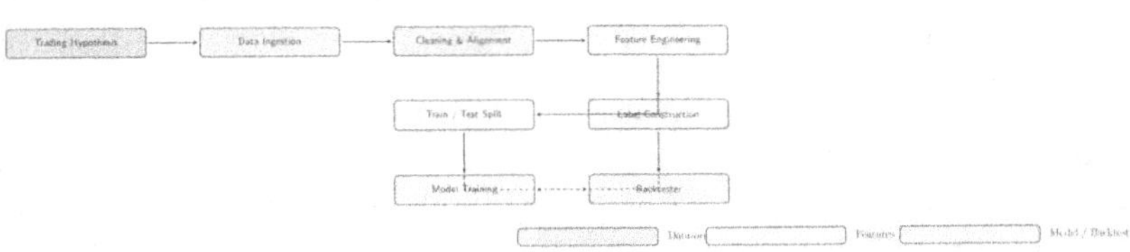

From Trading Story to Testable Hypothesis

Most bad research starts with the data and looks for patterns. Most good research starts with a question about how markets work, then asks whether the data supports that view.

A **trading story** becomes a **hypothesis** when you can state it in terms of observable quantities and falsifiable predictions.

Example: Value–Momentum Interaction.

- *Story:* "Cheap stocks that have recently started to outperform may be underpriced reversals rather than value traps."
- *Hypothesis:* Among stocks in the cheapest valuation decile at time t, those with positive 6–12 month momentum will have higher risk-adjusted returns over the next 1 month than those with negative momentum, after controlling for market and sector effects.

Notice that this hypothesis specifies:

- the *universe*: stocks,
- the *conditioning set*: cheapest valuation decile,
- the *features*: value metric, past 6–12 month return,
- the *label*: next 1-month (risk-adjusted) return,
- the *horizon*: one month forward,
- and the *comparison*: positive vs. negative momentum.

This level of specificity provides a direct blueprint for data and feature engineering.

Mapping Hypotheses to Data and Labels

Given a hypothesis, your next step is to ask three practical questions:

- **What do I need to measure?** (features and labels)
- **At what frequency?** (daily, intraday, tick, etc.)
- **With what safety guards?** (no survivorship bias, no look-ahead bias)

Features vs. Labels. In supervised learning terms:

- **Features** $X_{t,i}$ summarize all information available about instrument i at time t that your strategy may use to make a decision.
- **Labels** $y_{t,i}$ describe the outcome you wish to predict, measured over some future interval relative to t.

For a long-only equity signal:

$$X_{t,i} = \left(\text{valuation}_{t,i}, \text{momentum}_{t,i}, \text{volatility}_{t,i}, \ldots\right), \quad y_{t,i} = r_{t \to t+21d,i},$$

where $r_{t \to t+21d,i}$ is the (log) return from day t close to day $t + 21$ close.

Two design decisions are crucial at this stage:

Prediction Horizon. You must fix an explicit lag between when features are observed and when labels are measured. This horizon should reflect realistic trading:

- A high-frequency market-making strategy might predict the next 1–5 seconds of mid-price change.
- A medium-horizon equity strategy might predict the next 1–20 trading days of return.

Decision Clock. You must also define *when* in the day decisions are made:

- End-of-day strategies: features based on today's close, orders executed at tomorrow's open.

- Intraday strategies: features computed on 5-minute bars, decisions at each bar close, orders filled within the next bar.

These choices determine how you will align timestamps across data sources and avoid look-ahead bias.

Data Ingestion, Cleaning, and Alignment

Real market data is messy: missing prices, out-of-order timestamps, corporate actions, and changing ticker symbols. Before computing any "smart" features, you must solve these mundane issues reliably.

Data Ingestion and Storage

At ingestion time, focus on two principles:

- **Raw data is immutable.** Never overwrite the raw feed; store it as-compressed-as-needed but logically read-only.
- **Metadata is explicit.** Each file or table carries instrument identifiers, vendor codes, timestamps, time zones, and corporate action flags.

Typical data feeds include:

- trades and quotes (TAQ),
- bar data (e.g., 1-minute, 5-minute, daily OHLCV),
- reference data (splits, dividends, symbol changes),
- fundamentals (earnings, book value),
- alternative data (news, sentiment, web traffic).

For systematic research, it is worth defining a canonical internal schema: for each asset i and time t, what minimal set of fields will always be present (price, volume, corporate action adjustment factors, etc.)?

Cleaning and Corporate Actions

Cleaning should aim to preserve economic meaning, not to make the data "pretty". The typical steps on bar data are:

- **Filter obvious errors:** remove or correct prices that imply absurd returns (e.g., $> 90\%$ up and down within one second without corresponding trades), or volumes that are clearly erroneous.
- **Apply corporate action adjustments:**
  - Adjust historical prices for splits and large stock dividends so that return series are continuous.
  - Decide whether to adjust for cash dividends (for total-return series you will).
- **Handle missing bars:**
  - Distinguish between "no trade" and "missing feed".
  - For daily bars, an entirely missing day may reflect a holiday or suspension.

The key is to document every transformation: in production you must be able to redo it for new data, and in a forensic investigation you must be able to reconstruct the exact inputs to a historical model run.

Time Alignment and Universe Definition

Markets trade at different local times, and corporate actions may have effective dates that differ from announcement dates. To avoid subtle bugs:

- Convert all timestamps to a common reference (e.g., UTC), but *keep* the original timezone as metadata.
- Define a **research universe** and a **trading universe**. The research universe might include delisted securities (to avoid survivorship bias) while your live trading universe includes only currently tradable ones.

For cross-sectional strategies, you must also decide, at each time t, which instruments are eligible (e.g., minimum price, minimum average daily dollar volume, index membership). These eligibility flags themselves become useful features.

Feature Engineering: Cross-Sectional and Time-Series Views

With clean, aligned data in hand, we can construct features. It is helpful to categorize features by the kind of variation they exploit.

Time-Series Features

Time-series features describe how *one* instrument evolves over time. For instrument i:

- **Returns at multiple horizons:**

  $$r_{t,i}^{(k)} = \log P_{t,i} - \log P_{t-k,i},$$

  where $P_{t,i}$ is the adjusted close at time t and k might be 1 day, 5 days, 21 days, etc.

- **Volatility measures:**

  $$\sigma_{t,i}^{(k)} = \sqrt{\frac{1}{k}\sum_{j=1}^{k}\left(r_{t-j+1,i} - \bar{r}_{t,i}^{(k)}\right)^2},$$

  where $\bar{r}_{t,i}^{(k)}$ is the mean return over the past k periods.

- **Liquidity measures:**
  - rolling average volume over last k days;
  - average dollar volume $= P_{t,i} \times \text{volume}_{t,i}$;
  - bid–ask spread, often as a percentage of mid-price.

- **Microstructure signals:**
  - order book imbalance: $(\text{bid volume} - \text{ask volume})/(\text{bid volume} + \text{ask volume})$;
  - short-term order flow: ratio of buyer-initiated to seller-initiated trades.

These features answer questions like: *Is this instrument trending? Is it volatile? Is liquidity drying up?*

Cross-Sectional Features

Cross-sectional features compare many instruments at the *same* time t. They are used to *rank* stocks or contracts relative to each other.

Common cross-sectional constructions include:

- **Ranks:** transform raw values into percentile ranks within the universe:

$$\text{rankFeature}_{t,i} = \frac{\text{rank of } x_{t,i} \text{ among all } j}{N_t},$$

  where N_t is the number of available instruments at t.

- **Z-scores:** demean and standardize features across the cross-section:

$$z_{t,i} = \frac{x_{t,i} - \mu_t}{\sigma_t},$$

  where μ_t and σ_t are the cross-sectional mean and standard deviation at time t.

- **Relative-to-benchmark:** subtract sector or index averages:

$$x_{t,i}^{rel} = x_{t,i} - \bar{x}_{t,sector(i)}.$$

Cross-sectional normalization is especially important for machine learning models that will be trained on pooled data across time: it ensures that feature scales are comparable across dates and that the interpretation "high vs. low" is relative to the market state at each t.

Practical Feature Engineering Techniques

Beyond simple transformations, there are several practical techniques you will use repeatedly to make features robust and machine-learning-ready.

Winsorization and Outlier Handling

Market variables often have heavy tails: extreme returns, illiquid days with zero volume, and so on. Unchecked, these can distort regression fits and tree splits.

Winsorization at, say, the 1st and 99th percentile on each day t caps extreme values:

$$x'_{t,i} = \begin{cases} q_{0.01}(x_{t,\cdot}) & \text{if } x_{t,i} < q_{0.01}, \\ q_{0.99}(x_{t,\cdot}) & \text{if } x_{t,i} > q_{0.99}, \\ x_{t,i} & \text{otherwise,} \end{cases}$$

where q_p is the cross-sectional p-th percentile at t.

Key points:

- Perform winsorization *cross-sectionally* at each time t, not over the entire history at once; this respects time variation in distributions.
- For highly skewed quantities (e.g., market capitalization), log-transform first, then winsorize.

Scaling and Normalization

Many machine learning algorithms assume features are on comparable scales. You will commonly apply:

- **Standardization:** z-scores cross-sectionally, as above.
- **Min–max scaling:** map features to $[0, 1]$ within each cross-section.
- **Rank transforms:** replace raw values by their fractional rank; this makes features more robust to outliers and nonlinear monotonic distortions.

Important: scaling parameters (means, standard deviations, quantiles) should be estimated *only* from the training period when you later split into train and test sets. During historical backtests, you recompute them at each t using only information up to t.

Detrending and De-seasonalization

Some variables display slow drifts or strong seasonal patterns that may obscure the behavior you care about. Examples:

- market-wide valuation levels drift over years;
- intraday volume follows a U-shape: high at open and close, low midday;
- volatility often clusters following macro events.

You can make features more stationary by:

- subtracting a rolling mean or median over a long window;
- modeling and removing predictable seasonal components (e.g., average intraday pattern by 5-minute bar index);
- working with relative measures (e.g., current volatility divided by a 60-day average).

The objective is to focus learning on deviations from "normal" rather than on the drift of normal.

Handling Missing and Stale Data

In financial data, missing does not always mean "unknown"; it may mean "not traded" or "delisted". You should:

- Distinguish between:
  - *structural missingness*: the asset did not exist or was not listed yet;
  - *temporary missingness*: data feed interruption.
- Avoid forward-filling prices across long gaps; instead, use explicit flags:
  - binary features like "traded today" or "volume > 0";
  - missing indicators to tell the model that a value was imputed.

For cross-sectional strategies, you will routinely filter out instruments whose data is too stale (e.g., no trade for 10 days) from the trading universe at time t.

Label Construction Aligned with Trading

Label design is where research and trading meet directly: labels must reflect the P&L consequences of your decisions under realistic assumptions.

Return-Based Labels

The simplest label is a future return over horizon H:

$$y_{t,i} = \log P_{t+H,i} - \log P_{t+1,i},$$

if you assume decisions at t result in execution at $t+1$ and holding until $t+H$. Variations include:

- **Direction labels:** $y_{t,i} = \mathbf{1}\{r_{t \to t+H,i} > 0\}$ for classification.
- **Bucketed labels:** e.g., quintiles of future return, to focus on ranking rather than exact values.
- **Risk-adjusted labels:** returns in excess of a benchmark or factor model, so the model learns idiosyncratic rather than market-wide moves.

Execution- and Event-Based Labels

For microstructure or execution models, labels may not be returns at all:

- Probability that a limit order posted at price p at time t will fill within Δt.
- Expected slippage relative to mid-price for a market order of size Q.
- Probability of a price jump exceeding a threshold following a news event.

In these cases, your labels encode market *events* or execution outcomes, and features are constructed to be consistent with the information set at order submission time.

Train/Test Splits and Time-Respecting Data Sets

Once features and labels are defined, you must assemble them into matrices suitable for both machine learning and backtesting. The core object is:

$$\mathcal{D} = \{(X_{t,i}, y_{t,i}) : t \in \mathcal{T},\ i \in \mathcal{U}_t\},$$

where $\mathcal{U}_t$ is the eligible universe at time t.

To avoid look-ahead and overfitting:

- Use **time-based** splits (e.g., train on 2010–2016, validate on 2017–2018, test on 2019–2022).
- Ensure that any statistic used to scale or transform features at time t is computed only from data up to t.

We will later extend this to walk-forward validation, but even here the principle is the same: pretend you are moving forward through time, only using information that would have been available then.

Embedding the Workflow in Code and Documentation

A research workflow is not just ideas; it is code and documentation that make results reproducible and refutable. Three practices are especially useful:

- **Version control:** Store all research code (scripts, notebooks, configuration files) in a version-controlled repository. Tag key experiments (e.g., v1_momentum_value_2022Q4).
- **Parameterized experiments:** Avoid hard-coding dates, horizons, or universe definitions in many places. Use configuration files (YAML/JSON) that define:
  - data sources and sample period;

    - feature definitions and hyperparameters (e.g., look-back windows);
    - label definitions and prediction horizon;
    - train/validation/test splits.

  This makes it easier to rerun the same experiment with different hyperparameters or extended data.

- **Standardized schemas:** Define a common schema for:
    - feature tables: columns for `asset_id`, `timestamp`, and feature names;
    - label tables: same keys plus one or more label columns;
    - metadata: universe membership, eligibility flags, regime tags.

These structures let your downstream components—machine learning training routines and the backtester—consume data with minimal custom glue code.

This section has turned a loosely worded "trading story" into a concrete research pipeline:

- define precise hypotheses and prediction horizons;
- map them to observable features and realistic labels;
- ingest and clean raw market data with careful handling of corporate actions, time zones, and missingness;
- engineer time-series and cross-sectional features, with appropriate normalization, winsorization, and detrending;
- construct labels that reflect trading outcomes;
- assemble time-respecting train/test datasets in a standardized schema.

The resulting feature matrix and labels provide the inputs for the next stages of the algorithmic trading machine: machine learning models that estimate predictive relationships, and backtesters that determine whether those predictions can be translated into robust, tradable profits.

4.2 Machine Learning Models and Diagnostics

In the previous section we built a disciplined research workflow: starting from a trading hypothesis, we produced clean, time-respecting features and labels that can drive both a backtester and a predictive model. We now stand at the point in the pipeline where we must decide *how* to map those features to predictions about returns, directions, or events.

This section introduces supervised learning models that are widely used in trading, explains how regularization and model selection protect you from overfitting, and then focuses on diagnostics and interpretability—tools to tell genuine economic edge from accidental noise fitting.

Throughout, you should think of models as *components in a trading system*, not as black boxes to be maximized on a leaderboard. A slightly less accurate but transparent and stable model is almost always preferable to a fragile, opaque one.

From Features and Labels to a Predictive Task

Recall that our research workflow produces pairs

$$(X_{t,i}, y_{t,i}),$$

where $X_{t,i}$ is a vector of features for instrument i at time t and $y_{t,i}$ is a label aligned with the trading decision (e.g., next-day log return, a direction indicator, or a fill/no-fill outcome).

- When $y_{t,i}$ is *continuous* (returns, slippage, execution time), we have a **regression** problem.
- When $y_{t,i}$ is *discrete* (up/down, event/no-event, bucket), we have a **classification** problem.

In both cases we seek a function

$$f : X_{t,i} \mapsto \hat{y}_{t,i}$$

that takes feature vectors as input and returns predictions $\hat{y}_{t,i}$ that are informative for trading.

Linear and Generalized Linear Models: Baseline Workhorses

We begin with the simplest and most interpretable family: linear and generalized linear models (GLMs). These should be your first choice in almost any new project, for three reasons:

- They are computationally cheap, even in large cross-sections.
- They provide clear coefficient estimates that are easy to interpret.
- They form a strong baseline against which more complex models must prove their worth.

Linear Regression for Returns

For a regression task, linear models assume that the expected label is an affine function of features:

$$\hat{y}_{t,i} = \beta_0 + \beta^\top X_{t,i},$$

where β is a vector of coefficients, one per feature.

If $y_{t,i}$ is a future return and the elements of $X_{t,i}$ are standardized (for example, cross-sectional z-scores), we can interpret β_j as the expected change in the label per one-standard-deviation change in feature j, holding other features constant.

The coefficients are estimated by minimizing a loss function, typically the mean squared error (MSE):

$$\mathcal{L}(\beta) = \frac{1}{N} \sum_{(t,i)} \left(y_{t,i} - \beta_0 - \beta^\top X_{t,i}\right)^2,$$

where the sum runs over all training pairs.

Logistic Regression and GLMs for Probabilities

Often we care about the *probability* of an event rather than a raw value: for example, the probability that a stock will be in the top return decile next month, or that a limit order will fully fill within 30 seconds.

In these cases, generalized linear models link a linear score to a probability via a nonlinear transformation. The most common is *logistic regression*, which models

$$p_{t,i} = \mathbb{P}(y_{t,i} = 1 \mid X_{t,i}) = \sigma(\beta_0 + \beta^\top X_{t,i}),$$

where $\sigma(z) = \frac{1}{1+e^{-z}}$ is the logistic (sigmoid) function.

The loss function becomes the log-likelihood (or equivalently, cross-entropy):

$$\mathcal{L}(\beta) = -\frac{1}{N} \sum_{(t,i)} \left[y_{t,i} \log p_{t,i} + (1 - y_{t,i}) \log(1 - p_{t,i}) \right].$$

GLMs generalize this idea to other distributions and link functions (e.g., Poisson regression for counts), but the basic pattern is the same: a linear score passed through a known nonlinearity.

Why Start Linear?

In trading, linear and GLM models have several practical strengths:

- **Speed and scalability:** When you have millions of (t, i) pairs and hundreds of features, more complex models may be infeasible without heavy infrastructure. Linear models scale well.
- **Interpretability:** Coefficients can be inspected, constrained, or regularized; you can easily sanity-check if they align with economic intuition (e.g., higher valuation multiples leading to lower expected returns).
- **Regularization-friendly:** They combine naturally with L1/L2 penalties, which we discuss next.

Even if you ultimately deploy a nonlinear ensemble, you should almost always build and benchmark a linear model first.

Regularization: Controlling Complexity and Overfitting

With rich feature sets, a naive linear model can easily overfit noise. Regularization adds a penalty for complexity, shrinking coefficients and improving generalization.

Ridge (L2) Regularization

Ridge regression adds an L2 penalty on coefficients:

$$\mathcal{L}_{ridge}(\beta) = \frac{1}{N}\sum_{(t,i)}\left(y_{t,i} - \beta_0 - \beta^\top X_{t,i}\right)^2 + \lambda\|\beta\|_2^2,$$

where

$$\|\beta\|_2^2 = \sum_j \beta_j^2,$$

and $\lambda \geq 0$ controls the strength of the penalty.

Effects:

- Coefficients are shrunk towards zero, but rarely exactly zero.
- Correlated features share the load; ridge tends to distribute weights among them.
- The solution is more stable in the presence of multicollinearity (highly correlated predictors).

In trading, ridge regularization is a natural choice when you have many noisy variants of similar signals (e.g., returns at nearby horizons).

Lasso (L1) Regularization

Lasso adds an L1 penalty:

$$\mathcal{L}_{lasso}(\beta) = \frac{1}{N}\sum_{(t,i)}\left(y_{t,i} - \beta_0 - \beta^\top X_{t,i}\right)^2 + \lambda\|\beta\|_1,$$

where

$$\|\beta\|_1 = \sum_j |\beta_j|.$$

Effects:

- Many coefficients are driven *exactly* to zero.
- This performs implicit **feature selection**, choosing a sparse subset.
- With strong correlation between features, lasso tends to pick one representative and discard the rest.

Lasso is useful when you suspect that only a small subset of your engineered features actually carries predictive power, or when you want a compact, interpretable model.

Elastic Net: Combining L1 and L2

Elastic net combines both penalties:

$$\mathcal{L}_{EN}(\beta) = \frac{1}{N} \sum_{(t,i)} \left(y_{t,i} - \beta_0 - \beta^\top X_{t,i}\right)^2 + \lambda \left(\alpha\|\beta\|_1 + (1-\alpha)\|\beta\|_2^2\right),$$

where $\alpha \in [0, 1]$ interpolates between ridge ($\alpha = 0$) and lasso ($\alpha = 1$). For trading data, elastic net is often a robust default because:

- It still encourages sparsity (via L1), yielding simpler models.
- It handles correlated groups of features better than pure lasso (via L2).

Regularization and Economic Intuition

A crucial habit is to read regularization not just as a statistical trick but as *encoding prior beliefs*:

- L2 (*ridge*) encodes: "I believe coefficients should be small but dense; many features matter a little."
- L1 (*lasso*) encodes: "I believe only a few features matter; most should effectively be zero."

Ask whether these priors match your understanding of the strategy. For example, in a factor-style equity strategy where many small effects combine, ridge or elastic net with low sparsity may be appropriate. In an event-driven setup with a handful of key indicators, a sparser lasso-style penalty can make sense.

Nonlinear Models: Trees and Ensembles

Linear and GLM models assume that the relationship between features and label is (after any transformations) approximately linear. Markets, however, often exhibit nonlinearities and interactions: a signal might work only in low-volatility regimes, or only in small caps.

Tree-based models and their ensembles are powerful tools to capture such structure while still retaining a degree of interpretability.

Decision Trees

A decision tree recursively partitions the feature space into regions and fits a constant prediction in each region. For regression:

- At each node, pick a feature x_j and threshold τ that best splits the data into two subsets, minimizing some impurity measure (e.g., MSE).
- Repeat the splitting recursively on each subset to grow a tree.
- Leaves contain training examples that share similar feature profiles; the prediction for a leaf is the average label of samples in that leaf.

Advantages:

- They naturally capture interactions (e.g., "if volatility is low and value rank is high, then ...").
- They are somewhat interpretable: you can walk down a path and see the conditions that led to a prediction.

Disadvantages:

- Single trees are high-variance estimators and prone to overfitting.
- Performance is often mediocre compared to ensembles.

Random Forests

Random forests average many decision trees to reduce variance:

- Each tree is trained on a bootstrap sample of the data.
- At each split, a random subset of features is considered.
- Predictions are averaged (for regression) or voted (for classification).

In trading applications:

- Random forests can capture complex, nonlinear profiles of instruments and regimes.
- They are relatively robust to noisy features and can provide useful feature importance measures.

However, they can be computationally heavy if you have very large cross-sectional datasets, and their predictions can be difficult to calibrate for probability outputs without additional post-processing.

Gradient-Boosted Trees

Gradient boosting builds trees *sequentially*, each new tree correcting the residual errors of the current ensemble:

- Start with a simple model (e.g., a constant prediction).
- Fit a small tree to the residuals.
- Add this tree to the model with a learning rate η.
- Repeat for many iterations.

Modern implementations (e.g., XGBoost, LightGBM, CatBoost) are highly optimized and widely used in quantitative finance because they:

- achieve strong predictive performance on tabular data;
- handle heterogeneous feature types and missing values;
- expose many knobs (tree depth, learning rate, number of trees, subsampling) to control overfitting.

The downside is increased complexity: boosted trees are less interpretable than linear models, more sensitive to hyperparameter choices, and more computationally intensive.

Model Selection: Choosing and Tuning Models

Once you have candidate model families (linear, elastic net, random forest, gradient boosting), you must decide which combination of architecture and hyperparameters to use. This is *model selection*.

Hyperparameters vs. Parameters

It is useful to distinguish:

- **Parameters** are learned from data by optimization (e.g., β coefficients in linear models, split thresholds in trees).

- **Hyperparameters** are set by you and govern model capacity (e.g., regularization strength λ, tree depth, number of trees, learning rate).

Hyperparameters control how easily your model can overfit. A very deep tree or a gradient-boosted ensemble with thousands of rounds and tiny regularization can memorize noise in your sample.

Validation Schemes and Walk-Forward Selection

In time-series trading, you *cannot* shuffle data randomly when performing cross-validation; this would leak future information into the training set. Instead, selection must respect the temporal ordering (see the later section on walk-forward validation for a detailed treatment).

At a minimum for model selection:

- Use an early period for training, a later contiguous period for validation, and an even later period for final testing.
- For each candidate model/hyperparameter set, train on the training window and evaluate on the validation window.
- Choose the configuration with the best validation performance (according to trading-relevant metrics, not only statistical ones).

You may also use rolling-origin or expanding windows for more robust selection, but the key is always the same: no peeking into the future.

Performance vs. Complexity Trade-off

When comparing models, avoid automatically choosing the one with the very best validation metric. Instead, aim for a *good-enough* model with:

- stable performance across nearby hyperparameter choices;
- lower complexity (fewer features with nonzero weight, shallower trees, fewer boosting rounds);

- economically interpretable behavior.

In practice, you may:

- plot validation performance as a function of λ (regularization strength) or tree depth;
- pick a point near the "elbow" where additional complexity yields diminishing returns.

This reduces the risk that your chosen model is an accidental beneficiary of noise in the validation period.

Diagnostics: Beyond Headline Accuracy

Even a modest model can generate impressive-looking backtests on historical data if you are not careful. Diagnostics help you understand *how* your model is making money (or not), and whether its behavior is plausible.

We group diagnostics into prediction quality, trading relevance, and stability.

Prediction Quality: Error and Calibration

Standard statistical metrics remain useful:

- **For regression:**
  - Mean squared error (MSE) and root MSE (RMSE).
  - Mean absolute error (MAE), often more robust to outliers.
  - R^2 as a measure of explained variance, although in noisy markets this is often small.
- **For classification:**
  - Accuracy and confusion matrices.
  - ROC curves and area under the curve (AUC), especially for imbalanced classes.

But in trading, we care strongly about *calibration* and *tail performance*:

- A probabilistic model is *calibrated* if events predicted with probability p occur about p fraction of the time. Calibration plots (predicted probability vs. empirical frequency in bins) are invaluable for limit-order and risk models.
- For return forecasts, we care whether the sign of the prediction is more often correct for the largest absolute predictions (the tails) than for small ones. This can be investigated by binning samples by predicted magnitude and computing hit rate in each bin.

Trading-Relevant Metrics: Rank and P&L

For many cross-sectional strategies, the absolute level of predicted return matters less than the *ranking* of instruments. Diagnostics should reflect this:

- Rank correlation (Spearman) between predicted and realized returns within each date.
- Long/short portfolio simulations by prediction buckets (deciles or quintiles):
  - Form decile 10 (top predictions) vs. decile 1 (bottom predictions) and track the spread return over time.
  - This is a direct picture of how much incremental edge your model adds across the cross-section.

Even if we defer full backtesting to the next chapter, partial analyses like these help you see whether the model's "strongest" predictions actually correspond to economically meaningful outcomes.

Stability Across Time and Regimes

A model that works only in one narrow period is unlikely to survive deployment. Always examine:

- Performance by year, by volatility regime, by market phase (bull/bear).
- Stability of coefficients (for linear models) over time: retrain on sliding windows and track how β evolves.
- Stability of the rank-order of features by importance.

Large, erratic swings in model behavior are a warning sign: they may indicate overfitting, poor feature quality, or a strategy that is inherently too unstable for your risk appetite.

Interpretability: Understanding What Drives Predictions

Interpretability is not a luxury in quantitative trading; it is central to risk management and to the scientific method. You should be able to explain, at least qualitatively, why your model is behaving as it does.

Coefficients and Sign Checks for Linear Models

For linear and GLM models, start with simple checks:

- Are the signs of key coefficients consistent with your economic hypothesis? For a value factor, a higher valuation multiple should not have a large *positive* coefficient predicting higher returns, unless you have a very specific contrarian story.
- Are magnitudes plausible? A coefficient implying that a one-standard-deviation change in a feature leads to an enormous change in expected return may indicate scaling issues or overfitting.

You can also examine coefficients by regimes or subuniverses: for example, does momentum behave similarly in small caps and large caps, or are coefficients systematically different?

Feature Importance in Tree-Based Models

Tree ensembles provide several notions of feature importance, such as:

- **Split-based importance:** how often and how early a feature is used to split nodes, weighted by the resulting reduction in error.
- **Permutation importance:** the increase in validation error when a feature's values are randomly permuted, breaking its relationship with the label.

Permutation importance is generally more robust and directly tied to predictive value. Use it to:

- confirm that economically sensible features are driving predictions;
- identify features that contribute little and could be removed to simplify the model.

Partial Dependence and Marginal Effects

For nonlinear models, partial dependence plots (PDPs) and related tools show how the prediction changes as you vary one or two features, averaging over others. For a feature x_j, the partial dependence function is roughly:

$$\mathrm{PD}_j(z) \approx \frac{1}{N} \sum_{(t,i)} f\big(x_{t,i}^{(1)}, \ldots, x_{t,i}^{(j-1)}, z, x_{t,i}^{(j+1)}, \ldots\big).$$

In trading:

- PDPs can confirm that higher volatility indeed leads to lower expected position size or higher expected slippage in an execution model.
- They can reveal threshold effects (e.g., a signal only turning on beyond a certain value) or saturation (e.g., extremely cheap stocks not offering additional expected return).

Always interpret PDPs with caution: they average over the empirical joint distribution of features, and strong correlations can complicate interpretation. Still, they are a powerful sanity check.

Diagnostics as Hypothesis Tests

Finally, use interpretability tools to revisit your original hypotheses:

- If a feature that you believed was central to the strategy has negligible importance, you may need to refine the hypothesis or the feature construction.
- If the model is relying heavily on a feature you did not anticipate (e.g., a subtle liquidity proxy), investigate whether this reflects genuine economics or an artifact of data or labeling.

The objective is not to "trust the model blindly" but to use the model as one more lens through which to examine your trading ideas.

In this section we connected the research workflow's feature and label construction to a range of supervised learning models:

- Linear and generalized linear models as fast, interpretable baselines, with coefficients that can be read directly.
- Regularization (L1, L2, elastic net) as a principled way to control complexity, encode prior beliefs, and prevent overfitting.
- Tree-based models and ensembles (random forests, gradient-boosted trees) to capture nonlinearities and interactions in rich market data.
- Time-respecting model selection strategies that choose models and hyperparameters based on validation windows without leaking future information.
- Diagnostics and interpretability tools—from calibration and rank-based metrics to feature importance and partial dependence—that help distinguish genuine edge from curve-fitting and ensure model behavior remains economically plausible.

These models and diagnostics are not endpoints; they are tools in a broader loop of hypothesis, testing, and refinement. In the next section, we will couple them with an event-driven backtester and realistic execution models, closing the gap between statistical predictability and tradable performance.

4.3 Backtester Design and Execution Simulation

In the previous sections we learned how to turn trading ideas into features and labels, and how to fit supervised learning models that produce forecasts or decisions. The next question is deceptively simple:

> If I had run this strategy in the past, using only the information available at the time, what would have happened to my capital?

Answering this requires more than plugging predictions into a spreadsheet. Markets are asynchronous, orders interact with an order book, and execution prices depend on liquidity and our own trading. A serious algorithmic trading operation therefore needs a *research-grade backtester*: an engine that replays market history and simulates trades in a way that is faithful, deterministic, and reproducible.

This section explains how to design such a backtester. We will:

- define goals and guiding principles for backtests;
- describe an event-driven architecture and its main components;
- walk through the life cycle of a simulated trade;
- introduce execution and slippage models, from simple to microstructure-aware;
- discuss parameterization and stress-testing of these models.

Goals of a Research-Grade Backtester

A research-grade backtester is not a toy environment that shows you what you want to see. Its purpose is to *contradict* you when your idea is wrong and *temper* your optimism when your idea is right.

Three goals are non-negotiable:

- **Determinism:** Given the same inputs—data, parameters, random seeds—the backtest must produce exactly the same outputs. This is essential for debugging, peer review, and regulatory audit.

- **Time fidelity:** The simulation must respect the flow of time. No decision may depend on information that was not yet available at that simulated moment.

- **Execution realism:** Fill prices, quantities, and delays must reflect plausible interactions with the market, capturing slippage, spread, and liquidity constraints.

Everything in the design follows from these principles.

Event-Driven Architecture: An Overview

The natural way to enforce time fidelity is to drive the backtester by *events*. Market data arrives as a stream of events (quotes, trades, bar closes, corporate actions). The strategy reacts by emitting orders. Downstream components transform those orders into simulated executions and position changes, which in turn generate P&L updates.

Figure summarizes the architecture.

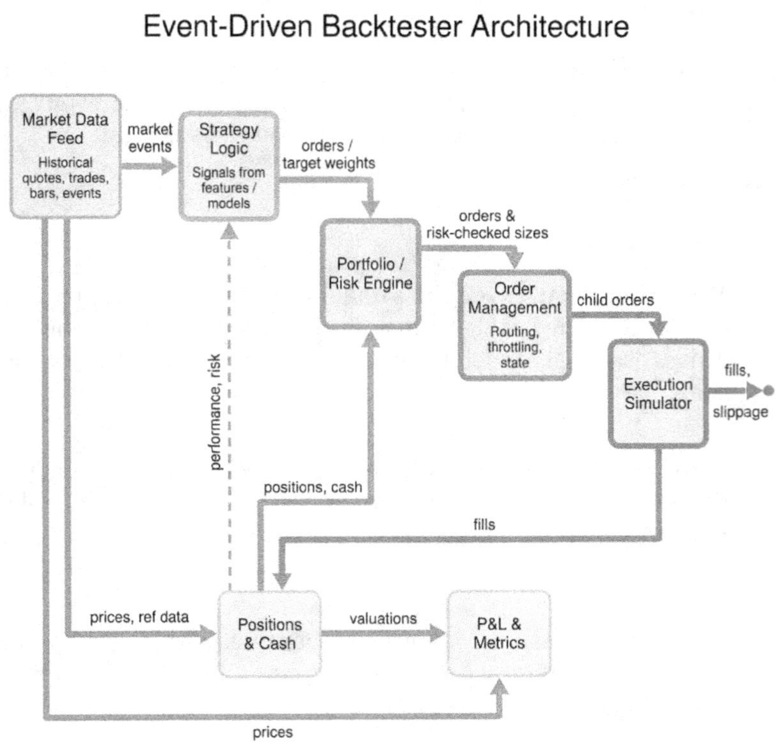

The main modules are:

- **Market Data Feed:** Replays historical events (ticks, bar closes, corporate actions) in chronological order.
- **Strategy Logic:** Reads current state (features, signals, positions, risk) and generates trading intents: orders or target portfolios.
- **Portfolio / Risk Engine:** Translates intents into concrete orders while enforcing risk limits, margin constraints, and capital allocation rules.

- **Order Management System (OMS):** Manages order lifecycles: splitting, queueing, cancellations, and replacement.
- **Execution Simulator:** Given historical trades/quotes and the current order book state (explicit or modeled), simulates fills, prices, and slippage.
- **State Stores:** Positions, cash, valuations, and P&L are updated as events and fills arrive.

Each module communicates via *events*: "new bar for AAPL at 10:00," "strategy requests to be 5% long AAPL," "order #123 partially filled for 500 shares at $145.10," and so on.

The Life Cycle of a Simulated Trade

It is helpful to walk through a single decision cycle, from the arrival of a data event to its impact on P&L.

1. Market Event Arrives

The data feed emits an event at time t. Depending on your data frequency and strategy, this could be:

- a *bar close* (e.g., 5-minute bar for a stock with OHLCV);
- a *quote update* (best bid/ask changed);
- a *trade print* (a trade occurred at price p and size q);
- a *corporate action* (split, dividend, symbol change).

The backtester updates internal references (current prices, corporate action factors) and emits a "market data" event to the strategy logic.

2. Strategy Computes Signals and Intents

Given the new data and the current state, the strategy:

- updates any features that depend on the new information (e.g., rolling volatility, momentum, order book imbalance);
- calls the predictive model to compute signals (e.g., next-period expected return, probability of fill);
- transforms these signals into trading intents, such as:
- target weights for each asset,
- desired trade list (buy/sell quantities),
- or direct order specifications (limit/market, price, size, time-in-force).

For a medium-horizon equity strategy on daily bars, this might occur once per day at the close: the strategy reads closing prices, updates signals, and outputs a target portfolio for the next day. For a market-making strategy, this might happen many times per second in response to quote changes.

3. Portfolio and Risk Engine Enforces Constraints

The portfolio/risk engine receives the strategy's intents plus the current positions and risk state (sector exposures, gross and net leverage, margin usage). It then:

- computes the *difference* between target and current holdings;
- checks risk constraints and adjusts or caps trade sizes (e.g., maximum position per name, maximum leverage, liquidity limits);
- may aggregate trades across related strategies to maintain a portfolio-level view.

The output is a set of *risk-checked orders*: for example, "buy 10,000 shares of XYZ at limit $25.10, good for 10 minutes; sell 5,000 shares of ABC at market."

4. Order Management and Routing

The OMS is responsible for taking these orders and managing their life cycle:

- splitting large parent orders into smaller child orders according to an execution schedule (e.g., VWAP-style participation throughout the next hour);
- imposing throttling to avoid trading too much in illiquid names (e.g., no more than 10% of recent volume per minute);
- deciding when to cancel and replace orders if they are not filling or if market conditions change.

In a backtester, these decisions are usually deterministic algorithms parameterized by knobs you can tune (e.g., participation rate, urgency level).

The OMS produces a stream of concrete child orders that are passed to the execution simulator.

5. Execution Simulation: Fills, Prices, and Slippage

The execution simulator is the component that connects your orders to market history. Given:

- the order details (side, size, limit price, time-in-force);
- the prevailing and future quotes and trades in the historical data;
- and any microstructure model parameters (market impact, queue position),

it returns:

- a sequence of fills (partial or complete);
- the effective execution prices and timestamps;

- any residual unfilled quantity (order expiry).

We will discuss execution models in more detail later, but at this stage the important point is that the simulator must:

- never fill a limit order at a price better than the historical best opposite quote available at that time;
- never assume liquidity that did not exist in the historical record, unless you deliberately model hidden liquidity as an assumption;
- apply your participation constraints; if your order is too large relative to volume, it should take longer to fill and move the price more.

6. Positions, Cash, and P&L Update

When the execution simulator reports fills, the backtester:

- updates share counts for each instrument;
- adjusts cash by the traded value plus or minus transaction costs (commissions, fees, taxes);
- updates realized P&L from closed trades;
- recomputes unrealized P&L by marking open positions to current market prices.

These updated positions and valuations feed back into both the portfolio/risk engine and the strategy, closing the loop. At any point, you can compute performance metrics (returns, drawdowns, turnover, slippage) on the simulated equity curve.

Design Choices: Caching vs. Streaming, Bars vs. Ticks

Implementing the above architecture forces you to make pragmatic design decisions.

Caching vs. Streaming Data

- A **streaming** backtester reads events sequentially from disk or a message queue, processing them one at a time and maintaining only the necessary current state in memory. This is resource-efficient and naturally enforces time ordering.
- A **cached** backtester loads larger chunks (e.g., several days of bars or quotes) into memory. This can be faster for exploratory research but requires discipline to avoid accidentally peeking into the future when computing features or execution statistics.

For latency-sensitive strategies or ones that depend on order book dynamics, a streaming, tick-based approach is usually necessary. For daily-bar strategies, caching daily data in memory is often acceptable.

Bars vs. Intrabar Events

A key simplification in many backtests is to aggregate ticks into *bars* (e.g., 1-minute or daily OHLCV) and assume that:

- signals and decisions occur at bar closes;
- execution occurs at the next bar's open, close, or VWAP.

This bar-based view is convenient, but you must be explicit about its assumptions:

- If you assume fill at the *next bar's close*, you are assuming you could have executed at the volume-weighted average of all trades in that bar without impact—often optimistic for large orders.
- If you assume fill at the *mid-price* of a bar (average of high and low), you implicitly assume perfect timing inside the bar, which is rarely achievable.

For strategies where intraday timing matters (e.g., ones reacting to news or quote changes), it is safer to simulate at the tick or quote level or at least use finer-grained bars and realistic execution models.

Execution and Slippage Models

Execution and slippage modeling is where microstructure enters the backtester. We will move from simple bar-based models to more detailed order book approaches.

Simple Bar-Based Execution

In the simplest setting (daily bars, small trades), you might use:

- **Close-to-close** execution: if you decide at today's close, you assume execution at tomorrow's open or tomorrow's VWAP.
- **Spread-based** slippage: assume you pay half the quoted spread for a market order:

  $$\text{fill price} = \begin{cases} \text{ask} - \alpha \times \text{spread} & \text{for sells,} \\ \text{bid} + \alpha \times \text{spread} & \text{for buys,} \end{cases}$$

  where α captures how aggressive you are (e.g., $\alpha = 0.5$ for mid-spread, $\alpha = 1$ for touching best quote).
- **Transaction cost surcharge:** add a fixed or variable cost proportional to notional traded (e.g., 5–20 bps round-trip).

These assumptions are rough but easy to implement and often sufficient when trade sizes are small compared to typical daily volume.

Volume-Participation Models

To model larger trades over intraday horizons, a common approach is to tie your trading schedule to observed market volume. For example:

- Choose a participation rate ρ (e.g., 5% of total volume).
- For each intraday bar b with historical volume V_b and price P_b, you allow yourself to trade up to ρV_b at an effective price of P_b plus a slippage term that increases with your participation.

A simple linear impact model might be:

$$\text{effective price for buys in bar } b = P_b \left(1 + \gamma \frac{q_b}{V_b}\right),$$

where q_b is your traded quantity and γ controls impact severity.

Key advantages:

- It automatically slows your execution in illiquid periods and accelerates it when volume is high.
- It discourages unrealistic trades that would require being a very large fraction of daily volume.

Order Book and Queue-Position Models

For high-frequency or execution-focused strategies, bar-based models are insufficient. You may instead simulate explicit interaction with a limit order book:

- Historical Level 2 data provides depth at each price level and timestamps for order book updates.
- When you submit a limit order, you are added to the back of the queue at that price.
- Fills occur only when incoming market orders and cancellations ahead of you deplete the queue.

A basic queue-position model involves:

- tracking your queue position in shares at the chosen price level;
- decrementing that position when trades occur at that price or when resting orders ahead of you are canceled;
- recording a fill when your position hits zero or when you decide to cancel.

This type of simulation can capture:

- partial fills and non-fills for passive orders;
- adverse selection: your passive buy order is more likely to fill just before the price moves down;
- queue-jumping dynamics when you cross the spread with marketable orders.

The trade-off is data volume and computational cost. Full order book backtests are significantly more complex and often reserved for specialized execution and market-making research.

Parameterizing and Stress-Testing Execution Models

Every execution model introduces parameters: participation rates, impact coefficients γ, queue-priority rules, spread assumptions, and so on. It is critical to distinguish:

- **Estimation:** fitting these parameters to historical execution and market data (e.g., regression of observed slippage vs. participation rate).
- **Stress-testing:** deliberately making them harsher than historical averages to explore how sensitive strategy performance is to execution frictions.

A sensible workflow is:

- Estimate baseline parameters from a training period where you have rich execution and intraday data.
- Run the backtest under:
  - baseline parameters;
  - pessimistic scenarios (e.g., impact $\times 2$, half the assumed liquidity, wider spreads).

- Compare key metrics: CAGR, Sharpe ratio, max drawdown, turnover, and slippage as percentage of gross alpha.

If small changes in execution assumptions erase most of the strategy's performance, you are likely dealing with a fragile edge that may not survive real markets.

Avoiding Subtle Sources of Bias

Backtester design is full of traps that can quietly inflate backtest performance. A few of the most important to watch for:

Look-Ahead in Signals and Features

Ensure that:

- Features at time t use only data up to t (plus any safe lag for reporting delays, such as fundamentals).
- Orders and positions are computed using signals that are available at decision time (e.g., yesterday's close, not today's close if you trade at today's open).

This is a joint responsibility of the research data pipeline and the backtester clock.

Look-Ahead in Transaction Costs

It is tempting to use average daily spread or average execution cost over a period to set transaction cost parameters. However:

- This effectively uses future information for each trade.
- Instead, transaction cost models should be calibrated on a training period and then applied *as is* in the backtest, or updated only with a realistic lag.

Survivorship and Selection Bias

Your backtester should be able to simulate trades in instruments that later delisted or became illiquid, not only those that survived to the present. This requires:

- using a reference database with historical constituents and delistings;
- correctly handling corporate actions and cash flows triggered by mergers or bankruptcies.

Finally, be cautious about tuning strategy rules after seeing backtest results (overfitting). This is addressed more fully in the chapter's final section on walk-forward validation and robustness tests, but the backtester is where such tuning can quietly creep in.

In this section we have transformed the concept of a backtest from a simple spreadsheet into a structured, event-driven simulation engine that:

- replays market data as a chronological stream of events;
- drives strategy logic, portfolio/risk checks, order management, and execution simulation;
- maintains positions, cash, and P&L in a deterministic, reproducible manner;
- incorporates execution models that range from simple bar-based approximations to detailed order book and queue-position simulators;
- allows parameterization and stress-testing of transaction cost and liquidity assumptions;
- guards against subtle biases such as look-ahead, survivorship bias, and optimistic execution assumptions.

A robust backtester is the experimental laboratory of the algorithmic trading machine. It lets you expose machine learning models and trading rules to the complexity of real market microstructure before any capital is put at risk. In the next section, we will close the research loop by describing walk-forward validation and robustness testing, which sit on top of this backtester to decide which strategies are truly ready for live deployment.

4.4 Walk-Forward Validation and Robustness Testing

The previous sections gave us the core building blocks of a systematic strategy:

- a disciplined research workflow and feature/label construction;
- supervised learning models that turn features into forecasts;
- an event-driven backtester that turns forecasts into simulated trades and P&L under realistic execution.

We now face a harder question: *How do we know that a strategy that performed well in backtest is likely to perform well in live trading?*

This section addresses that question. We will:

- explain why conventional, randomly shuffled cross-validation fails for time series;
- introduce *walk-forward validation* and related time-respecting schemes;
- show how to integrate hyperparameter tuning without contaminating test performance;
- develop robustness checks and stress tests that expose fragile dependence on optimistic assumptions;
- outline a pre-deployment checklist that combines statistical and economic evidence.

The goal is to separate strategies that only work on past data from those that have a reasonable chance of surviving live deployment.

Why Random Cross-Validation Fails in Time Series

In standard machine learning tasks, it is common to randomly split your dataset into training and test subsets, or to use K-fold cross-validation that randomly shuffles observations. This is *not* appropriate for trading.

Two key issues make the difference:

- **Temporal dependence:** Returns and features are not independent across time. Regimes, volatility clusters, and structural breaks mean that the future is not just a random reshuffle of the past.
- **Information leakage:** If you allow the model to train on data from both before and after a given point in time and then test on that same point, it can implicitly exploit patterns that are not yet "known" at that moment.

To see the danger, imagine randomly shuffling daily equity data from 2010–2024 and then training on 80% and testing on 20% of shuffled days. In such a setting:

- the model can inadvertently learn about the entire distribution of features and labels in 2020 and then be evaluated on 2011, even though, in reality, 2020 had not happened yet in 2011;
- structural breaks (e.g. pre- and post-crisis dynamics) are averaged out, hiding how the strategy behaves when regimes change.

This produces overly optimistic estimates of out-of-sample performance and hides instability. Instead, validation schemes in trading must respect the arrow of time.

Time-Respecting Validation: Basic Patterns

Time-respecting validation schemes preserve chronological order. The central idea is simple:

> Train a model on a contiguous block of past data, then evaluate it on a *later* block that the model has never seen.

Several patterns are widely used.

Single Train–Validation–Test Split

The simplest approach is to divide the full sample period into three contiguous segments:

$$\underbrace{\text{Train}}_{\text{e.g. 2010–2016}} \;\Big|\; \underbrace{\text{Validation}}_{\text{e.g. 2017–2018}} \;\Big|\; \underbrace{\text{Test}}_{\text{e.g. 2019–2022}}$$

- **Train:** Used to fit model parameters (e.g., regression coefficients, tree splits) and to rough-tune a small set of hyperparameter configurations.
- **Validation:** Used to choose among model types and hyperparameters, and to perform early stopping for more complex models.
- **Test:** Held out until the end and used once for a final performance estimate after all decisions are frozen.

This structure is easy to implement and often sufficient when the amount of data is limited. Its main downside is that performance estimates can be noisy: you are relying on one particular split that may or may not reflect future conditions.

Rolling-Origin (Walk-Forward) Validation

To better mimic live deployment, you can use *rolling-origin* or *walk-forward* validation. Here, you repeatedly move a training window forward in time and always test on the period just after that window.

For example, suppose you have daily data from 2010–2022. You might define:

- Training window: a rolling 5-year period.
- Test window: the next 1-year period.

You then construct folds as:

Fold 1:	Train 2010–2014, Test 2015
Fold 2:	Train 2011–2015, Test 2016
Fold 3:	Train 2012–2016, Test 2017
⋮	⋮
Fold k:	Train 2016–2020, Test 2021
Fold $k+1$:	Train 2017–2021, Test 2022

For each fold:

- Fit your model and any data transformations (scalers, PCA, etc.) on the training window only.
- Evaluate performance on the next test window, using your back-tester with no further retraining.

Aggregating across folds gives you a more robust view of:

- average out-of-sample performance;
- variability across market regimes;
- how the strategy behaves as you periodically retrain on new data.

This procedure closely mirrors how you would operate the strategy live: at each point in time you have a fixed historical sample, you calibrate the model, and then you trade for a while before updating the model again.

Expanding Window vs. Rolling Window

In a rolling window, the training sample size is fixed (e.g., 5 years), and the oldest data is dropped as you move forward. In an *expanding window*, you grow the training set over time:

Fold 1:	Train 2010–2012, Test 2013
Fold 2:	Train 2010–2013, Test 2014
Fold 3:	Train 2010–2014, Test 2015
⋮	⋮

Advantages and trade-offs:

- Rolling windows adapt more quickly to regime changes (they forget old data).
- Expanding windows use more data and may stabilize parameter estimates, but risk diluting the influence of recent conditions.

The choice should reflect your beliefs about the persistence of underlying economic relationships and the pace of structural change.

Hyperparameter Tuning Without Leakage

Hyperparameters (e.g., regularization strengths, tree depths, learning rates, impact coefficients) cannot be chosen by trial-and-error on the same data that you later treat as "out-of-sample." Doing so bakes hidden in-sample optimization into your evaluation.

The key is to introduce a *hierarchy of data partitions*:

- An **outer** split or walk-forward loop, whose test segments will be used for final performance assessment.
- An **inner** validation procedure, run only on the training portion of each outer fold, to choose hyperparameters.

Concretely, in each fold of a walk-forward experiment:

- **Split the training window again:** e.g., within Train[2010–2014], use 2010–2013 as inner-train and 2014 as inner-validation.
- **Hyperparameter search:** For each candidate configuration (say, L2 regularization $\lambda \in \{0.01, 0.1, 1\}$ and tree depth $d \in \{3, 4, 5\}$):
  - Fit the model on inner-train.
  - Evaluate using trading-relevant metrics on inner-validation (e.g., Sharpe, turnover-adjusted alpha).

- **Select configuration:** Choose the hyperparameters that perform best on inner-validation, possibly with a penalty for complexity.
- **Refit on full training window:** Using the chosen hyperparameters, retrain the model on the entire outer training window (2010–2014).
- **Evaluate on outer test window:** Now run the backtest on 2015 using this model. These test results are kept untouched in subsequent tuning.

Repeat this process for each fold and aggregate the outer test results. Hyperparameters may vary across folds if conditions change, which realistically reflects how you might re-tune the strategy over time.

Choosing Evaluation Metrics for Validation

In tuning and validation, you should use metrics that connect directly to trading performance and risk, rather than purely statistical loss functions.

Common metrics include:

- **Annualized mean return and volatility:** to compute Sharpe ratio or information ratio.
- **Maximum drawdown:** to understand worst-case capital loss.
- **Turnover and transaction cost burden:** to judge whether apparent alpha survives realistic trading frictions.
- **Hit rate in prediction buckets:** particularly for cross-sectional models, P&L by prediction decile or quintile.

Two practical recommendations:

- When performing inner validation, prefer *risk-adjusted* metrics (e.g., Sharpe) to pure return.

- Track several metrics simultaneously; a strategy that improves Sharpe marginally at the cost of dramatically higher turnover or drawdown may not be desirable.

Robustness Checks: Sensitivity to Key Knobs

Even a careful walk-forward backtest produces a single performance path under specific modeling assumptions. Robustness checks ask: *What happens if we perturb those assumptions?*

We focus on three families of perturbations: trading frictions, leverage and position limits, and data-level noise.

Transaction Costs and Slippage

Since execution costs are notoriously hard to estimate, you should treat them as a range rather than a point estimate.

For example, suppose your baseline backtest assumes a per-share commission plus a slippage model that adds 10 basis points (bps) for every 10% of bar volume traded. You can stress this by:

- scaling all cost parameters by factors such as $1.5\times$ and $2\times$;
- widening spreads or doubling the impact coefficient in your execution model;
- capping participation rates to lower levels (e.g., reducing maximum fraction of daily volume from 10% to 5%).

You then recompute key metrics:

- Does the strategy still have positive net alpha?
- How does the Sharpe ratio degrade as costs worsen?
- At what cost level does performance become indistinguishable from zero?

Strategies whose performance collapses under mild cost stress are unlikely to survive real-world frictions.

Leverage, Position Limits, and Liquidity Constraints

Similarly, test how sensitive performance is to risk and size assumptions:

- Reduce maximum gross and net leverage (e.g., from $3\times$ to $1.5\times$) and see how risk-adjusted metrics change.
- Introduce or tighten per-name and per-sector position limits.
- Impose stricter liquidity filters (e.g., only trade names with average daily dollar volume above a higher threshold).

If a strategy relies on very high leverage in illiquid names to achieve its backtest returns, that is a red flag.

Label and Feature Perturbations

Another form of robustness test perturbs the data itself:

- **Noise injection:** Add small, zero-mean noise to features or labels within plausible measurement error bands and re-train the model. Does performance materially change?
- **Delayed signals:** Shift features or signals by one or more bars to reflect realistic computation and execution latencies. For example, if a high-frequency feature would not actually be available at the exact decision time, delay its use and re-evaluate performance.
- **Coarse-graining:** Round features or predictions (e.g., to two decimal places) to test whether the strategy depends on unrealistically fine distinctions.

Robust strategies exhibit graceful degradation: small perturbations should not flip performance from strongly positive to strongly negative.

Scenario-Based and Regime-Specific Testing

Walk-forward validation already spreads evaluation over time, but it is useful to drill into specific scenarios:

- crisis periods (e.g., sharp drawdowns, volatility spikes);
- low-liquidity environments;
- trend-dominated vs. mean-reverting regimes;
- different interest-rate or macro regimes.

You can tag each time segment with regime labels (for example, based on realized volatility, credit spreads, or market trend) and then compute:

- average return and Sharpe in each regime;
- maximum drawdown and recovery time within each;
- contribution to total P&L by regime.

This analysis answers questions like:

- Does the strategy primarily make money in calm markets and suffer in crises?
- Does it act as a diversifier (e.g., profits in regimes when your core book suffers)?
- Are there regimes in which you should *not* deploy the strategy at all?

These insights are critical when integrating strategies into a larger portfolio.

Performance Attribution and Diagnostics

Robustness is not only about whether performance persists; it is also about understanding *where* performance comes from.

On top of the backtest results from walk-forward validation, you should perform performance attribution along several dimensions:

- **By signal strength:** Bucket trades by predicted return or score decile and compute P&L. Does most of the profit come from the highest-signal buckets?
- **By factor or feature group:** Decompose P&L by contributions associated with different families of features (e.g., value, momentum, quality, intraday order flow).
- **By asset group:** Attribution by sector, country, asset class, or liquidity bucket.
- **By execution quality:** Separate gross alpha (before costs) from realized alpha (after costs) and decompose the gap into spread, impact, and fees.

Healthy patterns include:

- profits concentrated where the model is most confident (top prediction buckets);
- consistent contributions across multiple, economically sensible feature groups;
- costs that are a manageable fraction of gross alpha (not dominating the economics).

Suspicious patterns include:

- most profits arising from trades with very small predicted edge (suggesting luck);
- heavy dependence on a narrow set of names, sectors, or illiquid instruments;
- cost structure that is extremely sensitive to optimistic execution assumptions.

Pre-Deployment Checklist

Combining all of the above, you can formulate a practical checklist for deciding whether a strategy is ready for live deployment, or at least for a cautious pilot.

At minimum, ensure that:

- **Time-respecting validation is complete:**
  - You have performed at least one walk-forward or rolling-origin evaluation over a meaningful length of time and regimes.
  - Hyperparameters were chosen using only past data in each fold.
- **Performance is robust:**
  - Strategy maintains acceptable risk-adjusted returns under reasonable cost and slippage stresses.
  - Performance does not depend on extreme leverage, concentration, or unrealistic liquidity assumptions.
  - Small perturbations to features, labels, and latencies do not destroy performance.
- **Behavior is understandable:**
  - You can explain in plain language where the edge comes from and in which regimes it should work.
  - Attribution by signal strength, factors, and asset groups aligns with the economic story.
- **Implementation is auditable:**
  - All data transformations, model fits, and backtests are version-controlled and reproducible.
  - Random seeds and configuration files are stored so that you can rerun any walk-forward experiment.

If a candidate strategy fails any of these checks, it should return to the research lab: reconsider hypotheses, features, models, or execution assumptions. If it passes, it may still deserve a cautious rollout (small capital, tighter risk limits, ongoing monitoring) rather than immediate full-scale deployment.

In this section we have placed the final layer on top of the algorithmic trading machine:

- Time-respecting validation schemes—particularly walk-forward and rolling-origin evaluation—that prevent information leakage and give a realistic picture of out-of-sample performance.
- Nested hyperparameter tuning procedures that avoid contaminating test results while allowing model complexity to adapt to market conditions.
- Robustness and stress tests that probe sensitivity to transaction costs, leverage, liquidity constraints, and data noise.
- Scenario and regime analyses that highlight how strategies behave under different market environments.
- Performance attribution and a pre-deployment checklist that tie statistical evidence back to economic intuition and implementation realism.

Together with the earlier sections on research workflow, machine learning models, and event-driven backtesting, these tools allow you to move from promising ideas to strategies that are not only profitable in historical simulation, but also hardened for the uncertainties of live trading.

Chapter 5

Portfolio Construction, Risk, and Execution

Signals are useless until they become positions, and positions are dangerous until they are risk-managed and well-executed. This chapter shows how to turn raw edge into a live, tradable portfolio: how weights are engineered under realistic constraints, how risk and costs reshape those weights, and how modern execution algorithms navigate fragmented, adversarial markets. By the end, you will see portfolio construction, risk control, and execution not as separate modules, but as one tightly coupled machine whose performance is determined at the weakest link.

5.1 Portfolio Optimization and Risk Modeling

In the previous chapters we treated signals mostly in isolation: how to design, backtest, and validate them. In live trading, however, you never trade a signal by itself. You trade a *portfolio* whose positions must satisfy capital, risk, and regulatory constraints, and whose performance depends as much on how you combine signals and manage risk as on the raw quality of the alpha forecasts.

This section builds the machinery that transforms a collection of security-level forecasts into a consistent vector of portfolio weights. Conceptually, you will need four ingredients:

- A precise *objective function*: what the optimizer is trying to maximize or minimize.
- A set of *constraints*: what portfolios are allowed or forbidden.
- A *risk model*: how portfolio risk is estimated from individual securities and common factors.
- An *optimization engine* that takes signals, risk, and constraints as inputs and produces implementable weights.

From Signals to an Optimization Engine

Assume that at a given decision time you have a vector of signals or expected returns

$$\hat{\mu} \in \mathbb{R}^N,$$

where N is the number of tradable instruments (e.g., stocks in your universe). The portfolio is described by weights

$$w \in \mathbb{R}^N,$$

where w_i is the fraction of capital allocated to asset i. In a dollar-neutral strategy, these weights may sum to zero; in a long-only strategy, they sum to one and are nonnegative.

At the most abstract level, the optimizer solves a problem of the form

$$\begin{aligned} \max_{w} \quad & \text{Objective}(w; \hat{\mu}, \Sigma, \dots) \\ \text{subject to} \quad & \text{Constraints}(w) \leq 0, \end{aligned}$$

where Σ is a covariance matrix (from your risk model) and the dots indicate any additional parameters (transaction costs, benchmark weights, etc.).

Immediately after introducing this abstraction, it is helpful to see how it fits inside the overall trading machine.

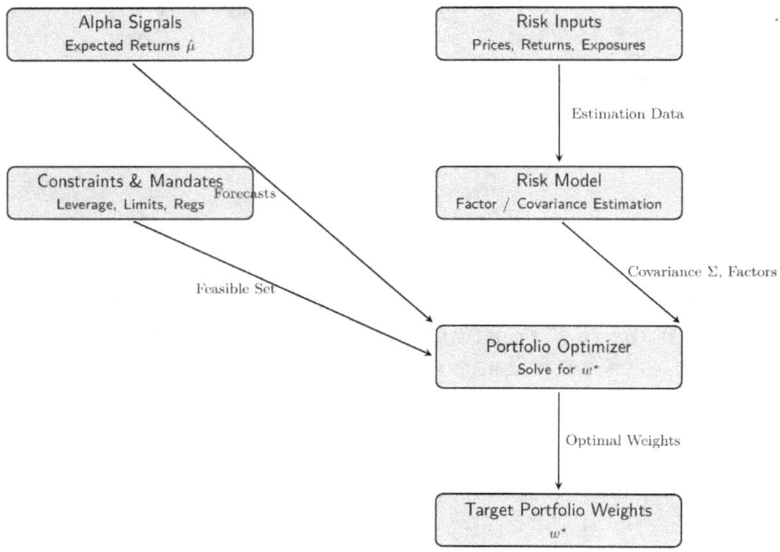

The rest of this section unpacks each piece: what objective you should use, what constraints matter in practice, and how to build the risk model (particularly Σ) that underlies the optimization.

Portfolio Objectives Beyond Naive Mean–Variance

The classical mean–variance framework proposes maximizing

$$\hat{\mu}^\top w - \frac{\lambda}{2} w^\top \Sigma w,$$

where $\lambda > 0$ is a risk aversion parameter. This is mathematically convenient but hides a few important choices.

Expected utility and risk-adjusted return

For small risks, maximizing a quadratic mean–variance objective is equivalent to maximizing expected utility for an investor with constant absolute risk aversion. In practice, you rarely know λ precisely, but you can think of it as controlling how aggressively you translate alpha into risk.

An alternative is to maximize a risk-adjusted performance metric, for example a proxy of the Sharpe ratio:

$$\max_{w} \frac{\hat{\mu}^\top w}{\sqrt{w^\top \Sigma w}}.$$

This is a fractional program (ratio of two functions). In many practical implementations, you turn this into a quadratic program by fixing the denominator (e.g., constrain $w^\top \Sigma w \leq \sigma^2_{target}$) and maximizing the numerator, or by maximizing a linearized approximation.

Benchmark-relative and tracking-error objectives

Most institutional portfolios are managed relative to a benchmark portfolio w^B (e.g., an index). In that case, the optimizer often targets *active weights*

$$w^A = w - w^B.$$

The relevant risk is not absolute risk but *tracking error*—the volatility of portfolio returns relative to the benchmark:

$$\mathrm{TE}(w) = \sqrt{(w - w^B)^\top \Sigma (w - w^B)}.$$

A common objective is

$$\max_{w} \ (\hat{\mu} - r\mathbf{1})^\top (w - w^B) \ - \ \frac{\lambda_{TE}}{2}(w - w^B)^\top \Sigma (w - w^B),$$

or, more simply, maximize expected excess active return subject to a tracking error constraint:

$$\begin{aligned} \max_{w} \quad & (\hat{\mu} - r\mathbf{1})^\top (w - w^B) \\ \text{subject to} \quad & (w - w^B)^\top \Sigma (w - w^B) \leq \mathrm{TE}^2_{max}. \end{aligned}$$

Including transaction costs and turnover

In an algorithmic trading system, it is not enough to choose a portfolio for today; you must consider the cost of moving from yesterday's holdings w^{old} to today's target w. A simple incremental objective adds a penalty for turnover:

$$\max_{w} \ \hat{\mu}^\top w \ - \ \frac{\lambda}{2} w^\top \Sigma w \ - \ \gamma \|w - w^{old}\|_1,$$

where $\|w \ - \ w^{old}\|_1$ is proportional to the traded volume (sum of absolute changes in weights) and γ controls how strongly you penalize trading.

More sophisticated models incorporate explicit, nonlinear transaction cost estimates (e.g., spread plus a concave impact component), but even a simple linear turnover penalty is a major step toward realistic portfolio construction.

Practical Constraints and the Feasible Set

Objectives tell the optimizer what it wants; *constraints* tell it what is allowed. In live trading, constraints are often more binding than the objective, and they strongly shape the final portfolio.

We can write the feasible set of weights as

$$\mathcal{W} = \{w \in \mathbb{R}^N : Aw \leq b, \ Cw = d\},$$

where A, b, C, d encode linear inequality and equality constraints. Common examples include:

Capital and leverage constraints

A basic long-only portfolio obeys

$$\sum_{i=1}^{N} w_i = 1, \quad w_i \geq 0.$$

In a long/short equity strategy, you might constrain gross and net exposure:

$$\sum_{i=1}^{N} w_i = 0 \quad \text{(market neutral)},$$

$$\sum_{i=1}^{N} |w_i| \leq L_{max} \quad \text{(gross leverage limit)}.$$

These ensure that leverage stays within mandate and financing limits.

Position and sector bounds

To avoid concentration in individual names, you impose box constraints:

$$\ell_i \leq w_i \leq u_i, \quad i = 1, \dots, N.$$

For example, $-2\% \leq w_i \leq 2\%$ for each stock.

Similarly, you can cap exposures at the sector or industry level. Let G be a matrix with $G_{kg} = 1$ if stock g belongs to sector k, else 0. Sector weights are $s = Gw$. You can impose bounds,

$$s_k^{min} \leq (Gw)_k \leq s_k^{max},$$

to limit sector tilts or ensure diversification.

Factor neutrality and mandate constraints

If your strategy is supposed to be pure stock selection rather than a macro bet, you may require neutrality to broad risk factors such as market, size, value, or momentum. If $B \in \mathbb{R}^{N \times K}$ is a matrix of factor exposures (each column is a factor, each row is a security), then the portfolio's factor exposures are

$$f = B^\top w.$$

You can enforce

$$f_k = 0 \quad \text{for selected factors } k,$$

or keep them within a band:

$$-\delta_k \leq f_k \leq \delta_k.$$

These constraints express your investment mandate (e.g., "market neutral", "beta-neutral", "sector-neutral") directly in the optimizer.

Turnover and trading limits

To control turnover, you can bound changes from old weights:

$$-\Delta_i^{max} \leq w_i - w_i^{old} \leq \Delta_i^{max},$$

or impose a budget on total turnover,

$$\sum_{i=1}^{N} |w_i - w_i^{old}| \leq \text{Turnover}_{max}.$$

You may also integrate per-name and per-day trading limits based on liquidity (e.g., at most a fixed percentage of average daily volume).

In code, these constraints are passed to the optimizer as matrices and vectors, but conceptually they define a shape in N-dimensional space—the feasible set $\mathcal{W}$ inside which the optimizer searches for the best portfolio.

Risk Models: From Covariances to Factors

So far, risk has appeared in the objective through a covariance matrix Σ. For a small universe, you could estimate Σ directly from historical returns. For a realistic universe with hundreds or thousands of names, naive sample covariance is unstable: it is noisy, often poorly conditioned or singular, and highly sensitive to estimation window choices.

The standard solution is to build a *risk model* that decomposes asset returns into a small number of common factors plus idiosyncratic noise.

Linear factor structure

Suppose asset returns are governed by

$$r = Bf + \epsilon,$$

where

- $r \in \mathbb{R}^N$ is the vector of asset returns,
- $B \in \mathbb{R}^{N \times K}$ is the factor exposure matrix,
- $f \in \mathbb{R}^K$ is the vector of factor realizations,
- $\epsilon \in \mathbb{R}^N$ is the vector of idiosyncratic returns, with $\mathbb{E}[\epsilon] = 0$ and $\text{Cov}(\epsilon) = D$ diagonal.

If the factors have covariance $\Sigma_f = \mathrm{Cov}(f)$, then the implied asset covariance is

$$\Sigma = B\Sigma_f B^\top + D.$$

This decomposition is powerful:

- The number of factors K is much smaller than N, so Σ_f is easier to estimate robustly than a full $N \times N$ covariance.
- Risk can be interpreted economically (e.g., "50% of my variance comes from the market factor, 20% from value, 10% from size, 20% idiosyncratic").
- Constraints on factor exposures $f = B^\top w$ naturally align with the covariance structure.

Types of factor models

There are two broad classes of factor models used in portfolio optimization:

Fundamental (or characteristics-based) factor models. Here, factors correspond to economically or fundamentally motivated themes:

- Style factors: value, momentum, size, quality, volatility.
- Industry or sector factors: GICS or NAICS-based groups.
- Country or region factors in global portfolios.

The exposure matrix B is constructed from fundamental or cross-sectional data (e.g., a value score or a standardized momentum score for each stock). Factor returns f and their covariance Σ_f are then estimated from historical returns using regression or time-series methods.

Statistical factor models. Here, factors are extracted statistically from the return covariance structure itself, for example by principal component analysis (PCA). You choose a number of factors K, compute the leading eigenvectors of the sample covariance, and let those define your factor loadings. These models often explain a large fraction of variance with a few factors but may be harder to interpret economically.

In practice, many commercial risk models blend fundamental structure (sectors and styles) with statistical techniques (e.g., shrinkage, PCA on residuals).

Estimating and stabilizing covariance

Even with a factor structure, you must estimate Σ_f and the idiosyncratic variances in D. Common stabilization techniques include:

- **Shrinkage**: blend the sample covariance with a structured target (e.g., identity or constant-correlation matrix),

$$\Sigma_{shrunk} = \alpha\Sigma_{sample} + (1-\alpha)\Sigma_{target}.$$

- **Exponential weighting**: give more weight to recent returns when computing covariances, which better captures current volatility regimes.
- **Clipping and floor/ceiling rules**: limit extreme variances or correlations that appear due to noise.

A numerically stable, positive-definite covariance matrix is essential for optimization; otherwise, the optimizer may produce extreme, unstable weights or even fail to converge.

Putting It Together: Optimization with a Factor Risk Model

With a factor model in hand, the mean–variance objective can be rewritten in terms of factor and idiosyncratic risk:

$$w^\top \Sigma w = w^\top (B\Sigma_f B^\top + D)w = (B^\top w)^\top \Sigma_f (B^\top w) + w^\top D w.$$

Here, $B^\top w$ is the vector of portfolio factor exposures. This decomposition reveals how much of your portfolio risk comes from common factors versus specific stock risk and allows you to control them separately.

Quadratic programming formulation

A widely used formulation—because it is convex and scalable--is a quadratic program (QP) of the form:

$$\begin{aligned} \max_{w} \quad & \hat{\mu}^\top w - \frac{\lambda}{2} w^\top \Sigma w - \gamma \|w - w^{old}\|_1 \\ \text{subject to} \quad & Aw \leq b, \\ & Cw = d, \\ & \ell \leq w \leq u. \end{aligned}$$

If you approximate the turnover penalty using a differentiable surrogate (e.g., split positive and negative changes or use a quadratic penalty), the problem remains a QP:

$$\max_{w} \quad \hat{\mu}^\top w - \frac{\lambda}{2} w^\top \Sigma w - \frac{\eta}{2} \|w - w^{old}\|_2^2.$$

Such problems can be solved efficiently for hundreds or thousands of assets using off-the-shelf numerical solvers. In an algorithmic trading system, this QP is embedded in an event-driven loop: each time new signals or risk estimates arrive, the optimizer recomputes the target weights, which are then passed to the execution layer.

The role of constraints in shaping solutions

Understanding how constraints interact with the risk model helps interpret the optimizer's output:

- **Box constraints** and sector caps limit concentration; the optimizer will spread risk across more names, even if some have slightly weaker alpha.
- **Factor neutrality** constraints can dramatically change the portfolio: if your raw signals are positively correlated with the market factor, enforcing market neutrality will cause the optimizer to add short positions in other high-beta stocks to offset this exposure.
- **Turnover limits** smooth the evolution of weights over time, making the portfolio more stable but slower to respond to changes in alpha or risk.

As you add realistic constraints, the "optimal" portfolio becomes less about the unconstrained Sharpe-maximizing weight vector and more about best exploiting your signals *within* operational and mandate boundaries.

Model Risk, Diagnostics, and Robustness

No risk model is perfect. If your covariance or factor exposures are materially mis-specified, the optimizer may choose portfolios that look attractive on paper but perform poorly out of sample. This is especially dangerous because optimizers tend to exploit any perceived structure in $\hat{\mu}$ and Σ, including noise.

Signs of an unstable or mis-specified model

Problems to watch for include:

- Extremely large long and short positions in individual names (within allowed bounds) that nearly cancel at the portfolio level.
- Excessive sensitivity of weights to small changes in input signals or in the risk model.
- Portfolios that load heavily on obscure or poorly estimated factors.

These are often symptoms of overfitting to noise in $\hat{\mu}$ or Σ.

Regularization and robustness techniques

To mitigate model risk, you can:

- **Add explicit regularization**: Penalize large weights (e.g., $\|w\|_2^2$) or large factor exposures ($\|B^\top w\|_2^2$) in the objective, which discourages extreme solutions.
- **Impose tighter box and turnover constraints**: These act as hard caps on how aggressively the optimizer can exploit noisy estimated alphas.
- **Stress-test**: Apply shocks to factor returns or volatilities and re-optimize to see how the portfolio changes. Large swings indicate fragility.

- **Use multiple risk horizons**: Compare risk estimates based on different lookback windows (short vs. long) to gauge stability.

Automated checks in an algorithmic trading system

In a fully automated trading machine, you should build diagnostic checks around the optimizer:

- Reject or downscale solutions with suspicious leverage, concentration, or factor exposures.
- Monitor realized volatility and factor exposures versus model predictions; sustained discrepancies may indicate a degraded risk model.
- Log optimization inputs and outputs for post-mortem analysis and to support backtesting with "frozen" risk models.

These checks close the loop between portfolio construction and live performance, ensuring that the optimization and risk modeling layer remains reliable as market conditions evolve.

5.2 Transaction Costs, Position Sizing, and Rebalancing

In the previous section, we treated the optimizer as if it could freely move the portfolio to any desired set of weights $w^\star$. In live trading, that freedom is an illusion. Every change in weights requires trading, and trading incurs *costs*. These costs erode your edge, limit the effective size of your bets, and force you to think carefully about how often—and how aggressively—you rebalance toward your target.

This section has three goals:

- To decompose transaction costs into explicit and implicit components and show how to approximate them with simple models.
- To connect *edge* (expected alpha) and *risk* (volatility) to *position sizing*, including the intuition of Kelly-style optimal bets and why we usually scale them down in practice.

- To design *rebalancing rules* that keep the portfolio aligned with signals without overtrading, using ideas like no-trade regions, turnover budgets, and staggered adjustments.

The guiding principle is that portfolio optimization, trading costs, and rebalancing must be treated as parts of one coherent problem.

What Transaction Costs Really Are

Transaction costs are the economic friction between your *current portfolio* and your *target portfolio.* When you move from weights w^{old} to w^{new}, you send orders to the market. Those orders are filled at prices that are, in expectation, less favorable than the mid-price you observe at decision time. The difference is what we broadly call "cost".

It is useful to break costs into four components:

- **Explicit fees and commissions:** Exchange fees, broker commissions, and any per-share or per-notional charges. These are usually small and predictable.
- **Spread cost:** The bid–ask spread is the most visible implicit cost. If you cross the spread with a market order, you buy at the ask or sell at the bid, immediately paying roughly half the spread versus the mid-price.
- **Market impact:** Large or aggressive orders tend to move the price against you. The more you try to trade relative to available liquidity, the worse your average fill price becomes.
- **Slippage and timing risk:** Even if you aim to trade at a certain benchmark price (e.g., the mid or the day's VWAP), delays, partial fills, and intraday volatility mean your actual execution can deviate.

These pieces combine into a per-share expected cost, typically expressed in basis points (bps) of traded notional or as a fraction of bid–ask spread. Your strategy's alpha must be large enough *after* these costs to maintain a positive edge.

Simple Parametric Cost Models

An algorithmic system cannot estimate costs from scratch for each trade; it needs a *model* that maps order characteristics to expected cost. The goal is not perfect prediction but a stable approximation good enough for optimization.

A basic cost decomposition

Consider buying a quantity Q of a stock with mid-price P, bid–ask spread s, and daily dollar volume ADV. A widely used stylized model decomposes cost per share (in dollars) into:

$$c(Q) = c_{spread} + c_{impact}(Q) + c_{fees}.$$

A simple choice is:

$$c_{spread} \approx \frac{s}{2},$$

assuming you cross the spread once.

Market impact can be modeled as a concave function of the *participation rate*

$$\phi = \frac{|Q|}{\text{ADV}},$$

for example:

$$c_{impact}(Q) \approx k\, P\, \sigma\, \phi^{\beta},$$

where:

- σ is recent daily volatility (in returns),
- k and β are positive constants calibrated from historical executions or taken from the literature (typical $\beta \in [0.4, 0.8]$).

This captures three key intuitions:

- More volatile stocks are more expensive to trade.
- Larger orders relative to ADV are more expensive, and cost grows faster than linearly in size (concavity).

- Costs scale roughly with price and volatility.

Fees can be added as a constant per share or per unit notional.

From share-level to portfolio-level cost

At the portfolio level, changing weights from w^{old} to w^{new} over total capital C implies an order for stock i of:

$$Q_i = C \cdot \frac{w_i^{new} - w_i^{old}}{P_i}.$$

Plug these Q_i into your per-share cost model $c_i(Q_i)$ to obtain total expected dollar cost:

$$\text{Cost}(w^{new}, w^{old}) = \sum_{i=1}^{N} |Q_i| \, c_i(Q_i).$$

Dividing by capital C yields cost in return space, which can be integrated into the optimizer's objective.

In practice, to keep optimization convex and tractable, you often approximate this nonlinear cost with a piecewise-linear or quadratic function of $|w_i^{new} - w_i^{old}|$. The key is to preserve two qualitative features: cost increases with trade size and does so in a way that discourages very large, illiquid trades.

Edge and Optimal Bet Size

Once you can approximate how much it costs to trade, you can ask: *how big should I trade a given signal?* Intuitively, if your signal is weak or noisy, trading it aggressively is unwise; if it is strong and reliable, you want to allocate more risk to it, up to the point where either risk limits or costs make further scaling suboptimal.

A single bet: Kelly intuition

Consider a stylized one-asset problem with no costs and repeated independent bets. At each period, you can invest a fraction f of capital in a bet with expected return μ and variance σ^2. Under certain assumptions, maximizing expected log wealth leads to the *Kelly fraction*:

$$f^\star = \frac{\mu}{\sigma^2}.$$

This formula embeds intuitive trade-offs:

- Higher expected return μ increases the optimal fraction.
- Higher variance σ^2 reduces it.

In practice, pure Kelly sizing is too aggressive because:

- μ and σ are estimated with error; overestimation of μ leads to oversizing.
- Investors care about drawdowns, not only long-run log wealth.

As a result, traders often use *fractional Kelly*, e.g., half-Kelly or quarter-Kelly, or apply Kelly logic only as a rough guide to the *relative* size of bets.

From one asset to many: risk budgeting

In a multi-asset setting with covariance matrix Σ and expected returns $\hat{\mu}$, Kelly's idea generalizes to:

$$w^\star \propto \Sigma^{-1}\hat{\mu},$$

which is precisely the unconstrained mean–variance optimal portfolio for a risk-averse investor with quadratic utility. In other words, the *structure* of the Kelly optimal weights is the same as the mean–variance solution; what differs is the interpretation of the absolute scale.

This suggests a practical approach:

- Use the optimizer (with a risk model) to find a risk-efficient way to exploit your signals.

- Then decide the *overall risk budget* (e.g., annualized volatility or expected drawdown) you are willing to tolerate.
- Scale the entire portfolio up or down to hit that budget, aware that your $\hat{\mu}$ and Σ estimates are noisy.

Incorporating costs into bet sizing

Costs reduce effective edge. If your signal implies a gross expected return of α_{gross} over the holding period but you expect to pay cost in trading to establish and later unwind the position, then the *net* expected return is

$$\alpha_{net} = \alpha_{gross} - \text{cost}.$$

In the Kelly framework, effective μ is replaced by α_{net}. If costs are high relative to raw alpha, net edge may be too small or even negative. This has two consequences:

- Some marginal signals that look slightly positive before costs should not be traded at all.
- For a given signal, there is an *optimal size* beyond which higher size increases cost more than it increases profit.

Within the portfolio optimizer, you can reflect this by:

- Penalizing turnover in the objective, making it costly to chase small changes in signals.
- Multiplying expected returns by a "haircut" factor that reflects typical costs in that asset, making illiquid names less attractive.

Rebalancing: When and How to Trade Toward Targets

So far, we have assumed that at each decision time we compute an optimal target portfolio $w_t^\star$. The question is: *Do we trade all the way to $w_t^\star$ immediately?* In a frictionless world, the answer is yes. In the presence of costs, the answer is usually no.

Rebalancing is about managing the path from w_{t-1} to $w_t^\star$ over time, balancing three forces:

- **Alpha decay:** Signals have finite horizon. If you delay trading too long, you miss the opportunity.
- **Risk control:** Deviations from target may increase risk or undesired exposures.
- **Transaction costs:** Trading too often or too aggressively wastes edge on costs.

No-trade regions

A useful first tool is the concept of a *no-trade region*. For each asset i, define a band around the current weight w_i inside which it is not worth trading, because the expected benefit from moving closer to target is smaller than the cost.

At a high level:

- If the difference $|w_i^\star - w_i|$ is small, and the asset is expensive to trade (large spread, low liquidity), you keep the current weight.
- You only trade when the gap between actual and optimal weight exceeds a threshold that makes the trade worthwhile.

Formally, one might define lower and upper bounds $\ell_i(w_i^\star)$ and $u_i(w_i^\star)$ such that:

$$\ell_i(w_i^\star) \leq w_i \leq u_i(w_i^\star) \quad \Rightarrow \quad \text{do not trade asset } i.$$

Outside this region, you trade back toward the boundary or partially toward the target. The size of the band should depend on both alpha strength and cost: stronger signals and cheaper trading justify narrower bands (more frequent rebalancing).

Turnover budgets

Another portfolio-level control is a *turnover budget*. Instead of allowing the optimizer to trade any amount as long as the net objective improves, you impose a hard or soft cap on the total amount traded per period:

$$\sum_{i=1}^{N} |w_i^{new} - w_i^{old}| \leq \text{Turnover}_{max}.$$

This forces the optimizer to *prioritize* trades:

- Positions with large alpha improvements per unit of cost are adjusted first.
- Smaller or lower-conviction trades are delayed or skipped.

You can interpret Turnover_{max} as the "bandwidth" of your trading infrastructure and risk appetite for costs.

Staggered and partial rebalancing

Even when you decide to trade, you do not need to go all the way from w to $w^\star$ in one step. *Staggered* or *partial* rebalancing spreads the move over several periods:

$$w_{t+1} = w_t + \lambda(w_t^\star - w_t),$$

with $0 < \lambda \leq 1$. Here:

- $\lambda = 1$ corresponds to immediate full rebalancing.
- $\lambda < 1$ trades only a fraction of the distance to the target each period.

Partial rebalancing has two benefits:

- It reduces instantaneous trading volume and thus impact and cost.
- It naturally smooths portfolio changes in response to noisy signals; if tomorrow's optimizer output changes direction, you have not yet fully committed to the previous target.

The downside is that you track the theoretical optimal portfolio more loosely, potentially leaving some alpha unexploited. Finding the right λ is an empirical question and should be studied in backtests that incorporate realistic cost models.

Intraday versus end-of-day targets

Many portfolios are optimized at a relatively low frequency (e.g., daily or hourly), while executions happen throughout the day. This creates a separation between:

- A *slow* layer: computes portfolio targets $w^\star$ using the latest alpha and risk estimates.
- A *fast* layer: executes child orders intraday, responding to real-time fills, liquidity, and short-term microstructure.

Rebalancing policies must bridge these layers:

- At the slow layer, you decide the desired end-of-day (or end-of-interval) portfolio.
- At the fast layer, you decide how to schedule and route the necessary trades over time, subject to participation caps and cost objectives.

This book will discuss execution algorithms and microstructure in later sections; here, the key point is that your notion of "turnover" and "rebalancing" should align with what your execution layer can realistically achieve without excessive impact.

Embedding Costs and Rebalancing into the Optimizer

Conceptually, you can think of transaction costs and rebalancing rules as sitting *around* the optimizer. In a more advanced design, you push them *inside* the optimization problem, so that portfolio choice, trading speed, and cost-awareness are solved jointly.

A generic formulation might look like:

$$\begin{aligned} \max_{w} \quad & \hat{\mu}^\top w - \frac{\lambda}{2} w^\top \Sigma w - \text{Cost}(w, w^{old}) \\ \text{subject to} \quad & w \in \mathcal{W}, \\ & \sum_{i=1}^{N} |w_i - w_i^{old}| \leq \text{Turnover}_{max}, \end{aligned}$$

where:

- $\hat{\mu}$ and Σ come from your alpha forecasts and risk model.
- Cost(w, w^{old}) is an approximate but realistic cost function.
- $\mathcal{W}$ encodes all your constraints (leverage, factor neutrality, sector bounds, etc.).

In implementation, you will often:

- Use a convex, solver-friendly approximation to Cost, such as a piecewise-linear or quadratic function of trade sizes.
- Convert absolute values $|w_i - w_i^{old}|$ into linear constraints using auxiliary variables, preserving convexity.
- Solve the resulting quadratic or linear program at each decision time.

This design naturally yields:

- Smaller trades in illiquid, high-cost securities.
- Less chasing of small changes in noisy signals.
- Portfolio paths that respect both risk and cost budgets.

Transaction costs, position sizing, and rebalancing are the glue between your theoretical optimal portfolio and the one you can actually trade in the market. Explicit and implicit costs eat into your edge and must be approximated with practical models. Edge and risk determine how large your bets should be, but estimation error and drawdown concerns usually lead you to scale down from theoretically optimal (Kelly-like) sizes. Rebalancing policies—no-trade regions, turnover budgets, and staggered adjustments—decide when and how to move toward optimizer targets without overtrading.

In a robust algorithmic trading machine, these elements are not afterthoughts. They are embedded in the optimization problem and automated in the system's control logic, ensuring that every trade is not only statistically justified by alpha and risk models, but also economically justified after accounting for cost and execution realities.

5.3 Smart Order Routing and Execution Algorithms

The previous sections answered two questions: *What portfolio do we want to hold?* (optimization and risk) and *How quickly and how much should we trade?* (position sizing and rebalancing under costs). This section addresses the next question in the chain:

> Given a desired change in the portfolio, *how do we actually trade in fragmented, electronic markets* to achieve that change with acceptable cost, speed, and risk?

Modern markets offer many trading venues (exchanges, dark pools, alternative trading systems) and many order types (market, limit, pegged, hidden, etc.). The trading machine must decide, in real time, *where* to send orders, *how fast* to trade, *which order types* to use, and *how to react* to partial fills and changing conditions. This is the role of *smart order routing* (SOR) and *execution algorithms*.

From Portfolio Targets to Venue-Level Orders

At each decision point, the portfolio and rebalancing layers produce a vector of target weights $w^\star$ and, by comparing to current holdings w, a vector of desired trades $\Delta w = w^\star - w$. Translated into shares or contracts, this yields a list of *parent orders*, one per instrument:

$$Q_i = \frac{C\,\Delta w_i}{P_i},$$

where C is total capital and P_i is the current reference price.

The task of the execution layer is to transform these parent orders into a stream of *child orders* routed across venues and time, while controlling three competing dimensions:

- **Cost:** Minimize implementation shortfall relative to a benchmark price (e.g., arrival mid, VWAP).

- **Speed (risk):** Avoid excessive exposure to price risk while the order is outstanding.

- **Information leakage:** Avoid revealing your trading intentions and becoming the target of adverse selection.

It is helpful to visualize how this relates to the rest of the trading machine.

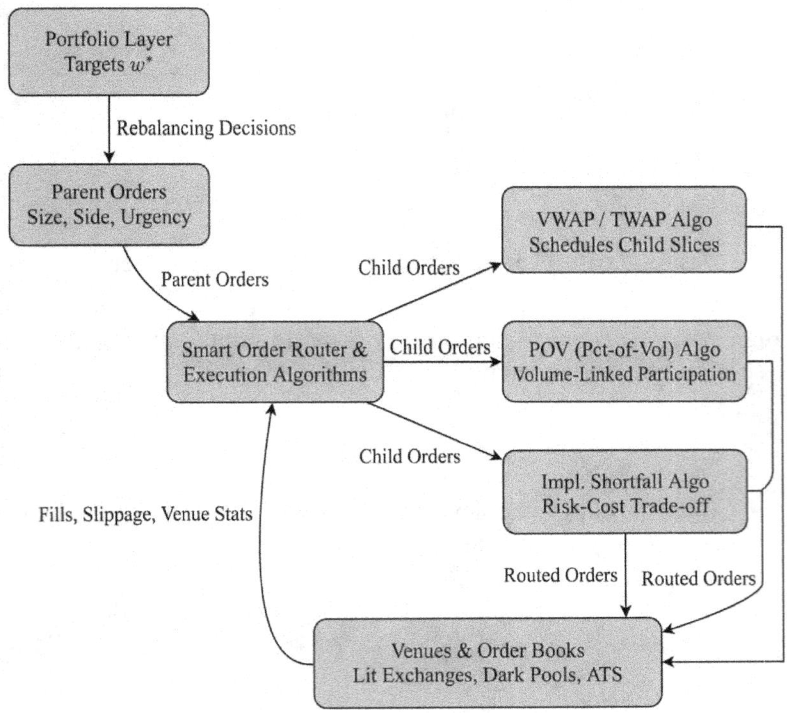

The remainder of this section explains how the smart order router and the main classes of execution algorithms operate, and how they expose parameters that the portfolio layer can tune.

Smart Order Routing as a Real-Time Decision Engine

A *smart order router* is an automated system that decides, for each parent order and at each decision moment, how to split and route child orders across venues. Conceptually, the SOR solves a sequence of small optimization problems:

> Given the remaining quantity to trade, current market data (prices, spreads, depth, fees), and a target trading schedule from the execution algorithm, what child orders should I send right now, and to which venues, to improve my expected execution quality?

Key inputs to the SOR include:

- **Order attributes:** symbol, side (buy/sell), remaining size, urgency, any constraints (e.g., participation cap).
- **Market state:** best bid and ask on each venue, available displayed depth by price level, historical and real-time volume, queue lengths, and volatility.
- **Venue characteristics:** fees/rebates, likelihood of hidden liquidity, latency to each venue, and any internal toxicity scores (probability of adverse selection).

The SOR must decide:

- How to divide the remaining size across venues.
- Whether to post passive limit orders (seeking the spread) or send aggressive orders (crossing the spread).
- How to manage cancellations and replacements as the book evolves.

From a system design perspective, the SOR exposes *parameters* (e.g., aggression level, maximum participation rate, routing preferences). These parameters can be chosen by the execution algorithm, which in turn is configured by the portfolio layer depending on strategy needs.

Execution Objectives and Benchmarks

Before diving into specific algorithms like VWAP, TWAP, POV, and implementation shortfall, it is crucial to understand what they are trying to optimize. Each algorithm targets a particular *execution benchmark* and reflects a trade-off between minimizing cost and controlling risk.

Common benchmarks include:

- **Arrival price (implementation shortfall):** The mid-price (or last traded price) at the moment the decision to trade is made. The goal is to minimize the difference between this price and the realized average execution price.
- **VWAP (Volume-Weighted Average Price):** The average price of trades in the market, weighted by volume, over a specified interval (e.g., the trading day). Matching or beating VWAP is common for "neutral" execution.
- **TWAP (Time-Weighted Average Price):** The simple average of prices over equal time intervals. Matching TWAP is equivalent to trading in equal slices over time.

Different strategies and mandates favor different benchmarks:

- A benchmark-tracking fund may prioritize VWAP-style executions to avoid predictable deviation from the index.
- A high-conviction, alpha-driven strategy may focus on minimizing implementation shortfall relative to the decision price, accepting more timing risk.

Schedule-Based Algorithms: VWAP and TWAP

VWAP algorithms

A VWAP execution algorithm attempts to trade at a pace proportional to the expected intraday volume profile. If $V(t)$ denotes market volume at time t, and you know the typical volume curve over the day (e.g., from historical averages), then the algorithm seeks to keep your participation rate roughly constant:

$$\text{Participation rate} \approx \frac{\text{Your traded volume up to } t}{\text{Market volume up to } t}.$$

If the total parent order size is Q and the predicted total volume for the day is $\widehat{V}_{day}$, then an approximate target participation rate is:

$$\pi = \frac{Q}{\widehat{V}_{day}}.$$

At each time step, the algorithm computes how much you *should* have traded by now given the predicted cumulative volume, compares it to what you have already traded, and sends child orders to catch up or slow down.

Intuition. VWAP is attractive when:

- You care about being "neutral" with respect to the day's trading, avoiding the appearance of front-running or slow execution.
- Your order is not so urgent that you must finish quickly, but not so small that you can trade it opportunistically without regard to the average.

However, VWAP ignores information in the current price path: if prices are moving favorably, it does not automatically speed up, and if prices are moving against you, it does not slow down, unless you add tactical overlays.

TWAP algorithms

A TWAP algorithm simply slices the order into equal parts over equal time intervals. For a parent order of size Q to be completed over horizon T with n intervals, each slice is:

$$q = \frac{Q}{n},$$

and at times $t_1, t_2, \ldots, t_n$ the algorithm submits a child order of size q.

Intuition. TWAP is:

- Simple and predictable.
- Insensitive to the actual volume traded in the market, which can be an advantage (you do not crowd with others) or a disadvantage (you may send too much volume in a thin period).

TWAP is often used in relatively liquid names for small orders, or in markets where reliable volume curves are not available. It is also a useful building block: more sophisticated strategies may adapt the slice sizes based on real-time conditions instead of keeping them equal.

Participation-Based Algorithms: Percentage of Volume (POV)

While VWAP and TWAP specify *how much* to trade over time, a *percentage-of-volume* (POV) algorithm specifies *how aggressively* to participate in whatever volume the market offers. The core parameter is a target participation rate π, for example 10%.

At each time step:

1. Observe the market volume traded since the last step, ΔV_t.
2. Compute your target volume for this interval, $\Delta Q_t^{target} = \pi \, \Delta V_t$.
3. Compare to the volume you actually traded; if you are behind, send new child orders to catch up, subject to risk and limit constraints.

POV is particularly useful when:

- You must avoid being too large a fraction of the tape to reduce impact and signaling (e.g., never more than 15% of volume).
- Market volume is uncertain and you prefer to adapt your pace in real time.

You can think of POV as a dynamic throttle: it adjusts your trading speed up or down as liquidity appears or disappears, while keeping your footprint bounded.

Implementation Shortfall Algorithms

VWAP, TWAP, and POV implicitly treat the target price path (VWAP or TWAP) as the main objective. *Implementation shortfall* (IS) algorithms instead explicitly target minimizing the difference between the arrival price and the realized execution price, taking into account both cost and risk.

Let:

- P_0 be the arrival price when you decide to trade (often the mid-price).
- $\overline{P}$ be your average execution price.
- Q be the signed total quantity (positive for buy, negative for sell).

The implementation shortfall in dollars is:

$$\text{IS} = Q(\overline{P} - P_0) + \text{Fees} + \text{Other costs}.$$

For a buy, $\overline{P} > P_0$ means you paid more than the arrival price (negative outcome); for a sell, $\overline{P} < P_0$ is similarly adverse.

An IS algorithm balances:

- **Market impact:** Trading faster, especially with aggressive orders, increases cost from impact and spread.
- **Price risk:** Trading slower leaves you exposed to the possibility that the market moves against you before you finish.

In practice, an IS algorithm uses a model of short-horizon price volatility and impact to choose a *trading schedule* that minimizes expected shortfall plus a penalty for risk of adverse moves. A typical approach:

1. Estimate volatility over the execution horizon.
2. Specify a risk aversion parameter: more urgent orders correspond to higher aversion to execution risk.
3. Solve for an optimal trajectory of child orders over time, often front-loading more trading for urgent orders.

The user (portfolio layer) usually controls an *urgency* knob:

- **Low urgency:** IS algorithm leans more on passive, slower trading to reduce impact.
- **High urgency:** Trades more aggressively and faster, accepting higher impact to reduce price risk.

Linking Execution Algorithms to Cost, Speed, and Risk

It is helpful to compare these algorithm families through the lens of the objectives from earlier sections:

- **Cost minimization:** Passive and schedule-based algos (VWAP, slow POV) focus on minimizing expected cost relative to a benchmark, but may incur more timing risk.
- **Risk control:** IS algos with high urgency or tightly bounded completion windows prioritize finishing quickly, reducing risk at the expense of higher cost.
- **Information leakage:** High participation POV or very predictable VWAP shapes may be detected by other market participants; sophisticated SORs randomize slice timing and venues to reduce this.

In a well-designed trading machine, the portfolio layer indicates:

- The *time horizon* over which the position is relevant (e.g., intraday vs. multi-day alpha).
- The *tolerance* for execution risk relative to forecast risk.
- Any *constraints* (e.g., must complete by close, cannot exceed 20% participation).

The execution layer then chooses and parameterizes the appropriate algorithm.

Venue Selection and Liquidity-Seeking Logic

So far we have discussed *how much* to trade and *how fast*. Where to trade is equally important. Smart order routing continuously evaluates potential venues:

- **Lit venues:** Transparent order books where your displayed limit orders contribute to quoted depth.

- **Dark pools and hidden orders:** Venues or order types where liquidity is not pre-displayed; fills may occur at mid or better prices, often with less signaling, but with uncertain fill probabilities.
- **Internalization / crossing:** Matching your orders against other flow (e.g., from your broker's clients) potentially yields better prices and lower fees.

Liquidity-seeking logic might:

- Probe dark pools with small orders before crossing the spread in lit markets.
- Route to the venue with the best combination of price, depth, and fees, adjusted for latency.
- Avoid venues with poor fill quality or high toxicity (frequent adverse price moves after your trades).

From an architectural point of view, venue selection is another optimization problem, but on a much shorter time scale and with more microstructural detail than the portfolio optimizer.

Monitoring, Feedback, and Continuous Calibration

Execution quality cannot be taken for granted. The trading machine must monitor its own performance and feed that information back into both the execution layer and the higher-level portfolio optimizer. Key metrics include:

- **Slippage:** Realized shortfall relative to chosen benchmarks (arrival, VWAP, TWAP), per order and aggregated over time.
- **Fill rates and latency:** How quickly and completely orders are being filled on each venue and with each algorithm.
- **Venue toxicity:** Statistical measures of adverse selection, such as the average post-trade price move following fills on a venue.

These metrics support:

- **Recalibration of cost models:** Updating parameters in the parametric cost functions used by the portfolio optimizer.
- **Routing adjustments:** Reweighting venue preferences and modifying SOR logic as market conditions or venue quality change.
- **Strategy evaluation:** Understanding whether apparent alpha in backtests survives after realistic execution costs.

Smart order routing and execution algorithms are the bridge between theoretical portfolio decisions and actual trades in the market. The portfolio and rebalancing layers specify *what* to trade and *how much risk* to take; the execution layer decides *where* and *how* to trade to balance cost, speed, and information leakage.

Schedule-based algorithms (VWAP, TWAP), participation-based algorithms (POV), and implementation shortfall algorithms represent different points in the cost–risk trade-off and target different execution benchmarks. A smart order router coordinates these tactics across venues, using real-time market data and feedback from past executions to make high-frequency decisions compatible with the higher-level objectives.

In a robust algorithmic trading machine, this connection is explicit: the optimizer's transaction cost models are informed by realized execution data, and execution parameters (urgency, participation caps, venue preferences) are set consistently with the portfolio's alpha horizon and risk limits. This closes the loop between abstract portfolio construction and the concrete microstructure of electronic markets.

5.4 Market Impact, Latency, and Microstructure

The previous section treated execution algorithms and smart order routing largely at the level of *schedules* (VWAP, POV, implementation shortfall) and *venues*. Underneath those abstractions lies the concrete machinery of the electronic market: the limit order book, matching rules, and the network of latencies between your trading system and the exchanges.

To design robust execution logic and realistic cost models, you must understand how your orders interact with this microscopic environment. In this section we:

- Describe the basic structure of a limit order book and how different order types interact with it.
- Explain how latency and queue position shape whether passive orders are filled and with what risk.
- Introduce stylized models of market impact and adverse selection, and show how they feed back into execution design and cost-aware optimization.

The Electronic Limit Order Book

Most modern electronic markets use a central limit order book (LOB). Conceptually, the LOB is a set of queues of limit orders waiting to trade at specific prices.

Quotes, depth, and the spread

At any instant, the visible state of the book consists of:

- A **bid side**: standing limit *buy* orders at different prices.
- An **ask side**: standing limit *sell* orders at different prices.

For each side, the book lists:

- **Price levels** $p_1, p_2, \ldots$ sorted from most to least aggressive. On the bid side, the highest bid price is most aggressive; on the ask side, the lowest ask price is most aggressive.
- **Depth** at each level: the total quantity (shares, contracts) waiting at that price.

The best bid and best ask define the inside market:

$$\text{Best bid } = p_1^{bid}, \qquad \text{Best ask } = p_1^{ask},$$

and the *bid–ask spread* is

$$s = p_1^{ask} - p_1^{bid}.$$

The mid-price,

$$m = \frac{p_1^{bid} + p_1^{ask}}{2},$$

is often used as a reference benchmark for costs and slippage.

Order types and matching rules

Two fundamental order types explain most microstructure behavior:

- **Limit orders**: specify a price and a quantity. A buy limit order at price p says, "buy up to this quantity at any price $\leq p$." If it cannot be executed immediately, it rests in the book.
- **Market orders**: specify a quantity and side but no limit price. A market buy order immediately executes against the best available asks, potentially walking up the book if the order is large.

Most exchanges implement price–time priority:

- Orders at better prices are matched first.
- Within the same price, earlier orders are matched before later ones.

This means your *queue position* at a given price level directly determines whether you get filled when an incoming order hits that level. Execution algorithms that rely on passive orders must therefore care about both *where* they quote (price) and *when* they arrive (queue priority).

Latency and Queue Position

Latency—the time delay between an event in the market and your system's response—is a central constraint in how you interact with the LOB.

Sources of latency

Round-trip latency includes:

- **Network latency**: physical distance between your servers and exchange matching engines; routing through intermediate nodes.
- **Processing delay**: time for your software stack to read, process, and act on market data.
- **Exchange latency**: time spent in exchange gateways and matching engines.

In fast markets, even microseconds or milliseconds can separate informed and uninformed participants. For your trading machine, this latency manifests as stale information and delayed reactions.

Queue position dynamics

Consider placing a passive buy limit order at the best bid. Your execution outcome depends on:

- The total depth ahead of you in the queue at that price.
- The rate at which sell market orders and more aggressive sell limits arrive and hit that bid.
- Cancellations ahead of you (which move you forward in the queue).

From your perspective:

- A **better queue position** increases the probability of getting filled before the price moves away.

- **Long queue positions** may mean you either need to improve your price (move up the book) or accept that a large part of your passive order will go unfilled.

Latency affects queue position in two important ways:

- By the time your order reaches the exchange, other participants may already have filled the front of the queue.
- If you attempt to cancel or modify an order after observing adverse market data, that cancel message may arrive *after* your order has already been executed.

Consequently, passive execution is a balance:

- Too passive: you risk not being filled or being picked off when prices move against you but you cannot cancel in time.
- Too aggressive: you cross the spread and incur immediate impact and spread cost.

A Stylized Picture of the Order Book and Impact

Before introducing models, it is useful to visualize the two key objects in this section: the shape of the order book and the relationship between trade size and price impact.

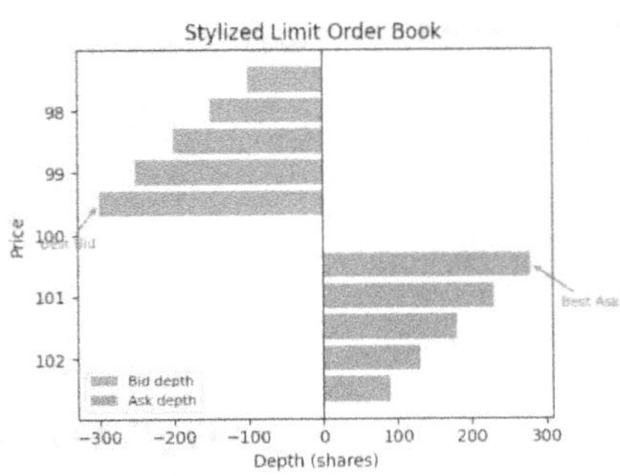

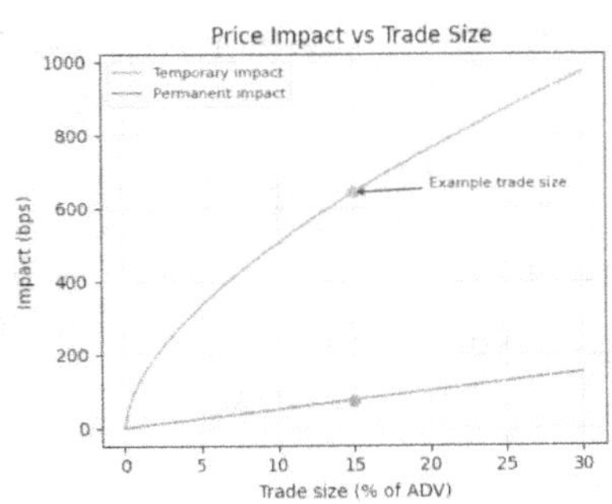

The left panel summarizes the state of liquidity at different prices; the right panel summarizes how trading a given fraction of daily volume might move the price.

Modeling Market Impact

When your order consumes liquidity from the book (typically with market or aggressively priced limit orders), it moves the price. Impact is usually decomposed into:

- **Temporary impact:** Short-lived price pressure that partially reverses once your trading stops.
- **Permanent impact:** The lasting component, often interpreted as the market digesting information about your trading (i.e., your order reveals information).

Impact as a function of trade size

A common stylized model expresses expected impact (in returns) as a function of trade size relative to average daily volume (ADV). Let:

$$\phi = \frac{|Q|}{\text{ADV}},$$

and model the total impact Δp (in basis points, bps) as:

$$\Delta p(\phi) = \underbrace{k_{temp}\,\phi^{\beta}}_{\text{temporary}} + \underbrace{k_{perm}\,\phi}_{\text{permanent}},$$

where:

- k_{temp} and k_{perm} are calibrated constants (impact per unit of size).
- $\beta \in (0, 1)$ captures the concave growth of temporary impact.

This reflects key empirical regularities:

- Doubling trade size less than doubles impact (concavity).
- Very small orders have nearly linear impact.

- Permanent impact is usually smaller and roughly linear in size.

Time and participation rate

Impact also depends on *how fast* you trade. Let:

- T be the execution horizon.
- ϕ_t be your instantaneous participation rate (fraction of market volume) at time t.

Impact models in the execution literature often express temporary impact as a function of participation rate, not just total size. Higher participation at a given moment consumes more of the visible depth and more strongly disturbs the price.

For execution design, the important qualitative lessons are:

- Spreading a given size over a longer time (lower participation) reduces impact but increases timing risk.
- Concentrating the trade (higher participation) reduces timing risk but increases impact and information leakage.

Adverse Selection and Toxicity

Not all fills are equal. Sometimes you passively buy at the bid and then the price moves up: you captured the spread and benefitted from the subsequent move. Other times you buy at the bid and the price immediately trades down: you were *picked off* by someone with better information. This is adverse selection.

Measuring adverse selection

A simple, intuitive metric for adverse selection is the average post-trade price change following your fills. For each execution j at time t_j and price P_j, define a short-horizon reference price $P_{j+\Delta}$ (e.g., mid-price a few seconds later). For a buy trade:

$$\text{Post-trade move}_j = \frac{P_{j+\Delta} - P_j}{P_j}.$$

If this is systematically negative, your buys are being followed by price drops; your passive orders are adversely selected.

Aggregating these moves by venue, order type, or counterparty type yields *toxicity scores* that guide routing decisions:

- Venues where post-trade moves are often adverse are "toxic"; you may reduce usage or change order types there.
- Venues with neutral or favorable post-trade moves are more benign.

Adverse selection vs. spread capture

Passive orders aim to earn the spread: buy slightly below the mid-price, sell slightly above. Adverse selection is the risk that information-rich counterparties only trade with you when it is good for them and bad for you. Execution design must balance:

- **Spread capture:** Using passive or midpoint orders to reduce cost.
- **Adverse selection risk:** Avoiding being the "liquidity provider of last resort" during informed price moves.

A common compromise:

- Use passive orders when volatility is low and order flow appears balanced.
- Switch to more aggressive or immediately executable orders when volatility spikes or when your models detect directional pressure.

How Microstructure Feeds Back into Execution Design

The models and measurements above are not academic; they directly inform the high-level choices made by your execution algorithms and, by extension, your portfolio optimizer.

Setting participation caps and urgency

Market impact and adverse selection estimates tell you how expensive it is to trade at different participation rates. This informs:

- **Maximum participation rate:** A cap such as "never exceed 15% of volume" in a given name, used by POV and IS algorithms.
- **Urgency parameters:** If you know that speeding up trading beyond a certain rate sharply increases impact, you may choose to accept more timing risk instead of pushing for ultra-fast completion.

These parameters should be calibrated by analyzing historical executions and fitting impact models against realized data.

Choosing between passive and aggressive tactics

Microstructure-aware models also guide the choice of order type:

- If spread is wide but book depth is ample and toxicity is low, passive orders at or inside the spread can be very cost-effective.
- If liquidity is thin, spreads are tight, or the order is very urgent, aggressive orders may be preferable despite higher instantaneous cost.

Execution algorithms can adapt in real time:

- Start passively; if fill rate is too low relative to target schedule, increase aggression (cross the spread or improve quotes).
- Monitor post-trade price moves to adjust reliance on particular venues or order types.

Feeding impact back into the optimizer

In earlier sections, transaction cost models were expressed as functions of trade size, volatility, and liquidity. Microstructure analysis provides the empirical basis for these models:

- Impact curves estimated from LOB and execution data define the cost of different trade sizes and participation strategies.

- Adverse selection metrics refine the expected cost of passive strategies and dark pool interactions.

These estimates should flow back into the portfolio optimizer:

- Illiquid or "toxic" names carry higher expected costs, reducing their attractiveness.
- Strategies that require frequent, large trades in such names may be down-weighted or rejected in backtesting.

Latency Constraints in Algorithm Design

Finally, latency considerations place hard constraints on what your algorithms can safely attempt.

Limits of reaction-based strategies

Algorithms that try to react to microstructure signals—such as fleeting quote improvements or small shifts in depth imbalance—must do so within a reaction time that is competitive with other market participants. If your end-to-end latency is significantly higher:

- You will often trade on stale signals.
- Your cancellations may arrive too late to avoid fills during adverse moves.

In that case, you should:

- Avoid strategies that rely on ultra-fast quote stuffing or fleeting depth signals.
- Prefer more stable, slower-moving signals (e.g., intraday volume patterns) that survive your latency.

Latency-aware order placement

Even with moderate latency, you can design tactics that are robust:

- Place passive orders at slightly less aggressive prices to reduce the risk of being picked off when you cannot cancel instantly.

- Limit order lifetime: automatically cancel and refresh quotes after a short duration, even without new signals, to avoid stale exposure.
- Use randomization in timing and placement to avoid becoming predictable.

These design choices increase resilience to adverse microstructure conditions at the cost of some spread capture.

Market impact, latency, and microstructure are the fine-grained realities that shape how your algorithmic trades interact with the market. The limit order book defines what liquidity is available at each price; latency and queue position determine whether your passive orders actually get filled and at what risk; and impact and adverse selection models quantify how your trading changes prices and how other participants respond.

A robust algorithmic trading machine does not treat these as afterthoughts. Instead, it:

- Uses LOB and execution data to estimate impact and adverse selection empirically.
- Embeds those estimates into both execution algorithms (choice of order type, schedule, and venue) and portfolio optimization (cost-aware sizing and rebalancing).
- Designs tactics and parameter choices explicitly around its own latency profile and microstructure footprint.

By closing this loop, you ensure that every part of the trading machine—from signals to portfolio weights to venue-level orders—is aligned not only with statistical forecasts, but also with the actual microscopic rules by which markets operate.

Chapter 6

Low-Latency Engineering and Infrastructure

Low latency is not a single optimization; it is a disciplined way of thinking about time as a first-class design constraint. In this chapter, we descend from Linux internals and wire-level networking, through kernel-bypass feed handlers and gateways, down to FPGA offload and colocation strategy, and back up into resilience patterns that keep the entire machine trading-even when components fail in the most inconvenient possible ways.

6.1 Operating Systems, Networking, and Time Sync

In the previous chapter we treated low latency mostly at the level of algorithms and architecture: how work is partitioned, how events flow through the trading machine, and how we measure performance. In this section we move one level down, to the foundations that decide whether those designs can actually run with deterministic, microsecond-level behavior in production.

There are three pillars:

- The operating system: how Linux schedules your threads, moves data, and responds to interrupts.
- The networking path: how bytes travel from the wire into user space and back out again.
- Time synchronization: how all of the above is anchored to a stable, shared notion of time.

If any one of these pillars is misconfigured, clever strategy code cannot recover the lost performance or determinism. The goal of this section is not to turn you into a systems administrator, but to give you enough understanding to reason about low-level choices, challenge defaults, and specify a reproducible baseline configuration for trading workloads.

A Layered View of the Low-Latency Stack

Before we dive into details, it is useful to visualize where latency and timestamps enter the picture. Figure shows a simplified layered architecture from the physical network interface up to your strategy code, with the time synchronization components aligned alongside.

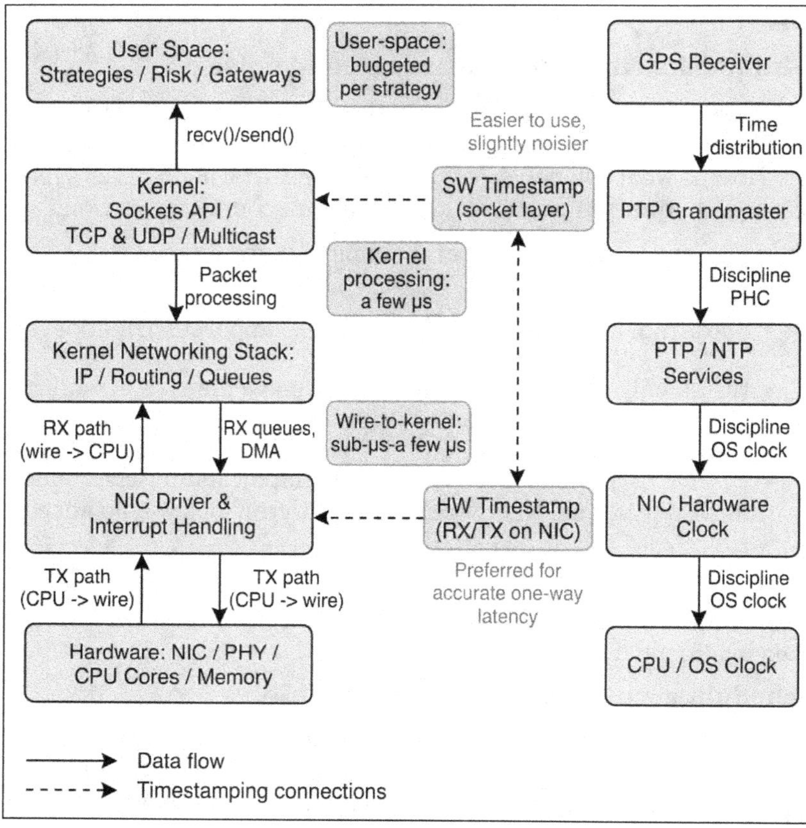

This picture will guide the rest of the section. We now work down the stack, from user space to hardware, then sideways into the time-synchronization components.

Linux Fundamentals for Trading Systems

Most low-latency trading stacks run on Linux, not because Linux is magically fast, but because it is open, configurable, and well supported by hardware vendors and exchanges. Out of the box, however, a stock distribution is optimized for general-purpose workloads: desktops, file servers, web servers. Your first task is to strip away unnecessary variability.

Minimal distributions and background noise

Every background service that occasionally wakes up a CPU core—logging daemons, automatic updates, desktop environments—adds jitter. Jitter is what you perceive when a packet that usually takes 5 μs to reach your strategy suddenly takes 50 μs, for no apparent reason.

The practical way to reduce jitter is simple but unglamorous:

- Start from a server-oriented, long-term support distribution.
- Install only what is needed to boot, manage the system, and run your trading stack.
- Disable or uninstall everything else: graphical interfaces, indexing services, unused network daemons, cron jobs you do not control.

From a trading perspective, the "features" you remove are often more valuable than the ones you add.

Scheduling, run queues, and CPU affinity

On a loaded machine, many processes want CPU time. The Linux scheduler multiplexes them. This is good for fairness, but bad for deterministic latency, because it means your hot-path thread can be descheduled right when a market data burst arrives.

Key concepts:

- **Run queue**: the set of runnable tasks for a given core. The more entries in the queue, the longer a task may wait.
- **Preemption**: the scheduler can interrupt a running task to let another run.
- **Affinity**: a mask that tells the kernel which CPUs a thread is allowed to run on.

For low latency you want:

- Dedicated cores for your most critical threads (feed handlers, gateways, risk checks).
- Those cores' run queues to contain as few other tasks as possible (ideally only one).
- Preemption of these threads to be rare and predictable.

In practice this means:

- Using Linux isolcpus / nohz_full boot parameters to isolate a set of cores from the general scheduler.
- Pinning critical threads to these isolated cores using sched_setaffinity or equivalent calls.
- Moving interrupts and background daemons off those cores.

An intuitive way to think about this: you are renting individual CPU cores as if they were private offices for your threads, rather than letting them hot-desk in a crowded open-plan space.

Interrupts, polling, and tail latency

When a packet arrives at the NIC, the hardware typically raises an interrupt to notify the CPU. The kernel then runs the interrupt handler, which pulls packets off the NIC's receive queues and passes them up the stack. This is efficient for low traffic, but it introduces variability:

- Interrupts may be coalesced (grouped) to reduce overhead, adding delay.
- Interrupt handlers can run on cores you thought were "free".
- Under heavy load, interrupt storms and context switches can dramatically inflate tail latency.

An alternative is to have a dedicated thread *poll* the NIC or socket—busy-waiting in a tight loop, checking for new packets. This burns a core but yields very stable latency.

Low-latency trading often combines both approaches:

- Interrupts wake up a poll loop or kernel thread when there has been a long idle period.
- Once traffic begins, the system switches to polling to minimize variance.

You will see this theme repeatedly: we are willing to trade average efficiency (more CPU cycles used) for lower maximum latency and less jitter.

Memory, huge pages, and NUMA awareness

Latency is not only about CPUs and packets. Memory access patterns also matter.

Huge pages. Modern CPUs fetch data from memory in cache-line-sized chunks, but the *virtual memory* system maps large regions of your address space in much bigger units called pages. Normal pages are typically 4 KB. Huge pages (also called large pages) can be 2 MB or more.

Using huge pages reduces the number of page-table entries the CPU must manage. Fewer entries mean fewer misses in the translation lookaside buffer (TLB), a small cache that holds the most recent virtual-to-physical translations. Fewer TLB misses mean more predictable memory access times. For large, long-lived data structures—order books, symbol tables, in-memory risk limits—configuring huge pages is a low-level but meaningful improvement.

NUMA. Many modern servers are Non-Uniform Memory Access (NUMA) machines: memory is physically divided into nodes attached to particular CPU sockets. Accessing memory local to a core's node is faster than accessing memory attached to another socket.

For a trading stack, you want to:

- Allocate the memory used by a given thread (and its NIC) from the same NUMA node.
- Pin the thread to cores on that node.

This keeps the CPU–memory–NIC triangle compact, reducing both latency and jitter introduced by cross-node traffic.

Networking Basics with a Trading Bias

At the network layer, your primary concern is how data moves between the exchange and your strategy:

- Market data feeds: usually UDP multicast or UDP unicast.
- Order entry: usually TCP or specialized binary protocols over TCP.

Here we highlight several aspects of networking that have outsized impact on latency.

TCP vs. UDP vs. multicast

- **TCP** provides reliable, ordered byte streams. It handles retransmissions, congestion control, and flow control in the kernel. This reduces complexity in your application code, but adds overhead and may introduce backpressure if buffers fill.
- **UDP** is a simple message-oriented protocol. It does not guarantee delivery or order. This reduces per-packet overhead and latency, but shifts responsibility to your feed handler to detect gaps and request retransmissions or fall back to snapshots.
- **Multicast** (usually over UDP) allows the exchange to send one copy of each packet to a group address; the network replicates it to many subscribers. This is efficient for disseminating the same market data to many participants, but can complicate network design and debugging.

From a latency standpoint, UDP and multicast are attractive because they go through a thinner code path. However, strategy correctness is paramount: missing or mis-ordering messages can cause far more damage than a few extra microseconds. In practice, exchanges choose the protocols; your task is to configure the stack to handle them well.

Small configuration details that matter

Several TCP/IP settings have direct impact on one-way and round-trip latency:

- **Nagle's algorithm** (TCP). Designed to batch small writes into larger segments, reducing network overhead. For order-entry gateways, this added delay is unacceptable. You typically disable Nagle by setting TCP_NODELAY on sockets, allowing small messages (orders, cancels) to be sent immediately.
- **Socket buffers**. The kernel maintains receive (RX) and transmit (TX) buffers per socket. If these buffers are too small, bursts of traffic may be dropped. If they are excessively large, data may sit in queues longer before being delivered or flushed. For low latency, you tune these sizes based on expected burstiness and link speed, seeking a balance between loss and latency.
- **Congestion control**. TCP sends probes to discover how much data the network can carry. Some congestion-control algorithms are more aggressive; others are smoother but slower. For order flow inside a well-engineered data-center network, it is common to use algorithms that ramp quickly and avoid long recovery times after packet loss.

These settings do not change the laws of physics, but they shape the microstructure of delay along the path.

Kernel and NIC tuning

Returning to Figure, we focus on the region between the NIC and the sockets layer. Here, several knobs affect both throughput and latency:

- **Interrupt coalescing**. The NIC can group several packets before raising an interrupt, reducing interrupt rate but adding delay. For low-latency feeds, you often minimize coalescing on the receive path, accepting more interrupts in exchange for faster packet delivery.
- **Receive-Side Scaling (RSS)**. On multi-core systems, RSS distributes incoming packets across multiple queues and cores. This improves throughput, but can complicate ordering guarantees and cache locality. For a single hot feed handler, you may want to steer all relevant traffic to one queue on one core.
- **Descriptor ring sizes**. NICs store packet metadata in ring buffers (descriptor rings). Oversized rings can hide congestion—

packets wait longer in queues before being processed. Undersized rings risk overflow and drops under bursty traffic. The goal is to size rings to comfortably handle expected bursts while keeping them short enough that queued packets do not accumulate large delays.

- **Offloads (checksum, segmentation, GRO/LRO).** The NIC and kernel can perform certain work on your behalf: computing checksums, combining small packets into larger ones (Large Receive Offload, LRO; Generic Receive Offload, GRO), or segmenting large packets for transmission. These offloads improve bulk throughput but may alter packet boundaries and introduce extra buffering. For latency-sensitive market data, you usually disable receive offloads so that each packet is delivered promptly and individually.

Notice that the same mechanisms that make a web server handle millions of connections—large buffers, aggressive coalescing, heavy use of offloads—are often harmful to the microsecond-level determinism desired in trading.

Time Synchronization as a First-Class Requirement

So far we have spoken of latency as if it were a single number. In reality, you care about the whole distribution, and you care about it *relative to a clock.* Without a precise notion of time, you cannot:

- Measure one-way latency from exchange to strategy.
- Correctly order events coming from multiple venues or systems.
- Satisfy regulatory requirements that specify timestamp accuracy.

Time synchronization is therefore not an afterthought; it is a critical part of the low-latency stack.

Sources of time: NTP, PTP, and GPS

Three acronyms dominate time synchronization in trading data centers:

- **GPS** provides an absolute time reference (UTC) via signals from satellites. A GPS receiver with a disciplined oscillator can act as an on-premises time source.
- **NTP** (Network Time Protocol) synchronizes system clocks over IP networks. It is widely used and easy to deploy but typically achieves accuracy in the tens of microseconds (or worse under load).
- **PTP** (Precision Time Protocol, IEEE 1588) is designed for sub-microsecond synchronization across local networks, using hardware timestamping at switches and NICs.

A common arrangement, reflected in Figure, is:

- A GPS receiver feeds a PTP grandmaster clock.
- The grandmaster distributes time to PTP-aware switches and servers.
- On each server, a PTP or NTP daemon disciplines both the NIC hardware clock and the CPU/OS clocks.

The goal is to keep all relevant clocks in the data center aligned to within a fraction of a microsecond.

Hardware vs. software timestamping

When a packet is received or transmitted, we can associate it with a timestamp:

- **Software timestamp**. The kernel stamps the packet when it passes through a particular layer (often the socket layer). This is easy to enable and works on most hardware, but the timestamp includes any queueing and processing delays that occurred before that point.
- **Hardware timestamp**. The NIC stamps the packet as close as possible to the physical layer, when it is received from or transmitted onto the wire. This requires NIC support and proper configuration but yields more precise, less noisy timing.

For tasks like measuring one-way latency from exchange to your host, or ordering events from multiple servers, hardware timestamps referenced to a common time source are much more reliable. In the diagram, these are indicated near the NIC hardware, with arrows leading back to the time-sync stack.

Clock alignment and latency measurement

Consider a feed handler timestamping incoming packets with the NIC clock, while the strategy thread timestamps decisions using the CPU's Time Stamp Counter (TSC). To compare these timestamps meaningfully, you must know the offset and skew between the two clocks—and keep them bounded over time.

Time-sync daemons perform three essential functions:

- Estimate the offset between local clocks and the reference (grandmaster).
- Estimate and correct for frequency drift (skew)—the tendency of oscillators to run slightly fast or slow.
- Apply adjustments smoothly to avoid sudden jumps that would confuse applications.

From the trading system's perspective, you want:

- A *traceable* chain from each timestamp back to a known time source.
- Quantified bounds on clock error (e.g., "this server is within ± 200 ns of UTC").
- Tools to monitor synchronization health and raise alerts when accuracy degrades.

Once you trust your clocks, you can take the latency budgeting ideas from earlier chapters and apply them rigorously: measure distributions at each hop (NIC, kernel, user space), track them over time, and quickly detect regressions when an OS upgrade or configuration change shifts the distribution.

A Baseline Low-Latency Configuration

Bringing the pieces together, here is a high-level checklist for a reproducible baseline suitable for many production trading workloads:

- **Operating system**
  - Minimal server Linux distribution with only required packages.
  - Isolated cores for feed handlers and gateways using isolcpus / nohz_full.
  - Critical threads pinned to specific cores and NUMA nodes.
  - Background daemons and interrupts moved off isolated cores.
  - Huge pages configured for large, long-lived data structures.
- **Networking**
  - Nagle's algorithm disabled (TCP_NODELAY) on latency-sensitive TCP sockets.
  - Socket and NIC buffer sizes tuned for expected burst sizes.
  - RX interrupt coalescing minimized on critical feeds.
  - RSS and queue steering configured so each hot path (feed, gateway) has dedicated queues on specific cores.
  - Receive offloads (GRO/LRO) disabled on latency-critical interfaces.
- **Time synchronization**
  - GPS-disciplined PTP grandmaster providing a local time reference.
  - PTP daemon on each host disciplining NIC and OS clocks.
  - Hardware timestamping enabled on relevant interfaces.
  - Monitoring of offset and delay statistics, with alarms on degradation.

This baseline will not win latency races by itself; elite shops push further with kernel bypass, FPGA offload, and custom network fabrics. But without a solid foundation in OS, networking, and time sync, those advanced techniques will sit on unstable ground. In the next sections we will build on this foundation to design feed handlers, gateways, and kernel-bypass architectures that fully exploit it.

6.2 Feed Handlers, Gateways, and Kernel Bypass

In the previous section we focused on the foundations: how the operating system, NIC, and time synchronization must be configured so that microsecond-level performance is even possible. We now move one step up the stack and design the *hot paths* that actually carry trading information:

- From the exchange wire into your strategy logic (the *ingress* path).
- From your strategy back out to the exchange (the *egress* path).

These paths are implemented by *feed handlers* and *order-entry gateways*. They are the arteries and veins of an algorithmic trading machine. Every extra memory copy, lock, or cache miss along these paths shows up as latency or jitter in your measurements.

The key design principle is simple to state but challenging to achieve: *treat the hot paths as special*. They do not look like general enterprise applications. They avoid unnecessary abstraction, allocate memory sparingly and predictably, and make deliberate use of hardware-aware techniques such as kernel bypass.

From Exchange Wire to Strategy: Feed Handlers

A feed handler is the component that:

- Receives raw market data packets from the exchange.

- Decodes the exchange-specific protocol.
- Updates in-memory representations of the order book and trades.
- Exposes a clean, low-latency view of this state to strategies.

Each of these steps can be implemented in ways that either respect or destroy your latency budget.

Parsing exchange protocols without wasting cycles

Market data protocols (ITCH, OUCH derivatives, FIX variants, proprietary binary feeds) are usually compact binary formats. The naive implementation pattern is:

- Copy packet bytes into a temporary buffer.
- Allocate a new object for each message.
- Parse fields into that object.
- Pass the object to downstream logic.

This is convenient but expensive:

- Each allocation stresses the allocator and the CPU caches.
- Each copy burns bandwidth and pollutes caches with transient data.
- The GC or allocator metadata introduces jitter when it performs internal housekeeping.

A low-latency feed handler instead:

- Parses messages *in place* from the receive buffer, using fixed offsets and simple pointer arithmetic.
- Reuses fixed-size structs drawn from a pool instead of allocating new objects.

- Encodes field access patterns so that the CPU can prefetch data efficiently (e.g., struct-of-arrays or carefully packed structs).

Intuitively, you want the feed handler to behave more like a finely tuned finite-state machine than like an object-relational mapper.

Order book data structures for constant-time updates

Once messages are parsed, they must update an in-memory model of the order book. The book must support:

- Very fast incremental updates (new orders, cancels, trades).
- Very fast reads of best bid/ask and nearby levels.
- Predictable performance under bursty conditions.

Because trading strategies tend to care most about the top few levels, and because exchanges often impose price grids (tick sizes) and depth limits, we can design data structures that are both efficient and bounded in size.

Common patterns include:

- **Price-indexed arrays.** If the number of price levels is known and bounded, we can map price $\rightarrow$ array index using a simple linear function and store per-level volume and metadata in fixed arrays. Updates and reads are then $O(1)$.
- **Two-tier structures.** Use a price-indexed array for a fixed window around the touch, and a secondary structure (e.g., a heap or tree) for deeper levels that are accessed less frequently.
- **Compact per-instrument state.** Store all per-instrument data (book, statistics, last trade) in contiguous memory to maximize cache locality when processing updates for that instrument.

The goal is not to minimize asymptotic complexity—book sizes are not large enough for that to dominate—but to minimize instruction count, cache misses, and branches on the hot path.

Sharing data with strategies: push, pull, or both?

Once the feed handler maintains an up-to-date book, strategies must see it. There are two extreme approaches:

- **Pull-based.** Strategies call methods or access shared memory to read the latest book state whenever they need it. This avoids copying and can be very fast if the data resides in CPU caches. However, strategies must know *when* to read, and concurrent access to shared structures must be managed carefully.
- **Push-based.** The feed handler sends event messages ("best bid changed", "trade occurred") to strategies via queues. This decouples the internal representation from the external view, but introduces additional message objects or copies and can increase queuing delay.

Most real systems use a hybrid:

- Feed handler updates are written into cache-friendly, shared-memory data structures.
- A simple event or sequence-number notification is pushed to strategies via a lock-free queue.
- Strategies, upon receiving the notification, *pull* the latest state by reading directly from shared structures.

This minimizes copying while providing strategies with a clean event-driven interface.

From Strategy to Exchange: Order-Entry Gateways

On the egress side, the order-entry gateway is the mirror image of the feed handler. Its job is to:

- Accept intents from strategies (e.g., "Buy 10 lots at price p").

- Apply local checks (risk limits, throttle rules).
- Translate intents into exchange-native messages.
- Manage the session (logon, heartbeats, sequence numbers).
- Handle acknowledgments, rejects, and other responses.

Because outgoing messages must flow through similar OS and NIC layers as incoming data, many of the same latency concerns apply.

Designing the gateway interface

The interface between strategies and the gateway should be:

- **Simple.** A small set of commands: new order, cancel, replace, maybe a generic "raw" message escape hatch.
- **Lock-free on the hot path.** Strategies enqueue intents into a single-producer/single-consumer (SPSC) ring buffer consumed by the gateway thread.
- **Allocation-free in steady state.** Intents and their metadata are drawn from pools or allocated per-strategy at startup.

The idea is to move all complex logic—routing, risk, throttling—into the gateway thread and keep the strategy-to-gateway boundary largely mechanical.

Sequencing, acknowledgments, and throttling

Unlike market data, which is broadcast and stateless from your perspective, order entry is stateful. The gateway must track:

- Local order identifiers and their mapping to exchange IDs.
- Outstanding orders and their lifecycles (working, filled, canceled).

- Exchange-level throttling rules (messages per second, outstanding cancels, etc.).

This state is updated both when:

- Strategies send new intents.
- The exchange sends back acknowledgments, rejects, and execution reports.

To preserve low latency and correctness:

- The same thread (or a tightly coupled set of threads) should handle both outgoing and incoming gateway messages for a given session, to avoid locking and reduce reordering risk.
- Throttle logic should be implemented as simple counters and time windows, updated in constant time.
- On overload, the gateway should apply backpressure to strategies (e.g., by filling queues or returning explicit rejections) rather than trying to smooth spikes in a way that hides latency.

Lock-Free Queues and Rings: The Glue Between Components

We have now identified three key logical components:

- Feed handlers (ingress).
- Strategies (decision-making).
- Gateways (egress).

To connect them without introducing locks or unbounded queues, low-latency systems often use *lock-free rings*—fixed-size circular buffers with carefully constrained producer/consumer patterns.

Single-producer/single-consumer rings

The simplest and fastest pattern is the SPSC ring:

- Exactly one thread enqueues (producer).
- Exactly one thread dequeues (consumer).

In this case, we can implement the ring using only two indices (head and tail) and memory barriers, without any locks or atomic read-modify-write operations. This yields very low and stable overhead per message.

Typical uses:

- Feed handler → per-instrument or per-strategy event queues.
- Strategy → gateway for order intents.

Multi-producer or multi-consumer situations

Real systems sometimes need fan-in or fan-out:

- Multiple feeds may update a synthetic instrument.
- Multiple strategies may send orders through a single gateway session.

In these cases you can:

- Introduce an extra layer of aggregation that preserves SPSC semantics (e.g., a dedicated aggregator thread).
- Use well-designed multi-producer/multi-consumer lock-free queues, accepting slightly higher overhead when necessary.

The guiding idea is to keep the number of truly shared, contended queues as small as possible, and to keep their size bounded so that latency does not grow unnoticed under load.

Introducing Kernel Bypass

So far we have assumed that packets travel from the NIC through the kernel networking stack into user-space sockets. Even with careful tuning (interrupt coalescing, RSS, buffer sizes), this path incurs some irreducible overhead:

- Transitions between user mode and kernel mode.
- Copies between kernel buffers and user-space buffers (or at least cache-line touching).
- General-purpose logic in the networking stack that you do not need for a specialized trading application.

Kernel bypass is an umbrella term for technologies that allow user-space code to access NIC queues directly, handling RX and TX in its own tight loops. Examples include DPDK-like frameworks and user-space RDMA libraries.

The basic idea is:

- Map the NIC's descriptor rings into user space.
- Allocate packet buffers in user-space memory.
- Run a polling loop that reads and writes descriptors directly, with no system calls on the hot path.

This approach:

- Eliminates many sources of jitter (no unpredictable interrupts, no preemptive kernel scheduling on the critical path).
- Reduces per-packet overhead to a small, stable number of CPU instructions.
- Gives you fine-grained control over queue steering, batching, and memory layout.

The trade-offs are significant: more complex code, more responsibility for correctness and security, and tighter coupling to specific hardware. But for extreme low-latency strategies, kernel bypass often yields measurable gains.

End-to-End Hot Path with Kernel Bypass

We now have enough pieces to draw the full data path from exchange to strategy and back, highlighting where kernel bypass and lock-free rings fit. Figure provides an end-to-end view.

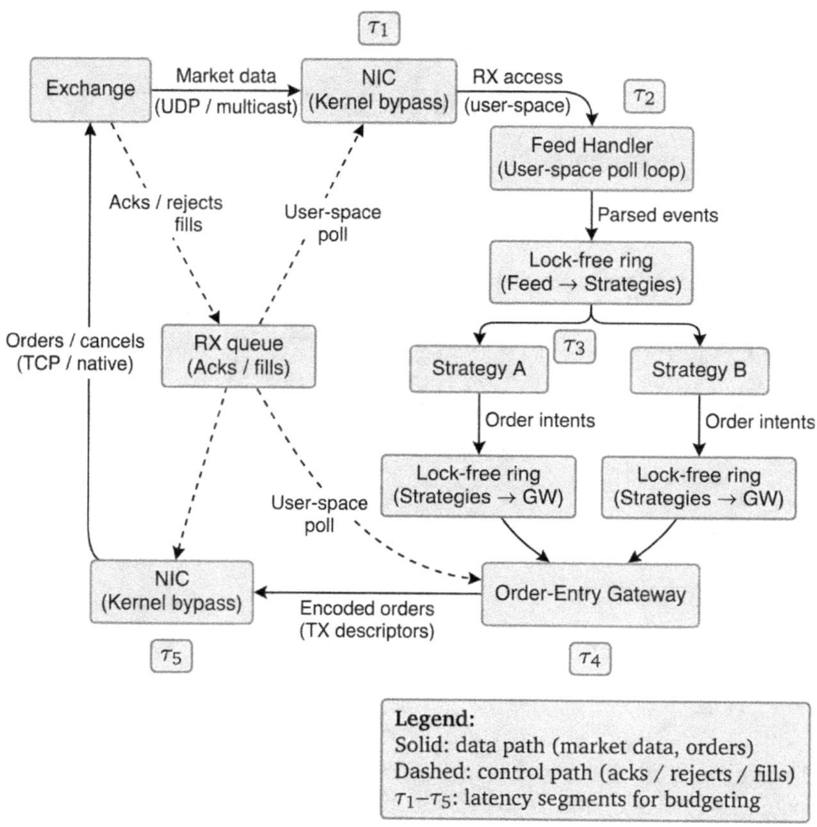

The figure highlights five latency segments τ_1 through τ_5. Your end-to-end wire-to-wire latency is approximately their sum, but in practice you will track their *distributions*, not just their means. Kernel bypass and lock-free queues aim to make each segment short and tightly distributed.

Latency Budgeting and Micro-Optimizations

To keep the hot path honest, you should treat latency as a *budget* to be allocated:

- τ_1: NIC and user-space poll loop (RX).
- τ_2: Parsing and book update.
- τ_3: Strategy logic and order decision.
- τ_4: Gateway encoding and risk checks.
- τ_5: User-space TX path and NIC.

Each segment can be profiled and optimized in isolation, but they interact via shared hardware resources (cores, caches, memory bandwidth). Micro-optimizations that matter in this context include:

- **Cache-aware data layouts.** Structuring data so that the fields needed together are contiguous, minimizing cache misses along the hot path.
- **Batch sizes.** Processing a small batch of packets or orders per loop iteration to amortize overhead, without building up harmful queueing delays.
- **Memory pools.** Pre-allocating and reusing objects (messages, intents) to avoid unpredictable allocator behavior during busy periods.

The guiding intuition is that any operation that happens on every message or every decision is worth scrutinizing. A single extra cache miss or conditional branch, multiplied by millions of events per second, can be the difference between a 10 μs and a 20 μs tail.

In this section we turned the low-level OS and networking foundations into concrete trading data paths:

- Feed handlers ingest raw exchange feeds, parse them with minimal copying and allocation, and maintain cache-friendly order books.
- Strategies see fresh market data via shared-memory structures and lock-free rings, and send intents back to the gateway through similarly lean queues.
- Order-entry gateways handle translation, risk, and session management while staying on the fast path via kernel-bypass NIC access and tight user-space loops.
- Kernel bypass removes kernel overhead from the hottest parts of the path, at the cost of greater engineering complexity and stronger coupling to hardware.

The result is an architecture where every hop along the wire-to-wire journey has been deliberately engineered to minimize copies, locks, and jitter. In the next section we will push further toward the metal, exploring hardware acceleration and colocation strategies that move parts of these hot paths directly into the network fabric itself.

6.3 Hardware Acceleration and Colocation Strategies

In the previous sections we treated low latency as a software and systems problem. We tuned Linux, shaped network paths, and built user-space feed handlers and gateways using kernel bypass and lock-free queues. At that point, you are squeezing most of the slack out of a general-purpose CPU-based design.

In many markets, that is enough: you are in the same ballpark as your competitors, and incremental software improvements still provide an edge. But there are regimes—especially in modern equity, futures, and FX matching engines—where nanosecond-scale differences change who trades first. In these regimes, sophisticated software alone cannot keep up with the physics of signal propagation and processor pipelines.

This section explores how and when to move work *into the fabric*:

- Using FPGAs and specialized NICs to perform latency-critical tasks closer to the wire.
- Designing measurement infrastructure that can resolve latencies at sub-microsecond resolutions.
- Shaping your physical topology and colocation strategy to shrink propagation delay itself.

The emphasis throughout is not on chasing the lowest possible headline latency, but on doing so *without* surrendering control, debuggability, or the ability to evolve your strategies.

What It Means to Push Work into the Fabric

So far, all of your business logic lived on CPU cores, with the NIC responsible only for moving packets in and out. "Pushing work into the fabric" means moving parts of this logic into hardware that sits earlier in the data path:

- **On the NIC**, using programmable pipelines or vendor-provided offloads.
- **In the FPGA**, usually on a card that combines NIC + FPGA or on a separate FPGA board connected by a high-speed link.
- **In the network**, using PTP-aware switches, time synchronization fabric, and topology choices that reduce propagation distance.

There are three broad motivations:

1. *Latency*. Hardware can perform some operations with lower and more stable latency than a CPU plus operating system.

2. *Determinism.* Well-designed hardware pipelines have very tight latency distributions—minimal jitter and almost no outliers.
3. *Offload.* Removing repetitive tasks from the CPU frees cores and cache for more complex strategy logic.

The central trade-off is flexibility: hardware is harder to change than software. The art lies in deciding which parts of your pipeline are stable enough and simple enough to move into hardware.

FPGA-Based Acceleration: What Belongs in Hardware?

Field-Programmable Gate Arrays (FPGAs) allow you to implement custom digital circuits that can be reconfigured after manufacturing. They excel at streaming, fixed-function tasks with strict timing requirements—exactly the nature of many low-latency trading operations.

However, not all tasks are equally suitable for FPGA implementation. A useful rule of thumb is:

> If the logic must be easily changed based on research, keep it in software; if the logic must be *always* fast and is structurally stable, consider hardware.

Concretely, three categories often benefit from FPGA offload.

Feed decoding and normalization

Every trading stack must:

- Deserialize packets from one or more exchange-specific binary formats.
- Validate message integrity (lengths, checksums).
- Normalize identifiers (symbols, instrument IDs) to internal representations.

This work is repetitive, simple in structure, and very close to the wire. An FPGA can:

- Parse packets in a streaming fashion as bits arrive.
- Discard malformed packets before they reach the CPU.
- Emit already-normalized, compact records into on-board memory or a PCIe-accessible ring buffer.

From the CPU's perspective, the FPGA becomes a source of high-level, clean events (e.g., "price level updated to $100.25, size 20") rather than raw packets. This can shave multiple microseconds from the ingress path and significantly reduce variability due to software parsing.

Simple order book maintenance

Some FPGA-based systems go a step further and maintain a basic order book on the card itself. The idea is to:

- Maintain volumes at each price level, at least for the top-of-book or a fixed depth window.
- Possibly compute derived quantities such as best bid/ask, spread, or simple imbalance measures.

Because the order book update rules are strictly specified by the exchange and rarely change, they are good candidates for a pipelined hardware implementation. The FPGA can thus provide the CPU with a continuously updated top-of-book snapshot and a small set of statistics without the CPU having to process every tick.

This design can be particularly effective for very simple, reactive strategies (e.g., top-of-book market making, basic cross-venue arbitrage) where the strategy logic primarily depends on a narrow slice of state.

Pre-trade risk checks

Regulations and internal policies often require that every outgoing order passes certain checks:

- Maximum order size.
- Per-instrument or per-bucket position limits.
- Fat-finger checks: price not too far from last or from reference.

Many of these checks can be expressed as simple arithmetic and comparison operations on counters and current prices. Implemented on FPGA:

- The risk pipeline can sit directly on the outbound path, ahead of the NIC's transmit logic.
- Orders exceeding limits are dropped or flagged before they ever reach the wire.
- Per-venue or per-strategy counters are updated deterministically with each accepted order and fill.

This reduces the risk of software bugs bypassing risk checks and can guarantee that even in CPU overload situations, basic controls remain in place.

Partitioning Logic Between FPGA and CPU

Once you identify candidate tasks for offload, the next question is architectural: how should you partition logic between CPU and FPGA?

A productive mental model is the *hardware-software boundary* as an API:

- The FPGA exports a simple, well-defined event stream upward: decoded messages, pre-processed book events, risk verdicts.
- The CPU sends only a constrained set of commands downward: configuration parameters, strategy intents encoded in a fixed schema, risk limit updates.

To keep this boundary stable over time:

1. **Push invariants into hardware.** Anything mandated by exchange specs or long-lived risk policies belongs in the FPGA.
2. **Keep heuristics in software.** Anything that may change as you refine models or react to market structure belongs on the CPU.
3. **Separate data movement from decision-making.** Hardware excels at moving and transforming data in fixed ways; CPUs excel at control flow and complex decision trees.

For example, your FPGA might maintain a top-of-book for each instrument and compute a small set of features (spread, depth imbalance) exposed to the CPU. Strategies then use these features, plus historical and cross-market context, to decide when and how to trade. This permits strategy evolution without constantly resynthesizing FPGA bitstreams.

Specialized NICs and On-NIC Processing

FPGAs are not the only way to offload work. Many modern NICs, even without a full FPGA fabric, offer programmable packet pipelines and hardware features relevant to trading:

- **Hardware timestamping.** As discussed earlier, NICs can stamp packets with their arrival/transmission time at the physical layer, aligned to PTP or GPS-synchronized clocks.
- **Flow steering and filtering.** NICs can direct different kinds of traffic (multicast groups, TCP ports, specific message types) into distinct receive queues, each bound to a different CPU core or process.
- **Receive-side scaling and load distribution.** Hardware hashing can distribute traffic for scalable processing, which you can combine with your own queueing strategies.
- **On-NIC parsing or matching.** Some high-end NICs and SmartNICs expose programmable match-action tables (similar to SDN switches), allowing simple header parsing and packet classification.

These capabilities can reduce software overhead without requiring a full custom FPGA design. For example:

- *Time-critical controls.* You can implement basic rate limiting or drop policies in NIC filters, ensuring that certain traffic never even reaches your application if it violates patterns.
- *Queue-per-strategy designs.* Flow steering can route different multicast groups or TCP sessions into separate queues that map one-to-one with feed handler or gateway threads, enhancing cache locality and reducing contention.

The design judgment here is similar to the FPGA case: find fixed, stream-like operations that benefit from being implemented as close as possible to the wire.

Latency Measurement and Profiling at Sub-Microsecond Scales

As soon as you begin investing in hardware acceleration, you must also invest in better *measurement.* Otherwise, you cannot tell whether your complex FPGA project actually improved things, or if a misconfigured PTP daemon is quietly dominating your latency budget.

Key concepts:

One-way vs. round-trip latency

- **Round-trip latency** measures the time from sending a message (e.g., an order) to receiving a corresponding response (e.g., an acknowledgment or fill). It is straightforward to measure entirely at the client side, but conflates outbound path, matching engine processing, and inbound path.
- **One-way latency** isolates a single direction (e.g., feed arrival from the exchange, or order propagation to the exchange). Measuring it requires synchronized clocks at both ends or at well-defined reference points along the path.

Hardware timestamping and disciplined clocks allow you to build realistic one-way latency distributions, which are crucial for understanding where hardware acceleration is paying off.

Histograms and tail distributions

Average latency is almost irrelevant in latency-sensitive trading. Instead, you care about:

- The median and high percentiles (e.g., 99th, 99.9th) of latency distributions for each segment of the path.
- The shape of the tail: do you see infrequent but huge outliers, or a tight, compact distribution?

A typical measurement pipeline might:

1. Timestamp market data packets at the NIC and again upon entering strategy code.
2. Timestamp order intents at strategy exit, at the FPGA or NIC TX, and at the exchange gateway (if you have logs).
3. Aggregate these into histograms over time windows, broken down by venue, instrument, and even message type.

This is where your earlier investment in precise time synchronization pays off. Without a common time base, you cannot meaningfully compare these measurements over different systems or across software/hardware boundaries.

Separating systemic jitter from rare outliers

A careful reading of latency histograms often reveals multiple components:

- **Baseline jitter**. Small, frequent fluctuations due to cache effects, small queueing, or normal OS behavior.

- **Burst-driven shifts.** Periods where an exchange emits bursts of data or stress events cause temporary congestion.
- **Pathological outliers.** Huge spikes, perhaps due to GC cycles, firmware bugs, or momentary loss of synchronization.

FPGAs and on-NIC offloads are particularly effective at reducing baseline jitter and eliminating many *classes* of outliers (e.g., those arising from OS scheduling). Large systemic delays due to network congestion or exchange-internal queuing must be addressed via different means, including colocation and network engineering.

Physical Topology and Colocation

Up to this point, our efforts have been about reducing the *processing* delay: how long it takes your systems to react once a packet arrives. There is another unavoidable component: *propagation delay*—the time it takes light (in fiber or copper) to travel between you and the exchange.

In fiber, light travels at roughly two-thirds of its vacuum speed, or about 5 ns per meter. This implies:

- 5 m of extra cable: ~ 25 ns.
- 100 m across a data center: ~ 500 ns.
- 1 km within a metro area: $\sim 5\ \mu s$.
- 1000 km cross-country: ~ 5 ms.

When your internal software latencies are in the single-digit microsecond range, these propagation times are no longer negligible. This is why colocation—the practice of placing your servers in the same facility or campus as the exchange matching engine—has become standard in high-frequency trading.

Distance budgets and cross-connects

Think of your physical layout as another form of latency budget:

- **Inside the rack.** Short twinax cables between NICs and top-of-rack (ToR) switches; a few meters, tens of nanoseconds.
- **Rack to ToR switch.** Typically tens of meters; hundreds of nanoseconds.
- **ToR to exchange cage.** Depending on the facility, tens to hundreds of meters; up to a microsecond.
- **Between data centers or cities.** Kilometers to hundreds of kilometers; microseconds to milliseconds.

Colocation policies and physical cross-connect choices determine how much of this distance you can control. For example:

- A direct cross-connect from your rack to the exchange's matching engine cage minimizes intermediate hops.
- Using a shared service provider or extra patch panels may add small but measurable length and extra switching elements.

At the nanosecond to microsecond scale, even the routing of fibers within a building can matter.

Internal network design

Within your own cage or suite, network design also affects latency:

- **Top-of-rack switches.** Low-latency switches with cut-through forwarding minimize per-hop delay compared to store-and-forward devices.
- **Fan-out for multiple servers.** Feeding the same multicast market data to several trading servers may require a small internal fabric; its latency and jitter characteristics must be considered in your budgets.
- **Redundant paths.** For resilience you may use dual ToR switches or diverse cross-connects. The backup path should be engineered to have predictable latency, even if slightly higher, so that failover events do not produce wild timing behavior.

The general principle mirrors our software designs: keep the hot path short, direct, and predictable; move complexity and redundancy onto slower, less time-critical paths.

Evolving Toward a Hybrid Software–Hardware Stack

Embedding hardware acceleration and colocation into your trading platform is best viewed as an *evolution*, not a big-bang rewrite. A pragmatic progression might look like:

1. **Mature the software stack.** Ensure your Linux tuning, kernel bypass, and feed handler/gateway designs are solid and well-instrumented. You should know your current latency distributions and where time is spent.
2. **Adopt advanced NIC features.** Enable hardware timestamping, flow steering, and appropriate offloads. This often yields substantial gains at relatively low engineering cost.
3. **Prototype selective FPGA offloads.** Start with the least strategy-dependent tasks—e.g., feed decoding or basic risk checks—and maintain a software fallback path for validation and debugging.
4. **Refine colocation and topology.** As your internal processing delays shrink, revisit your physical layout, cross-connects, and network design to ensure propagation delay is not the dominant term.
5. **Consider deeper integration only when justified.** More aggressive concepts—full hardware order books, on-FPGA strategies—should be undertaken only when you have clear evidence that the incremental gains outweigh the complexity and loss of flexibility.

Throughout, maintain a strict separation between:

- **Latency-critical hot paths**, where hardware and specialized software cooperate to minimize and stabilize delay.

- **Control and observability planes**, where you invest in rich logging, configuration management, and monitoring—even if they run at much higher latencies.

This separation enables you to push the former closer to the physical limits of the fabric without losing the ability to understand, debug, and govern the system as a whole.

This section extended the low-latency engineering story beyond CPUs and kernels into the hardware and physical domains:

- FPGAs and specialized NICs can offload stable, streaming tasks—feed decoding, simple book maintenance, pre-trade risk—achieving sub-microsecond, highly deterministic behavior.
- Partitioning logic between FPGA and CPU requires careful definition of a stable hardware-software boundary, with invariants pushed into hardware and strategy heuristics retained in software.
- Precise latency measurement, using hardware timestamps and disciplined clocks, is essential to validate gains and to separate baseline jitter from true outliers.
- Colocation and careful internal network design reduce propagation delay, which becomes increasingly important as processing delays shrink into the microsecond range.
- A staged evolution from pure software to hybrid software–hardware architectures helps preserve flexibility and debuggability while progressively harvesting hardware-driven latency gains.

In the final section of this chapter, we will reintroduce an equally important constraint: resilience. Ultra-fast systems that fail or misbehave under stress can be more dangerous than slower, well-behaved ones. We will explore how to combine the aggressive optimizations in this chapter with fault tolerance and robust recoverability.

6.4 Fault Tolerance and Resilience Engineering

The previous sections of this chapter were deliberately aggressive: we stripped the operating system to its essentials, bypassed the kernel, pushed logic onto NICs and FPGAs, and placed our servers as close as possible to the exchange. All of these choices reduce latency, but they also narrow safety margins. A single misbehaving component can now disrupt an entire trading day in microseconds.

Low latency without resilience is a liability. In this section we step back and ask: *How can we ensure that our ultra-fast trading machine fails safely, recovers predictably, and remains auditable?* The answer lies in treating fault tolerance and resilience as first-class design goals, not afterthoughts patched onto an existing low-latency stack.

We will proceed in four stages:

- Identify typical failure modes in low-latency trading systems.
- Introduce resilience patterns: redundancy, health checks, circuit breakers, backpressure, and graceful degradation.
- Discuss state and data management: what must persist, what can be reconstructed, and how event sourcing and CQRS help.
- Show how to combine these ideas into an architecture that maintains both speed and correctness.

Failure Modes in Low-Latency Trading Systems

To design resilience, begin by being honest about how things actually fail. In a modern low-latency environment, common failure modes include:

- **Process crashes.** A feed handler, strategy, or gateway segfaults due to a bug or unhandled exception.
- **Kernel panics and OS freezes.** A driver bug, misconfigured kernel-bypass stack, or resource exhaustion brings down the entire host.

- **NIC resets or link flaps.** Firmware issues, cabling problems, or misconfigured switches temporarily drop connectivity.
- **Exchange disconnects.** Session-level logouts, throttling sanctions, or exchange-side failures sever or degrade connectivity.
- **Pathological performance events.** Garbage collection pauses in supporting services, memory fragmentation causing allocation stalls, or cache-thrashing workloads that suddenly inflate latency.
- **Time sync failures.** PTP daemons losing lock, clock drift beyond specified bounds, or conflicting time sources leading to inconsistent timestamps.

Notice two broad categories:

- **Hard failures** where a component stops or disappears (crashes, disconnects).
- **Soft failures** where a component continues to operate but with degraded quality (latency spikes, corrupt state, inaccurate timestamps).

Resilience engineering must address both. It is not enough to "keep running"; you must ensure that the system does not silently produce invalid behavior while appearing healthy.

Redundancy and Instance-Level Resilience

The most basic resilience pattern is *redundancy*: run more than one instance of a critical component so that the failure of any single instance does not halt trading.

Hot–hot and hot–warm configurations

Two canonical modes are:

- **Hot–hot.** Two (or more) instances are fully active and processing the same input in parallel. If one fails, the others continue without a role change. This is common for feed handlers and risk engines.

- **Hot–warm.** One instance is active; another is running but not in the critical path (e.g., connected but not submitting orders). Upon failure of the active instance, the warm instance promotes itself and takes over. This is common for gateways bound to single sessions or throttled connections.

Hot–hot provides better failover characteristics (no switchover time) but requires careful design to avoid duplicate side effects; hot–warm is easier to reason about but has a small gap during promotion.

Instance-level design choices

For each logical role-feed handler, strategy, gateway, risk engine-define:

- How many instances run in parallel.
- Which inputs they share (e.g., same multicast group, same exchange session) and which they do not.
- How responsibilities are partitioned (e.g., instrument subsets, venue subsets).

Key principles:

- **No single point of failure on the hot path.** A single host, NIC, or process crash should not render you blind to the book or unable to cancel risk-critical orders.
- **Deterministic failover rules.** Promotion and demotion policies must be explicit, deterministic, and tested. For example: "If gateway A has not sent a heartbeat for 100 ms, gateway B attempts to log in using its reserved session credentials."
- **Split physical domains.** Where practical, place redundant instances in different racks, power domains, and network paths to avoid correlated failures.

Redundancy costs money-in hardware, rack space, and exchange connections-but for material strategies it is a non-negotiable part of operational risk control.

Health Checks, Circuit Breakers, and Backpressure

Redundancy helps when something *fails completely*. Many production incidents, however, arise when components degrade gradually or misbehave while still technically "up". Addressing this requires three complementary mechanisms.

Health checks

A health check is a small, periodic probe that tests whether a component is both *alive* and *performing adequately*. For a low-latency trading component, health is multi-dimensional:

- **Liveness.** Is the process running? Is it accepting messages on its queues?
- **Connectivity.** Are exchange sessions up? Are heartbeats being exchanged on time?
- **Latency.** Are message processing times within budgeted thresholds (e.g., 99th percentile below 50 μs)?
- **Data freshness.** Is the local book up to date relative to exchange sequence numbers?
- **Time sync.** Is the clock offset within acceptable bounds?

Health checks should be designed as low-overhead, out-of-band queries:

- Expose metrics (latency percentiles, queue depths, last-seen sequence numbers) via shared memory or a lightweight endpoint.
- Have supervisors or peers poll them periodically.

If any metric exceeds a preset threshold, the system can trigger protective actions.

Circuit breakers

A circuit breaker is a control that stops or limits trading activity under suspicious conditions. Examples:

- **Per-strategy breakers.** Disable a strategy if its P&L or inventory moves outside expected bounds within a short interval, or if it sends too many orders without fills.
- **Per-venue breakers.** Halt new orders to a venue if latency or reject rates spike, suggesting exchange-side issues.
- **Global breakers.** Stop *all* trading if time synchronization is lost or if core risk systems become unavailable.

A key design principle is *fail fast, fail safe*: if you are not confident that the system is behaving correctly, it is better to stop trading and investigate than to continue in uncertainty.

Backpressure

Backpressure is the system's way of saying "slow down" to its own components. In a low-latency architecture, this often takes the form of:

- Bounded lock-free queues between components (feed handler $\rightarrow$ strategy, strategy $\rightarrow$ gateway). When queues fill, producers block or shed work.
- Rate limiters at the strategy–gateway boundary: strategies that attempt to exceed allowed message rates are throttled or temporarily disabled.
- Dynamic load shedding, where non-critical tasks (e.g., detailed logging, secondary analytics) are reduced or disabled under heavy load to preserve capacity for the hot path.

By designing for backpressure, you avoid uncontrolled queue growth that silently inflates latency and memory usage. Instead, pressure is surfaced explicitly and can trigger higher-level responses (such as circuit breakers or auto-scaling of supporting components).

State, Caching, and Rebuildability

So far we have mainly discussed processes and flows. Underneath, every trading platform manages substantial state:

- **Reference data.** Instrument definitions, tick sizes, trading calendars.
- **Risk limits.** Per-strategy, per-venue, and global limits and configurations.
- **Session state.** Logon status, sequence numbers, outstanding orders.
- **Market state.** Local order books, recent trades, derived statistics.
- **Internal state.** Parameters and state variables used by strategies (e.g., indicators, alpha signals).

For resilience, you must decide for each category: *What must survive a crash, and what can we reconstruct?*

Durable vs. reconstructible state

- **Durable state** is information that must not be lost and may be expensive or impossible to recreate accurately from external sources. Examples: risk limit configurations, order ID mappings, regulatory logs.
- **Reconstructible state** is information you can rebuild from external streams and durable logs. Examples: order books (from market data), strategy indicators (from historical trades and quotes).

A sound design minimizes the amount of state that *must* be made durable in real time, reserving durable persistence for critical control and audit data. Everything else should be derived or cached, so that:

- Processes can restart quickly by replaying recent events.
- Cache corruption does not compromise overall correctness; it merely requires a rebuild.

Local caches and replicas

Low-latency components often keep local copies of reference data and state to avoid remote lookups on the hot path. For example:

- A gateway may cache per-instrument risk limits and per-client configurations.
- A strategy may cache instrument parameters and static metadata.

To keep these caches resilient:

- Establish a *single authoritative source* for each type of reference data (often a central configuration service or database).
- Propagate changes as events or snapshots, not ad hoc scripts, so that every cache can be rebuilt by replaying the same change stream.
- Define what happens when the authoritative source is unreachable: do you freeze existing limits, fall back to conservative defaults, or halt trading?

The goal is to ensure that local caches improve performance but do not become hidden single points of failure or inconsistency.

Event Sourcing and CQRS for Trading Systems

One architectural approach that fits trading particularly well is *event sourcing* coupled with *Command Query Responsibility Segregation* (CQRS).

Event sourcing

In an event-sourced system:

- The primary record of truth is an ordered log of immutable events (e.g., "order X created", "order X partially filled", "limit Y updated").
- System state is derived by replaying these events, either in real time or offline.

For trading, your event log typically includes:

- All incoming market data events you consider relevant (possibly filtered).
- All order-related commands and acknowledgments (including rejections and cancellations).
- All changes to configuration and risk limits.

The advantages are substantial:

- **Deterministic replay.** You can reconstruct the exact state of the system at any past time, for debugging or backtesting.
- **Auditability.** Regulators and internal risk managers can trace the causal chain from data to decision to order.
- **Recovery.** After a crash, you can restore state by replaying events from the last checkpoint.

The challenge is designing the event schema and log infrastructure so that it can keep up with market data rates without itself becoming a new bottleneck. This is where CQRS enters.

CQRS: separating commands and queries

CQRS separates the responsibilities of:

- **Command side.** Handles state-changing operations (e.g., new order, cancel, risk limit update) and writes them to the event log.
- **Query side.** Maintains one or more read-optimized views (e.g., position summaries, risk dashboards) built by consuming the same event stream asynchronously.

Applied to trading:

- **Hot path components** (feed handlers, strategies, gateways) participate in the command side, appending compact events to a log as they act. These events are written in a way that minimally disturbs their latency budgets (e.g., via batched, asynchronous I/O to local or replicated storage).

- **Support systems** (risk dashboards, compliance tools, analytics) consume the log on the query side, building their own materialized views without affecting or slowing down the hot path.

This segregation allows you to achieve both:

- High-speed, low-jitter behavior on the trading hot path.
- Rich, flexible reporting and analysis capabilities off the hot path.

Combining Speed and Integrity: A Composite Architecture

We can now outline an architecture that integrates low latency with resilience:

- Multiple feed handlers per venue, running in hot–hot mode on different hosts and NICs, consuming the same multicast groups. Each maintains its own order books and writes market data events into a replicated event log.
- Strategies subscribing to feed handlers via lock-free queues, with per-strategy circuit breakers and bounded queues to enforce backpressure.
- Redundant gateways per venue, in hot–warm or carefully designed hot–hot arrangements, managing sessions and enforcing pre-trade risk. Each gateway writes all commands and exchange responses into the event log.
- Time synchronization services monitored continuously; if clock error exceeds a threshold, global circuit breakers disable trading.
- A central event store, replicated and partitioned as needed, acts as the backbone of state reconstruction and offline analysis.
- Query-side services (risk dashboards, compliance, P&L reporting, backtesting harnesses) consume the event log asynchronously, never blocking or slowing the hot path.

Testing is as important as design. A resilient trading platform must be regularly subjected to:

- **Failure injection.** Intentionally kill processes, reset NICs, or simulate exchange disconnects in controlled environments to validate failover behavior.
- **Load and burst tests.** Replay historical high-volatility days to ensure that backpressure and circuit breakers behave as intended.
- **Recovery drills.** Practice rebuilding entire environments from event logs and snapshots to verify recovery times and data integrity.

The objective is not to prevent all failures-that is impossible-but to ensure that when failures happen, the system behaves in *predictable, bounded* ways, and that you can understand and reconstruct what occurred.

In this section we reframed low-latency engineering in the light of operational risk:

- We cataloged common failure modes in high-speed trading systems, from crashes and NIC resets to time-sync issues and pathological latency spikes.
- We introduced redundancy patterns (hot–hot, hot–warm), health checks, circuit breakers, and backpressure as tools to keep the system within safe operating bounds.
- We distinguished between durable and reconstructible state, arguing that most market and internal state should be derivable from event streams rather than maintained as opaque, fragile caches.
- We described how event sourcing and CQRS can provide both deterministic replay and rich analytics while keeping the trading hot path lean.

- We outlined a composite architecture that combines ultra-fast feed handlers, strategies, and gateways with a robust control and audit plane.

A trading machine built along these lines does not merely trade quickly; it trades quickly *and* remains intelligible, governable, and recoverable. This combination-speed with integrity-is what ultimately sustains an algorithmic trading business over years rather than milliseconds.

Chapter 7

DevOps, Governance, and Operational Excellence

Speed without discipline is how trading systems die. In this chapter, we turn a working strategy engine into a production-grade trading machine by wiring it into automation pipelines, hardened runtime environments, deep observability, and rigorous governance. You'll learn how elite shops ship changes dozens of times per day without blowing up, how they keep regulators and risk managers comfortable, and how they design operations so that even on the worst trading day of the year, the machine stays honest, explainable, and online.

7.1 CI/CD, Containers, and Infrastructure as Code

In the previous chapters we treated the trading system primarily as an architectural object: a network of research tools, backtest engines, live gateways, and risk controls. In production, however, that architecture is not static. Code changes daily, models are retrained, exchanges change their protocols, risk limits are adjusted, and infrastructure is patched or resized.

This constant change is where many otherwise sophisticated trading organizations fail. Spreads are tight, latencies are small, and a single undisciplined deployment can undo months of P&L. DevOps practices—continuous integration and delivery (CI/CD), containers, and infrastructure as code (IaC)—provide the backbone that lets you change the machine quickly *without* destabilizing it.

In this section we will:

- Define a canonical CI/CD pipeline for algorithmic trading systems.
- Explain why containers are the natural unit of deployment for research, backtesting, and live trading.
- Show how infrastructure as code lets you create, modify, and audit trading infrastructure like any other versioned artifact.
- Tie these pieces together in a trading-specific deployment strategy that respects market hours and risk limits.

From Ad-Hoc Releases to a CI/CD Backbone

At a high level, a CI/CD pipeline is a factory for safely turning changes into running systems. Whenever a developer, quant, or analyst changes something that could affect trading behavior—source code, configuration, a model file, even a dependency version—the pipeline ensures three things:

1. The change is *traceable*: you know who changed what, when, and why.
2. The change is *testable*: it is automatically validated through a battery of checks appropriate to its risk.
3. The change is *deployable*: once it passes checks and is approved, it can be promoted to production in a controlled, repeatable way.

In a non-trading web application, failing a deployment might mean a few minutes of downtime or a broken page. In trading, it can mean erroneous orders, capital losses, or regulatory breaches. CI/CD in this context is less about speed for its own sake, and more about *reliably* moving changes through an increasingly strict sequence of environments: development, staging, and production.

A Canonical Trading CI/CD Workflow

A typical end-to-end workflow for a trading organization looks like this:

1. **Change authored**: a developer modifies an exchange connector; a quant updates alpha logic; a risk manager updates a limit configuration; or a data engineer adjusts a transformation step.
2. **Change committed and pushed**: the change is pushed to a shared version control system (e.g., Git), usually through a feature branch and a merge request.
3. **Continuous Integration (CI)**: an automated system detects the new commit and launches a pipeline of checks:

- compilation or static type checking,
- unit tests (e.g., order book handlers, risk check functions),
- integration tests (e.g., strategy engine + risk layer + order router),
- simulation backtests over canonical scenarios (normal days, high-volatility days),
- static analysis and security scans.

4. **Artifact build**: if all CI checks pass, the system packages the software into versioned artifacts, typically container images, and publishes them to a registry.
5. **Staging deployment**: the new containers are automatically (or semi-automatically) deployed into a staging environment that mirrors production but does not trade real money.

6. **Validation in staging**: additional checks run in a realistic context:

- paper trading against live or recorded market data,
- performance and latency measurements,
- regression comparisons to previous model or strategy versions.

7. **Promotion and release**: after human review and sign-off where appropriate (e.g., model governance), the specific artifact versions that passed staging are promoted to production through a controlled deployment strategy (blue/green or canary).

This is a *machine* for change: consistent, inspectable, and improvable over time.

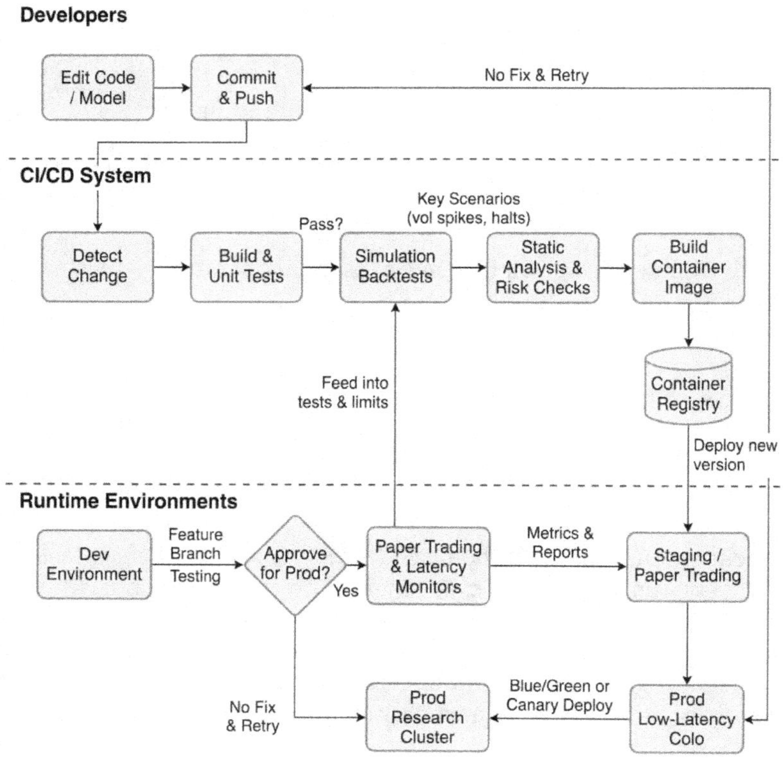

The rest of this section unpacks how this factory is constructed and how containers and infrastructure as code provide the building blocks.

Version Control as the Single Source of Truth

Everything that can change the behavior of the trading system should be under version control:

- strategy and engine source code,
- configuration files (risk limits, venue lists, mappings),

- infrastructure definitions (IaC templates),
- CI/CD pipeline definitions,
- data-processing scripts and schema definitions,
- pointers to model artifacts and data snapshots (with large binaries stored in appropriate artifact stores).

This discipline allows you to answer essential operational questions:

- What exactly changed before P&L degraded on a given day?
- Which risk parameters were in force when an order was rejected?
- Which version of the exchange protocol adapter was live during a venue outage?

Branching and merging policies (e.g., *feature branches*, *release branches*) ensure that experimental work does not directly contaminate stable releases. Access controls on repositories and mandatory code review reflect segregation-of-duties requirements discussed in governance chapters: the person who writes the code is typically not the only person who can approve it for production.

Automated Testing: From Unit Checks to Simulation Backtests

Once version control events trigger CI, the key question becomes: what tests should we run, and in what order?

Unit and Component Tests. These confirm that small pieces of the system behave as intended in isolation:

- Top-of-book and depth-of-book reconstructions from raw feed messages.
- Order state machines (new, partially filled, filled, cancelled).
- Individual risk checks (e.g., max order size, price collars).

They run quickly and catch obvious regressions before more expensive tests start.

Integration Tests. These combine components along realistic paths:

- A simulated client order flows through strategy logic, pre-trade risk, and routing to an exchange adapter.
- A quote change triggers the event loop, model evaluation, and order recalculation.

Here you are testing the *contracts* between modules, not just their internal logic.

Simulation Backtests in CI. Backtesting is discussed extensively elsewhere in the book, but in the CI context the aim is narrower: quickly check that new code or models do not behave catastrophically under standard scenarios. Typical patterns include:

- Short, representative date ranges: a quiet day, a volatile day, a day with a known trading halt.
- Reference benchmarks: for each scenario, store the P&L, turnover, drawdown, and risk metrics for a *baseline* version.
- Automatically compare new results to the baseline, with tolerance thresholds.

This does not replace deep research-grade backtesting; instead, it acts as a safety net to prevent obvious degradation from reaching staging or production. Since simulation backtests can be parallelized, a well-designed CI system can run dozens of such scenarios quickly on a cluster.

Security and Static Checks in the Pipeline

In addition to correctness and performance, trading systems must satisfy security and compliance constraints. The CI pipeline is a natural place to embed automated checks, such as:

- Static analysis for common coding errors and concurrency issues.
- Dependency vulnerability scans for known issues in third-party libraries.
- Policy checks on configuration files (e.g., maximum leverage, disabled venues).

These checks reduce the burden on human reviewers and create a tamper-evident trail: if a risky change bypassed or failed automated checks, the pipeline logs will show it.

Containerization: Reproducible Runtimes Everywhere

Testing is only as good as the similarity between the environments where tests run and the environment where trades execute. Containers provide a way to package a trading application with its operating system libraries, language runtime, and dependencies into a single, versioned artifact.

Why Containers Fit Trading Naturally

Consider the different places your trading code must run:

- a quant's laptop during exploratory analysis,
- a backtest cluster replaying months of market data,
- a staging environment paper-trading against live feeds,
- a low-latency gateway in a colocation facility,
- a research cluster training models or computing risk.

Without containers, each of these environments might have subtle differences in library versions, system settings, or tools. Bugs appear and disappear in ways that are hard to reproduce. With containers:

- The same image used in CI is deployed to staging and production.

- Upgrades to language runtimes (e.g., a new Python or Java version) can be tested by building separate images and rolling them out selectively.
- Rollbacks become predictable: you redeploy the previous, known-good image.

In practice, a trading firm will define a small number of *base images* (for example, a low-latency C++ gateway image, a Python research image, a Java risk dashboard image) and build specific components on top of them.

Packaging Strategy Code and Connectors

A container image for a trading strategy typically includes:

- the strategy and engine binaries or scripts,
- the configuration loader and schema validations,
- venue adapters and protocol codecs,
- logging and metrics agents,
- minimal system libraries tuned for latency or throughput needs.

The image is referenced by a unique tag (often including a Git commit hash and build number), which is recorded by the CI/CD system along with the exact tests it passed. This creates a tight link between code, tests, and runtime.

Staged Deployments and Market-Aware Rollouts

Once you can reliably build containers, the next challenge is controlling *when* and *how* new versions are rolled out.

Staging: A Dress Rehearsal for Production

The staging environment mirrors production topology as closely as possible:

- identical configurations except for API keys and account identifiers,

- the same orchestration system (e.g., Kubernetes) and deployment descriptors,
- similar data feeds, either from live sources (with orders disabled) or recorded sessions.

New images are first deployed to staging. The system runs paper trading sessions, comparing live decision streams against baselines. Latency, risk metrics, and error rates are monitored. Only after this dress rehearsal succeeds and receives human sign-off does the pipeline permit promotion to production.

Blue/Green and Canary Deployments

In many markets, you cannot afford to stop trading entirely while you deploy a new version. Two common strategies address this:

Blue/Green. Maintain two parallel production environments:

- *Blue*: the currently active production version.
- *Green*: the new candidate version, fully deployed but initially not receiving traffic or trading.

After final checks, you switch order flow atomically from Blue to Green, often by changing a routing rule or a configuration in an orchestrator. If a problem appears, you revert the routing. Because both environments are up, the cutover can be nearly instantaneous.

Canary. Instead of switching all traffic at once, you direct a small fraction—perhaps one instrument, one venue, or a small slice of volume—to the new version. You monitor performance and risk metrics closely:

- fill rates,
- realized spread,
- slippage relative to benchmarks,
- error/reject counts.

If the canary behaves as expected, you gradually increase its share. If not, you cut it off and investigate. In trading, it is common to implement canaries at the *instrument* or *strategy instance* level: a new model is first applied to a limited symbol set or a small notional cap.

Respecting Market Hours and Risk Limits

Deployments must be scheduled with an awareness of market conditions:

- Avoid deploying near major macroeconomic announcements, known high-volatility events, or during opening/closing auctions.
- For 24/7 markets (e.g., crypto), define internal "maintenance windows" where you tolerate temporarily reduced capacity.
- Include pre-deployment checks (e.g., is global volatility above a threshold?) that can automatically defer rollouts.

Risk systems can integrate with the deployment tooling to enforce these gates: for example, forbidding rollout of a new version if certain aggregate risk metrics are already elevated.

Infrastructure as Code: Declaring the Trading Machine

So far we have treated infrastructure as a substrate on which containers run. Infrastructure as code (IaC) extends the same discipline we apply to source code and containers to networks, machines, and storage.

What is Infrastructure as Code?

IaC tools let you describe your infrastructure in declarative templates. Instead of manually:

- creating virtual machines,
- configuring networks and firewalls,
- provisioning storage and databases,

- setting up load balancers and DNS entries,

you write a specification that says, in effect, *"this is what I want the world to look like."* The IaC engine compares this desired state to the current state and applies the necessary changes.

Crucially, these templates are:

- *versioned* in the same repositories as code,
- *reviewed* through the same merge-request processes,
- *tested* and applied through CI/CD pipelines.

Trading-Specific Infrastructure Elements

In a hybrid trading architecture, IaC may define:

- On-premises colocation racks: server counts, roles, and network segments.
- Cloud research clusters: autoscaling groups, spot instance policies, storage volumes.
- Data pipelines: message queues, stream processors, and data lake structures.
- Connectivity: VPNs or dedicated links between cloud and colo, firewall rules, and routing.

Because the definitions are declarative, you can reliably:

- spin up a *clone* of production (scaled down) for testing major changes,
- tear down unused environments to save costs,
- audit who changed which firewall rule or resource configuration and when.

Auditable, Repeatable Environments

IaC plays an important role in governance and compliance:

- When regulators or internal auditors ask, "What was your infrastructure on date t?" you can reconstruct it from template history.
- When a post-mortem identifies a bad configuration (e.g., too-permissive network access), you can fix it in code and propagate that fix consistently.
- When spinning up a new region or venue, you reuse approved patterns (modules, templates) instead of designing from scratch.

Combined with containerization and CI/CD, infrastructure becomes another controlled dimension of the trading system, rather than a bespoke, manually assembled environment.

Putting It All Together: The DevOps Backbone

CI/CD, containers, and infrastructure as code are mutually reinforcing:

- Version control and CI enforce that any change—code, configuration, model, or infrastructure—must pass automated tests and reviews.
- Containers ensure that the environments in which those changes are tested and deployed are consistent and reproducible.
- IaC ensures that the underlying compute, network, and storage resources are themselves defined, versioned, and auditable artifacts.

The result is a practical DevOps backbone for algorithmic trading:

- You can move from idea to live trading in smaller, safer increments.
- You can reconstruct exactly what logic, model, and infrastructure made each decision.
- You can respond to incidents with precise rollbacks and targeted fixes.

- You can demonstrate to stakeholders—risk managers, regulators, and investors—that the trading machine is not a fragile collection of scripts, but an engineered system with change under control.

Later sections will build on this backbone by layering observability, model governance, and operations practices, completing the picture of a trading machine that is not only profitable in backtests, but robust, explainable, and maintainable in the real world.

7.2 Observability, Model Registry, and Data Versioning

In the previous section we built a DevOps backbone for the trading system: CI/CD pipelines, containerized runtimes, and infrastructure as code. That backbone ensures that changes move through environments in a controlled way.

However, to operate a live trading machine responsibly you also need to *see* and *remember* what the system is doing. When P&L unexpectedly drops, when a model behaves oddly, or when a regulator asks how a particular decision was made, you must be able to reconstruct the full story:

- Which **code** version was running?
- Which **model** and hyperparameters were used?
- Which **data** was the model trained on and what market data did it observe at decision time?
- What **signals** did the system emit about its own health and performance?

This section introduces an observability and governance layer that answers these questions systematically. The key idea is to treat code, models, and data as first-class, versioned assets and to connect them to rich operational telemetry.

We proceed in three steps:

- Define observability for trading systems: logs, metrics, and traces.
- Introduce the model registry as a system of record for every trained model.
- Explain data versioning and lineage, and how they tie back to both models and production decisions.

When combined with the CI/CD machinery from the previous section, these capabilities create a fabric of transparency and reproducibility across the trading machine.

Observability: Seeing the Trading Machine in Motion

Why Observability Matters in Trading

In a typical web application, observability focuses on uptime and latency: are pages loading quickly, and are errors under control? In algorithmic trading, the questions are richer and more tightly coupled to economics and risk:

- Are order latencies stable across venues, or has a particular exchange slowed down?
- Are models producing outlier scores or signals in certain regimes?
- Are we seeing more order rejects, cancels, or partial fills than usual?
- Did our risk limits or circuit breakers trigger, and why?

Observability in this context must therefore capture both *technical* and *trading* behavior. The standard decomposition into logs, metrics, and traces is a useful mental model.

Logs: What Happened?

Logs are time-stamped, usually textual records of discrete events. Each log entry answers, in some level of detail, the question "what just happened?" For a trading system, important log classes include:

- **Order lifecycle logs**: order submissions, acknowledgements, partial and full fills, cancels, rejects, replacements.
- **Risk and control logs**: limit checks passed or failed, kill-switch activations, parameter changes.
- **Model decision logs**: input features, model version identifiers, scores, and selected actions (e.g., buy/sell decision and size).
- **System events**: restarts, configuration loads, connection drops, reconnections.

A common pattern is to separate logs by *purpose*:

- High-volume, structured logs suitable for downstream analytics.
- Lower-volume, human-readable logs aimed at debugging and incident response.

For reproducibility, certain logs must be *immutable* and retained for long periods (this overlaps with audit trail requirements discussed later in the chapter). Others can be sampled or aggregated.

Metrics: How Much, How Often, How Fast?

Metrics are numeric time series, typically collected at regular intervals or per event. They allow you to observe trends, set thresholds, and trigger alerts. In trading systems, representative metrics include:

- **Latency metrics**:
  - order send-to-acknowledge time per venue,
  - tick-to-decision time (from market data arrival to strategy decision),
  - model inference time per call and per model version.
- **Throughput and volume metrics**:

  - orders per second per strategy and venue,
  - traded notional and turnover,
  - number of model inferences per second.

- **Quality metrics**:
  - fill ratios and partial fill rates,
  - reject rates (by reason code: price outside collar, risk limit exceeded, etc.),
  - realized spread and slippage relative to benchmarks.

- **Health metrics**: CPU, memory, and network usage, queue lengths, backlog in data pipelines.

Metrics are typically aggregated and visualized as dashboards, with alert rules that fire when conditions deviate from historical norms or defined thresholds. For example, an alert might trigger if:

- median order latency on Venue A exceeds 2 ms for more than 60 seconds,
- reject rate for Strategy X doubles relative to its 30-day median,
- model inference time for Version 17 exceeds 5 ms at the 95th percentile.

Traces: Where Did the Time Go?

Traces follow requests as they traverse multiple components, attaching a correlation identifier to each step. In a trading context, a "request" is often an order, a quote event, or a model inference.

For example, a trace for a single client order might include:

- Receipt at the API gateway.
- Validation and normalization.
- Strategy evaluation and signal computation.
- Pre-trade risk checks.

- Routing to a specific venue adapter.
- Send to the exchange and acknowledgement.

Each step in the trace records:

- timestamps,
- component name and code version,
- key contextual attributes (instrument, venue, account, strategy).

Traces answer questions like:

- Is latency dominated by strategy computation or by network round-trip?
- Do certain instruments or venues exhibit pathologically slow processing?
- Did a particular microservice or gateway contribute to an outage?

In practice, traces and logs are often stored in specialized backends, but the essential requirement at the architectural level is consistent propagation of correlation IDs and context.

Connecting Observability to Trading Reality

Observability only becomes valuable when connected to trading semantics:

- Dashboards are organized by *strategy*, *venue*, and *instrument group*, not just by container or host.
- Alerts differentiate between technical failures (e.g., process crash) and economic anomalies (e.g., realized spread collapses, sudden slippage increases).
- On-call playbooks use logs, metrics, and traces to rapidly answer "Is it just Market X? Just Strategy Y? Or the entire system?".

The next step is to link this observability fabric to structure around models and data.

Model Registry: Governance for Statistical Logic

So far we have treated “the model” as a black box inside strategy code. In a production trading machine, models are evolving assets: retrained on new data, evaluated with new metrics, and sometimes rolled back. A *model registry* is a system of record that formalizes this lifecycle.

What is a Model Registry?

A model registry stores and manages metadata and artifacts for each model version. Conceptually, each registered model version includes:

- a unique identifier (e.g., MODEL_X_v17),
- pointers to the exact model artifact (weights file, serialized object, or compiled binary),
- the code version that produced it (Git commit hash, branch, repository),
- training configuration: hyperparameters, optimization settings, feature definitions,
- training data snapshot identifiers (from the data versioning system, discussed below),
- evaluation metrics on standardized benchmarks and backtests,
- lifecycle state: *candidate, approved, deprecated*, etc.,
- governance metadata: who trained it, who reviewed it, when it was promoted or retired.

The registry may be implemented using specialized tools or with a combination of databases and artifact stores, but the architecture-level requirement is that *every* model used in production has a traceable, immutable record.

Tie-In with CI/CD and Deployment

In the CI/CD pipeline, training and validation jobs produce candidate models. Instead of directly deploying these artifacts, the pipeline:

- stores the model artifact in a dedicated storage system,
- registers it with the model registry, including all the metadata above,
- runs standardized evaluation tasks and logs results to the registry,
- transitions the model's lifecycle state based on automated checks and human review.

Only models marked as *approved* (possibly with additional tags like *for instrument universe A* or *for low-volatility regime*) are eligible for deployment. Strategy containers, when starting up, query the registry:

- by model name and deployment context, to obtain the correct version ID,
- and then fetch the corresponding artifact from storage.

At runtime, each inference or decision event logs the *model version ID* as part of its context. This simple step—passing a model ID through the system—is crucial for later analysis and audit.

Approval Workflows and Risk Considerations

The model registry provides a natural place to encode governance workflows. A typical pattern:

- Quant research teams can register new candidate models but cannot directly mark them as *approved for production*.
- A separate risk or model review committee examines performance metrics, stability, and sensitivity analyses.
- Approval decisions are recorded in the registry, possibly with conditions (e.g., limited to paper trading for a month, or limited to specified markets).

The CI/CD system integrates with the registry so that:

- deployment jobs validate that referenced models are in an appropriate lifecycle state,
- canary deployments attach explicit model versions and log them distinctly,
- rollbacks can be orchestrated by switching to a previous model ID in configuration, without code changes.

In this way, the model registry is not just a catalog; it is a control surface for statistical logic in the trading machine.

Post-Mortems and Model Drift Analysis

When performance degrades or anomalies occur, the registry enables structured analysis:

- Identify which model versions were active in the problematic period.
- For each version, compare training and validation metrics to realized performance metrics assembled from observability systems.
- Examine the training data snapshot to see whether recent regimes were underrepresented.

This feedback loop—from production metrics back into model and data governance—is essential for managing model drift and ensuring that retraining strategies are appropriate.

Data Versioning and Lineage

Models and code cannot be fully understood without understanding the data they consume. In trading, data is not a static asset: market data, reference data, and features evolve over time. Bugs in data pipelines can be as damaging as bugs in model logic.

Data versioning aims to answer three core questions:

- **Reproducibility**: Can we reconstruct exactly the dataset that was used to train a given model or run a given backtest?

- **Lineage**: For any derived dataset or feature, can we trace back to its raw sources and transformations?
- **Comparability**: When we compare performance across experiments or production periods, are we sure we are not accidentally mixing different data definitions?

Classes of Data in Trading Systems

It is helpful to distinguish several data categories:

- **Market data**: trades, quotes, order book snapshots, market depth, auction imbalances.
- **Reference data**: instrument definitions, corporate actions, tick sizes, trading hours, currency conversions.
- **Derived features**: moving averages, volatility estimates, order-flow imbalance, microstructure measures.
- **Labels and targets**: future returns over holding periods, realized volatility, event indicators (earnings, news).
- **Operational data**: logs and metrics produced by the trading system itself.

Each category may have its own storage and retention strategy, but the *versioning* principles should be consistent.

Snapshotting and Identifying Datasets

Data versioning systems typically represent datasets as immutable *snapshots*. A snapshot is:

- defined by filters (e.g., instruments, date range),
- bound to a schema version (column names, types, semantics),
- associated with a content hash or unique identifier reflecting its exact contents.

Training and backtesting jobs record, for each run:

- the identifiers of input snapshots (e.g., MARKET_DATA_-SNAP_2020_2022_v3),
- any derived transformations (as code versions and configuration),
- output dataset identifiers (for features and labels).

These identifiers are then stored in:

- the model registry (for models),
- experiment tracking systems (for research runs),
- or directly in CI/CD logs (for automated validation pipelines).

Later, when you need to reproduce a training run or investigate a discrepancy, you use these identifiers to retrieve the exact same data.

Lineage Graphs: From Raw Feeds to Model Inputs

Data lineage describes how datasets are produced from their inputs. You can think of it as a directed graph:

- nodes are datasets (raw or derived),
- edges are transformations (e.g., cleaning, feature engineering).

For example:

```
Raw Market Data (v1)
  |
  +---> Cleaned Quotes (v1.1)
          |
          +---> Top-of-Book Features (v2.0)
                  |
                  +---> Training Dataset for MODEL_X_v17
```

This lineage graph supports several operational questions:

- If we discover a bug in a transformation (e.g., wrong handling of corporate actions), which datasets and models are affected?

- If we want to retire a dataset, what downstream artifacts depend on it?
- When a regulator asks how a particular prediction was formed, can we show the chain from raw data to model input?

Technically, lineage can be captured via metadata systems, data catalogs, or custom pipelines, but conceptually it must be *automatically* recorded as transformations run, not manually reconstructed after the fact.

Production-Time Data and Decision Reconstruction

So far we have focused on offline data used for training and backtesting. For decision-time reconstruction you also need to capture:

- the stream of market data actually observed at the time of each decision (e.g., quotes and trades within a short window),
- any derived features or signals computed on-the-fly,
- the specific model version and configuration in effect.

You do not necessarily store full-depth books for every symbol at all times in a directly queryable form, but you must retain enough information—or be able to replay from raw feeds—to reconstruct the local context around any decision of interest.

This is where observability and data versioning intersect:

- Observability provides structured logs that record references to data snapshots and model versions for each decision.
- Data versioning ensures that the referenced snapshots are stable, immutable entities that can be retrieved later.

Together, they provide a path from a single order in production back to:

- the precise feature vector presented to the model,
- the training data that produced the model,
- and the transformations applied along the way.

Treating Code, Models, and Data as First-Class Versioned Assets

Let us step back and synthesize the picture across the last two sections.

Unified Asset View

The trading machine is composed of three interdependent asset classes:

- **Code**: strategy logic, risk checks, infrastructure definitions.
- **Models**: statistical or machine learning components that map features to signals.
- **Data**: raw feeds, transformed features, labels, and operational telemetry.

Each asset class:

- is under version control or an equivalent registry,
- has lifecycle states (experimental, candidate, approved, deprecated),
- leaves an audit trail of who changed what, when, and why.

CI/CD pipelines orchestrate changes in these assets and deploy them into containerized environments instantiated via infrastructure as code. Observability instruments these running systems and feeds back into the governance of code, models, and data.

Reconstruction and Accountability

With this fabric in place, reconstructing past behavior becomes straightforward:

- Start with an observed event: an order, a model decision, or a P&L anomaly.
- Use logs and traces to identify:

  - which container and code version handled it,
  - which model version ID was invoked,
  - which contextual data identifiers (snapshots, feature sets) were involved.
- Consult the model registry for:
  - the training configuration and data snapshots for that model version,
  - evaluation metrics and approval history.
- Use the data versioning system and lineage graphs to:
  - reconstruct the training and decision-time data,
  - analyze whether data issues contributed to the outcome.

This capability underpins not only internal diagnostics and continuous improvement but also external accountability to regulators, clients, and investors.

Preparing for the Next Layers: Compliance and Operations

The observability and governance structures described here are not optional embellishments. They are prerequisites for the topics that follow in this chapter:

- In the next section on compliance, security, and audit trails, we will reinterpret some of these mechanisms through the lens of regulations and legal obligations.
- In the final section on trade operations and continuity, we will use observability and versioned assets to design effective runbooks, incident response procedures, and disaster recovery strategies.

By treating code, models, and data as first-class, versioned assets and by instrumenting the system with rich observability, you transform the trading machine from an opaque box into an explainable, governable engine—one that can be improved systematically without sacrificing control.

7.3 Compliance, Security, and Audit Trails

In the previous sections we treated the trading machine as an engineered artifact: changes flow through CI/CD pipelines into containerized runtimes, and observability, model registries, and data versioning provide a detailed picture of what the system is doing and why.

We now place a different lens over the same machine: that of regulators, risk officers, and security teams. From this perspective, it is not enough that a strategy is profitable or technically elegant. The system must:

- enforce regulatory and internal *controls* before and after trades,
- restrict and monitor who can do what through *least-privilege access*,
- and maintain *immutable evidence* of its actions through robust audit trails.

This section explains how to align the trading architecture with regulatory, legal, and security expectations by embedding these concerns into the technical design, rather than treating them as external paperwork.

Regulatory Themes as Engineering Requirements

Different jurisdictions and regulators (SEC, CFTC, FINRA, MiFID II, and others) have their own detailed rules, but several common themes appear repeatedly:

- **Best execution**: firms must seek the most favorable terms reasonably available for their clients.
- **Market abuse prevention**: systems must detect and prevent manipulative or disruptive practices (e.g., spoofing, layering).
- **Risk controls**: pre- and post-trade risk limits, kill switches, and exposure monitoring must be in place.

- **Record-keeping and transparency**: orders, trades, communications, and algorithmic decisions must be logged and retrievable.
- **Governance and accountability**: firms must know who designed, approved, and modified their trading algorithms and risk parameters.

These themes translate directly into engineering constraints on the trading system. The key shift is to view regulations as design inputs, not after-the-fact checks. For example:

- Best execution informs how routing logic is designed and what data it must consider (prices, liquidity, fees, latency).
- Market abuse prevention shapes the behavior of internal surveillance and pattern-detection tools.
- Risk controls dictate that *no* order can reach the market without passing certain gates.
- Record-keeping requirements drive retention policies and audit trail structures.

Once expressed this way, regulatory themes integrate naturally with the CI/CD, observability, and versioning infrastructure already in place.

Controls in the Trading Path: Risk and Certification

Pre-Trade Risk Checks and Limit Controls

Pre-trade risk checks are automated controls that evaluate every order before it leaves the firm. They are typically implemented as a mandatory layer between strategy logic and exchange connectivity. Common checks include:

- **Order-level limits**:

  - maximum order size (shares, contracts, notional),
  - price collars relative to prevailing market prices,
  - instrument eligibility (e.g., blocklist for certain tickers).

- **Client- and account-level limits**:
  - daily notional caps,
  - sector or asset-class concentration limits,
  - leverage and margin constraints.

- **Firm-wide controls**:
  - aggregate position and P&L limits,
  - maximum participation rate in a given symbol or venue,
  - throttles on order message rates to prevent flooding.

Architecturally, these checks should:

- be centralized enough that *all* routes to the market must pass them,
- be configurable via versioned, auditable policies (not hard-coded constants),
- log both *pass* and *fail* results, including the triggering parameters.

By encoding limits as data (e.g., YAML or database tables under version control) and loading them at runtime, you can:

- review and approve limit sets before deployment,
- roll back to prior configurations,
- and reconstruct exactly which limits were in effect at any given time.

Kill Switches and Emergency Controls

A *kill switch* is an emergency mechanism to stop trading quickly under abnormal conditions. It can be triggered automatically (by risk metrics, system failures, or external market events) or manually (by humans). In practice, you often implement multiple layers:

- Strategy-level kill: disable a specific strategy instance or instrument universe.
- Venue-level kill: stop sending orders to a particular exchange or broker.
- Global kill: halt *all* electronic trading from the firm or a business unit.

Engineering requirements for kill switches include:

- **Fast**: switching off must be near-instant relative to trading frequencies.
- **Reliable**: the mechanism must be simple, well-tested, and independent of the components it controls where possible.
- **Auditable**: who pressed the switch, why, and what state changes occurred must be logged.
- **Reversible under control**: re-enabling trading should require appropriate authorization and leave an audit trail.

These controls should be integrated with observability systems: for example, alerts that certain volatility thresholds are exceeded can suggest that kill switches be considered, but the final actuation and its justification should be explicit and recorded.

Algorithm Certification and Change Management

Many regimes require that new or modified algorithms undergo a formal review before going live. Technically, this certification process can leverage the CI/CD and model registry infrastructure:

- each strategy or model version has:

  - associated backtest and simulation results,
  - stress-test outcomes (e.g., extreme volatility, illiquidity),
  - documentation of intended behavior and controls;

- a reviewer (distinct from the author) examines this package and records an approval decision,
- critical changes (e.g., to risk logic or routing) may require additional sign-offs (e.g., from risk or compliance),
- the approved version IDs are the *only* ones the deployment system is allowed to promote to production.

This implements segregation of duties in technical terms: developers cannot unilaterally deploy high-risk changes. Instead, approvals become structured steps in the CI/CD pipeline, and resulting states are tracked in registries and configuration repositories.

Security Architecture: Least Privilege and Zero Trust

Compliance concerns address *what* the system should do. Security architecture governs *who* can do what, and under what conditions. For algorithmic trading, a practical approach is to adopt "zero-trust" principles:

> Do not assume that any network, device, or process is trustworthy by default; instead, explicitly authenticate and authorize every action.

Identity and Access Management (IAM)

Identity and access management provides a structured way to define:

- **Identities**: humans (developers, quants, operators, risk officers) and non-humans (applications, services, containers).
- **Roles**: sets of permissions corresponding to job functions (e.g., *Developer*, *Release Manager*, *Risk Analyst*, *Ops On-Call*).

- **Policies**: explicit rules defining which roles may perform which actions on which resources.

Least-privilege access means that each identity receives only the minimal set of permissions needed to perform its functions. For example:

- A research quant may:
  - read historical market data and logs,
  - run experiments in isolated environments,
  - submit merge requests for code and model changes;
- but may *not*:
  - deploy directly to production,
  - change firm-wide risk limits,
  - modify audit log retention policies.

Similarly, production microservices:

- authenticate to other systems using service identities (not shared passwords),
- can only access the specific databases, queues, or APIs they need,
- are prevented by policy from reading, say, research-only datasets or unrelated client accounts.

All policy changes themselves should be versioned and reviewed, just like code.

Network Segmentation and Environment Isolation

To limit the blast radius of compromises or bugs, the infrastructure should be segmented into distinct network zones, often aligned with the environments from the CI/CD system:

- **Research**: many users, broad access to data, no direct connection to markets.

- **Staging**: topology close to production, but only test accounts and paper trading.
- **Production**: tightly locked down, minimal interactive access, whitelisted connections to exchanges and brokers.

Segmentation is enforced with firewalls, routing rules, and access-control policies; for example:

- SSH or shell access to production machines may be heavily restricted or disallowed entirely, replaced by controlled operational APIs and runbooks.
- Data exfiltration paths from production to research are constrained; for example, only aggregated, anonymized metrics may leave certain zones.
- Sensitive secrets (API keys, private keys, credentials) are stored in dedicated secret-management systems, not in code repositories or plain configuration files.

This physical and logical separation aligns well with the observability and IaC patterns: each environment has its own monitored infrastructure, but the definitions are consistently managed in code.

Protecting Secrets and Cryptographic Material

Trading systems rely on a variety of secrets:

- exchange and broker API keys,
- private keys for signing messages or establishing secure channels,
- database passwords,
- credentials for third-party data providers.

Sound practice includes:

- storing secrets in dedicated vault services with strong access controls,

- using short-lived tokens where possible rather than long-lived static keys,
- rotating secrets regularly and automatically where supported,
- never embedding secrets in code, container images, or human-readable logs.

Access to the vault is itself governed by IAM policies, and access attempts are logged. When combined with observability, this enables detection of unusual patterns (e.g., unexpected secret access from a given service or time).

Audit Trails and Immutable Evidence

Regulators, clients, and internal oversight functions often need to answer questions such as:

- Why did the system submit this order at this time and price?
- Which models, parameters, and limits were in place?
- Who changed configuration settings shortly before an incident?

Audit trails and records retention answer these by preserving *evidence* of system behavior and administrative actions.

What to Log for Audit Purposes

While observability captures a broad range of telemetry, audit logging focuses on events with compliance, legal, or governance significance. Typical categories include:

- **Trading events**:
  - inbound client orders and instructions,
  - internal strategy decisions (including model version IDs and key signals),
  - outbound orders and routing decisions,
  - execution reports and trade allocations.

- **Risk and control events**:
  - limit check evaluations (pass/fail, limit values),
  - kill-switch activations and deactivations,
  - breaching and restoration of thresholds (e.g., P&L, exposure).
- **Administrative and configuration events**:
  - changes to risk limits and routing rules,
  - deployments and rollbacks (code, models, infrastructure),
  - changes to IAM roles and access policies.
- **Security events**:
  - authentication successes and failures for privileged operations,
  - use of break-glass or emergency accounts,
  - access to sensitive data or secrets.

Every audit event should include:

- a precise timestamp (with time zone and, where relevant, microsecond resolution),
- actor identity (human or service),
- relevant context (instrument, account, strategy, environment),
- old and new values for changes,
- and a correlation identifier to link to related logs, metrics, and traces.

Ensuring Integrity: Append-Only Storage and Hashing

For audit logs to be credible, it must be infeasible for operators or attackers to tamper with them without detection. Common techniques include:

- **Append-only logs**: systems write events to storage that does not support arbitrary deletion or modification by normal processes.
- **Write-once media**: for long-term retention, some firms use write-once-read-many (WORM) storage or other technologies guaranteed to prevent alteration.
- **Cryptographic hashes**: logs are hashed in sequence (e.g., as a hash chain), such that modifying an event breaks the chain and is detectable.
- **Redundant copies**: logs are replicated across systems and locations, increasing resilience and raising the bar for undetected manipulation.

These properties need not be exposed directly to trading components; instead, logging libraries and infrastructure handle integrity, while applications simply emit structured events.

Retention, Retrieval, and Performance

Regulatory requirements typically specify retention periods (often several years) for trading-related records. Practically, this suggests a tiered approach:

- **Hot storage**: recent logs kept in easily searchable stores for rapid incident response and operations (e.g., last 30–90 days).
- **Warm storage**: compressed, indexed archives for investigations and performance reviews.
- **Cold storage**: long-term, immutable archives primarily for regulatory compliance, with slower retrieval times acceptable.

To make retrieval efficient:

- standardize schemas and identifiers across systems (e.g., consistent order IDs, strategy IDs, model IDs),
- maintain indexes on commonly queried fields (instrument, account, time range),

- provide tools and runbooks that guide analysts through typical investigations in a repeatable way.

Because observability and audit logging share many mechanisms, it is often best to architect a shared logging and event pipeline with distinct retention and access policies for operational vs. audit use cases.

Bringing It Together: A Governed, Defensible Trading Machine

Let us summarize how the themes of this section integrate with the DevOps and observability layers already established:

- **Controls as code**: pre-trade risk checks, kill switches, routing policies, and limit configurations are defined and versioned like code. CI/CD pipelines validate and deploy them, and observability verifies their behavior in production.
- **Least-privilege access**: IAM, network segmentation, and secret management ensure that humans and services have the minimal necessary capabilities, and all sensitive actions are logged.
- **Immutable evidence**: audit trails capture trading, risk, configuration, and security events in durable, tamper-evident stores, tied back to code, model, and data versions.

This does more than keep the regulator satisfied. For the trading firm itself, the same mechanisms:

- reduce the likelihood and impact of operational errors,
- shorten the time needed to investigate incidents and anomalies,
- and enable a culture of continuous improvement grounded in facts rather than anecdotes.

In the final section of this chapter, we will zoom all the way out to day-to-day trade operations: how orders move from creation to settlement, how reconciliations detect breaks, and how continuity plans keep the trading machine running under stress. The compliance, security, and audit structures described here will serve as essential scaffolding for those operational processes.

7.4 Trade Operations, Reconciliations, and Continuity

Up to this point, we have focused on how to *build* and *govern* the algorithmic trading machine: CI/CD pipelines move code and models into production; observability and data versioning let us understand what the machine is doing; compliance and security embed controls and auditability.

This section shifts perspective to the daily reality of running that machine. We follow the life of a trade from the moment a signal is generated to final settlement, then examine how operations teams verify that internal records match the outside world, and finally discuss how they keep the system alive—or safely shut it down—through failures and stress events.

Throughout, the emphasis is on the interaction between technology, process, and people.

The Order-to-Settlement Lifecycle

At a high level, every trade flows through six stages:

1. **Order creation** (front office / trading engine).
2. **Routing and execution** (brokers / venues).
3. **Post-trade enrichment and allocation** (middle office).
4. **Clearing** (central counterparties, prime brokers).
5. **Settlement** (custodians, cash movements).
6. **Books and records update** (back office, accounting).

Each stage is handled by different systems and teams, often across multiple organizations and time zones. Understanding this lifecycle is crucial because:

- operational risk accumulates at each handoff,
- reconciliations must span the whole chain,
- continuity plans must respect dependencies (you cannot restart settlement if clearing has not completed).

1. Order Creation

On the trading side, an order begins as a combination of:

- **Strategy intent**: a decision to change a position (e.g., buy 10 000 shares of X, or reduce exposure to a sector).
- **Client or portfolio context**: which account(s) the trade belongs to, mandates or restrictions, and investment guidelines.
- **Execution parameters**: order type (limit, market, VWAP, POV), time in force, maximum participation rate, urgency.

Within the algorithmic engine, a signal is translated into a concrete order object. This order passes through pre-trade risk checks and controls, as described in the previous section, and—if accepted—enters the routing layer.

2. Routing and Execution

The routing layer decides *where* and *how* to execute:

- choice of broker or venue (exchange, alternative trading system, dark pool),
- slicing logic (child orders over time and across venues),
- interaction with liquidity (aggressive vs. passive posting, midpoint order types, etc.).

From an operational viewpoint, this stage produces:

- outbound electronic messages to brokers or venues,
- acknowledgements, partial fills, full fills, and rejects returning over FIX or native protocols,
- per-order and per-venue statistics on latency and fill quality.

These events are logged and fed into real-time monitoring dashboards. They also form the raw material for post-trade allocations and reconciliations.

3. Post-Trade Enrichment and Allocation

Once executions are received, the middle office applies several transformations:

- **Enrichment**: adding commission schedules, taxes, and fees; tagging trades with internal reference data (desk, trader, strategy).
- **Allocation**: splitting block fills across underlying client accounts or portfolios based on agreed rules (pro-rata, target weights, etc.).
- **Confirmation**: generating trade confirmations to counterparties and clients, often via FIX or SWIFT messages, or through broker platforms.

Here, technology must integrate with portfolio management systems, client reporting tools, and reference data stores. Errors in these steps may not affect execution itself but can create downstream breaks in positions or cash.

4. Clearing

In most listed markets, trades are novated to a central counterparty (CCP) that becomes the buyer to every seller and the seller to every buyer. Clearing members (often prime brokers) stand between the firm and the CCP, managing:

- netting of positions and cash obligations,
- margin requirements and collateral movements,

- reporting obligations to clearing houses and regulators.

From the firm's perspective, clearing generates:

- cleared trade reports (often aggregated),
- margin calls and collateral statements,
- confirmations of positions at the CCP level.

Operations teams must reconcile internal positions and P&L against these external views.

5. Settlement

Settlement is the actual exchange of securities and cash:

- custodians move securities between accounts,
- cash is transferred between bank accounts or through payment systems,
- corporate actions (dividends, splits) are applied to positions.

Settlement may occur on different cycles (e.g., T+1, T+2) depending on the market and instrument, so operations must track multiple open days simultaneously.

6. Books and Records Update

Finally, back-office systems update:

- official books and records (general ledger, sub-ledgers),
- exposure and risk reports at the firm and portfolio levels,
- regulatory reports and client statements.

At this stage, the execution and settlement chain is "closed" for that trade—provided reconciliations show no inconsistencies.

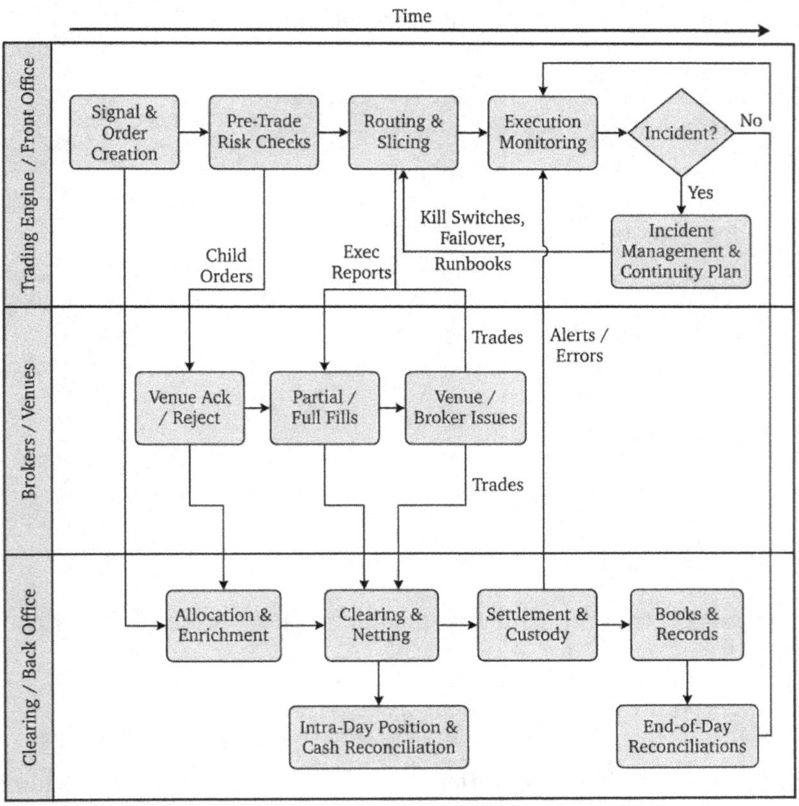

Reconciliations: Keeping Internal and External Views in Sync

Reconciliations are systematic comparisons of two independent sets of records. In trading operations, they are the primary tool for detecting and resolving *breaks*—discrepancies between what you think has happened and what the external world records.

Types of Reconciliations

There are several recurring reconciliation types:

- **Trade and execution reconciliation**:

- internal execution logs vs. broker / venue statements,
- share quantities, prices, and timestamps.

- **Position reconciliation**:

- internal positions vs. prime broker, CCP, and custodian positions,
- per-instrument and per-account levels.

- **Cash reconciliation**:

- internal cash balances vs. bank statements,
- including unsettled trades, fees, interest, and corporate actions.

- **Fee and commission reconciliation**:

- expected commissions and fees vs. charged amounts,
- across venues, brokers, and instruments.

- **Corporate action reconciliation**:

- internal application of dividends, splits, rights issues, etc.,
- vs. custodian and issuer records.

Each reconciliation compares:

- a *source of truth* from outside the firm,
- against the firm's internal books and records.

Automation is essential given the volume and frequency of trades, but human judgment remains crucial for resolving complex breaks.

Common Break Patterns in Algorithmic Trading

Algorithmic strategies can generate particular kinds of breaks:

- **High message rates**: partial fills and cancels across many venues can produce complex execution patterns, increasing the chance of missing or misprocessed messages.
- **Latency and race conditions**: local views of positions may temporarily diverge from external views, especially in high-frequency contexts.
- **Corporate actions and reference data changes**: strategies holding many symbols may be affected by late or inconsistent application of splits or symbol changes.
- **Time-zone and calendar mismatches**: global strategies spanning markets with different holidays and settlement cycles may misalign settlement dates.

Well-designed reconciliations take these patterns into account, using tolerances and rules appropriate to each asset class and strategy.

Designing Automated Reconciliation Processes

Whether implemented in specialized tools or custom pipelines, effective reconciliation systems share several characteristics:

Standardized identifiers. Consistent global IDs for:

- orders and executions,
- accounts and portfolios,
- instruments (mapping multiple vendor IDs to a canonical symbol).

Without this, matching records between systems becomes fragile and manual.

Deterministic matching rules. Clear, documented logic for pairing internal and external records, for example:

- match on (trade date, instrument, quantity, price, account) with tolerances for rounding,

- fallbacks when exact matches fail (e.g., group by instrument and net quantity).

Incremental, frequent runs. Reconciliations are not only end-of-day activities. Many firms run:

- *intra-day* reconciliations for key strategies and venues,
- *end-of-day* reconciliations across all products,
- *T+1 or later* reconciliations once all counterparties have finalized reports.

Break categorization and workflow. When breaks are detected, the system should:

- classify them (e.g., timing difference, price discrepancy, missing trade, booking error),
- assign them to responsible teams or individuals,
- track their status (open, investigating, resolved, waived) with timestamps and comments.

This turns reconciliation from a fire-fighting exercise into a managed process with clear ownership.

Humans in the Loop

No matter how automated the matching, break resolution often requires:

- contacting brokers or custodians to clarify discrepancies,
- adjusting internal bookings or correcting reference data,
- deciding whether a small discrepancy is material or can be waived.

Operational runbooks (discussed below) guide these actions: what information to collect, what systems to check, how to document resolutions. Over time, recurring break patterns can inspire structural fixes in upstream systems, improving data quality and reducing operational risk.

Business Continuity and Disaster Recovery

Trading systems operate in an environment where outages and failures are inevitable:

- hardware and network failures in data centers,
- software defects and misconfigurations,
- connectivity problems with exchanges or brokers,
- broader incidents such as power outages, natural disasters, or cyberattacks.

Business continuity (BC) and disaster recovery (DR) plans define how the firm:

- keeps critical services running through disruptions,
- safely degrades or suspends trading when necessary,
- restores normal operations and reconciles state afterwards.

Defining Criticality and Recovery Objectives

Not all components of the trading machine are equally critical. It is useful to classify systems and functions by:

- **Recovery Time Objective (RTO)**: how quickly a system must be restored.
- **Recovery Point Objective (RPO)**: how much data loss (in time) is tolerable.

For example:

- Low-latency gateways and order-routing components:
- RTO: seconds to a few minutes,

- RPO: near-zero; state (open orders, positions) must be preserved or reconstructible.

- Historical analytics or research clusters:

- RTO: hours,

- RPO: some recent data loss may be tolerable if it can be reloaded later.

- Reporting and batch risk systems:

- RTO: by start of next trading day,

- RPO: end-of-day states must be preserved.

These classifications inform architectural choices about redundancy, backup frequency, and failover strategies.

Geographic Redundancy and Failover

To mitigate localized outages, firms often deploy:

- **Primary and secondary data centers** for low-latency components (e.g., in two colocation facilities near an exchange),

- **Cloud regions** for research and batch processing, with cross-region backups,

- **Redundant network links** to exchanges, brokers, and data providers.

Failover strategies can be:

- **Active–passive**: one site handles all production traffic, while another stands by. On failure, traffic is switched to the passive site, which has kept state synchronized or can quickly reconstruct state from logs and snapshots.

- **Active–active**: multiple sites handle traffic concurrently with load balancing and cross-site state replication. This improves resilience but adds complexity, especially in keeping risk and position views consistent.

The CI/CD and IaC patterns from earlier in the chapter help here: standardized deployment and configuration across sites simplifies failover and reduces configuration drift.

Backups and State Reconstruction

Effective DR depends on being able to reconstruct critical state:

- open orders and their current statuses,
- positions and cash balances by instrument and account,
- configuration and limit settings.

Mechanisms include:

- continuous replication of databases to secondary sites,
- frequent snapshots of stateful systems (e.g., every few minutes for order books and positions),
- write-ahead logs and event streams that can be replayed into a fresh instance.

Because trading engines are already instrumented for observability and audit, many of the events needed for reconstruction—orders, fills, limit changes—are already recorded. The key is to ensure that:

- these logs are complete and consistent across components,
- tooling exists to replay or use them to rebuild state in a deterministic way,
- reconstruction procedures are documented and tested.

Continuity for External Dependencies

Continuity planning must also account for failures outside the firm:

- If an exchange halts trading or a broker experiences issues, how does the system respond?
- If a data provider is unavailable or sends corrupt data, do strategies automatically pause or switch to backups?
- Are there alternative execution venues or routing options for critical instruments?

Automated health checks, combined with observability metrics, can:

- detect abnormal error or reject rates for a venue,
- trigger routing changes or kill switches for affected flows,
- and raise alerts for operations teams to evaluate wider impacts.

Runbooks and Incident Management

Even with redundancy and automation, incidents will occur. The difference between a contained event and a disaster often lies in how well the organization responds. Runbooks and incident-management processes provide structure and clarity under pressure.

What is a Runbook?

A runbook is a documented procedure for handling a specific operational task or incident type. It typically contains:

- **Triggers**: conditions under which the runbook should be used (e.g., "venue reject rate > X% for 5 minutes").
- **Diagnosis steps**: what systems and dashboards to check, what logs to query, what tests to run.
- **Actions**: safe, prioritized steps to mitigate or resolve the issue (e.g., throttling orders, failing over to another site, activating kill switches).
- **Escalation paths**: who to call, in what order, and when to escalate to senior management or clients.

- **Post-incident tasks**: reconciling state, notifying stakeholders, opening a post-mortem.

Runbooks should be concise and precise, designed to be used by on-call staff under time pressure.

Incident Severity and Communication

Not all incidents are equal. A typical severity scheme might include:

- **SEV-1**: firm-wide trading impact or major client exposure; requires immediate attention from senior leadership.
- **SEV-2**: significant impact to a subset of strategies, venues, or clients.
- **SEV-3**: localized issues with limited trading impact; handled by on-call staff with minimal escalation.

For each severity level, the incident-management process specifies:

- expected response times,
- required communication channels (internal chat, conference bridge, email summaries),
- frequency of status updates,
- when and how to inform clients or regulators, if necessary.

Observability systems feed into this process by highlighting symptoms (e.g., spikes in latency, error rates) and by measuring recovery progress.

Post-Mortems and Continuous Improvement

After closing an incident, a structured post-mortem aims not to assign blame but to learn:

- What exactly happened, and in what order?
- Where did detection, diagnosis, or response take too long?

- What blind spots in observability, governance, or automation contributed?
- What code, configuration, or process changes would prevent recurrence or reduce impact?

The outputs of post-mortems often include:

- new or updated runbooks,
- enhanced monitoring or alerts,
- changes in CI/CD tests (e.g., adding regression tests for the failure mode),
- modifications to limits, controls, or deployment practices.

In this way, the DevOps, observability, and governance frameworks described earlier become engines for operational learning. The trading machine becomes more resilient over time, not just technically, but organizationally.

Bridging Engineering and Operations

This chapter has traced a path from:

- building and deploying trading systems safely (CI/CD, containers, IaC),
- observing and governing them (logs, metrics, traces, registries, data versioning),
- satisfying regulatory and security requirements (controls, least-privilege, audit trails),
- to running them day to day (operations, reconciliations, continuity).

In a mature firm, these are not separate concerns. Instead:

- operations staff participate in the design of observability and controls,
- engineers write runbooks and on-call procedures informed by production experience,
- risk and compliance teams help define limits, approval workflows, and audit requirements,
- and post-mortems feed directly into backlog priorities for development.

The algorithmic trading machine, viewed through this lens, is not a static system but a living socio-technical organism. Its success depends as much on disciplined operations and governance as on clever models or low-latency code.

www.ingramcontent.com/pod-product-compliance
Lightning Source LLC
LaVergne TN
LVHW052033200926
848481LV00005B/1664
9798896652427